ELECTION STUDIES

ELECTION STUDIES

What's Their Use?

Edited by

Elihu Katz with Yael Warshel

Preface by
Kathleen Hall Jamieson

Westview
PRESS

A Member of the Perseus Books Group

Copyright © 2001 by Westview Press, A Member of the Perseus Books Group

Published in 2001 in the United States of America by Westview Press, 5500 Central Avenue, Boulder, Colorado 80301–2877, and in the United Kingdom by Westview Press, 12 Hid's Copse Road, Cumnor Hill, Oxford OX2 9JJ

Find us on the World Wide Web at www.westviewpress.com

Library of Congress Cataloging-in-Publication Data
Election studies : what's their use? / [edited by] Elihu Katz with Yael Warshel.
    p. cm.
Includes bibliographical references and index.
ISBN 0-8133-6635-6 (alk. paper)
1. Elections—Research.   I. Katz, Elihu, 1926–   II. Warshel, Yael.

JF1001. E33 2000
324.9—dc21

00-063299

The paper used in this publication meets the requirements of the American National Standard for Permanence of Paper for Printed Library Materials Z39.48–1984.

PERSEUS
POD
ON DEMAND   10   9   8   7   6   5   4   3   2   1

CONTENTS

LIST OF FIGURES
AND TABLES

Figures

Tables

PREFACE

Writing in *The Federalist* No. 57, James Madison specified that the "aim of every political constitution" was to obtain "for rulers men who possess most wisdom to discern, and most virtue to pursue, the common good of society." Much has changed since Madison's time. The founders would have been surprised by Americans' almost universal right to ballot, by the audacity of candidates taking their case directly to the people, and by the technology that enables packaged images of those who aspire to lead to be carried to mass audiences so effortlessly.

The processes used to choose a president have varied across the history of the United States. For example, in 1888 the Scottish scholar and statesman James Bryce noted that "an American election is held to be, truly or falsely, largely a matter of booming." Booming took the form of "processions, usually with brass bands, flags, badges, crowds of cheering spectators." Such goings-on pleased "the participants by making them believe they are effecting something; it impresses the spectators by showing them that other people are in earnest, it strikes the imagination of those who in country hamlets read of the doings in the great city." By contrast, most Americans today experience presidential campaigns in the quiet of our living rooms or dens.

Throughout U.S. history elections have performed important functions, including ratifying the notion that this is a democracy in which the president is elected and not born to the office and providing citizens of voting age with a voice that equalizes, for the moment at least, the rich and poor, the educated and less educated. Each has a single vote. Elections also build accountability into the political system. Those who were unhappy with the Clinton-Gore years had the opportunity to vote against the vice president in 2000 when he sought the presidency in his own right. In an age in which political promises are preserved in audiovisual form, promises unkept are ammunition for attack ads-in-waiting when the promise-maker seeks reelection.

For as long as there have been elections, there have been observers who studied them. Some make sense of the process by which we elect by sifting through the historical record. Others, who are represented in this book, divine the meaning of elections by surveying the sentiments of voters and voyeurs. Underlying their labor is the assumption that elections are both consequential and interesting, that forces not apparent to the casual observer may be uncovered by rigorous and systematic study.

In the United States this process has produced a rich body of scholarship, some of it produced by the authors whose work is included here. The editors of this volume are Elihu Katz and Yael Warshel, who is a graduate student at the Annenberg School. Katz has done pioneering work with Paul Lazarsfeld on the interpersonal influences at play in political decisionmaking, with Jacob J. Feldman on the effects of the Kennedy–Nixon debates, and with Daniel Dayan in exploring the phenomenon of "time out" that is created by some media events.

The essays in this volume were commissioned to guide the research team at the Annenberg Public Policy Center in the construction of a rolling cross-sectional survey of the American electorate. That project has benefited measurably from the discussions in this book of where election studies have come from and where they are capable of going.

Kathleen Hall Jamieson

ACKNOWLEDGMENTS

The editors wish to thank the scholars who spoke at the Fall 1999 elections colloquium entitled "What's a Good Election Study, and What Are Election Studies Good For?" including Sam Popkin and Kathy Frankovic, who could not accept our invitation to join in this written version. We offer apologies for our relentless badgering to those whom we persuaded to transform their spoken remarks into the following chapters.

The aim of the colloquium was to contribute to the design and analysis of voting studies in the forthcoming U.S. presidential election, and particularly to the major study undertaken by Kathleen Hall Jamieson and the Annenberg School for Communication at the University of Pennsylvania. Indeed, proposals offered by two of the colloquium participants, Richard Johnston and Merrill Shanks were incorporated into the design of that study. The Jamieson study also underwrote the expenses of the colloquium.

We also wish to thank Richard Johnston and Mark Brewin, who were kind enough to help repair an earlier version of the Introduction, and Barbara Grabias, who helped with administrative aspects of the colloquium and with technical aspects of the production of the manuscript. Lee Benson and Henry Teune offered collegial encouragement. John C. Thomas did thoughtful copyediting. Saskia Fischer and Courtney Hamilton assisted with proofing.

This is the point at which to note that although the colloquium consisted of experts, each with his or her own vantage point on voting studies, the editors disclaim any special expertise in this field. They were simply interested hosts, joining in the applause, trying to serve as representatives of all of the nonexperts who are invited to read this book.

INTRODUCTION

ELIHU KATZ AND YAEL WARSHEL

Social science has been keeping watch on the voting behavior of American citizens for over half a century. Beginning with the presidential elections of 1936 (and even earlier, if geographical and historical methods are admitted), teams of sociologists and political scientists have tried to analyze contemporary voting behavior—not just of the polity as a whole, but of groups and of individuals. The Columbia University studies of the 1940s (Lazarsfeld et al., 1944/1948; Berelson et al., 1954) were the first to track the intentions and decisions of voters from the primaries and nominating conventions through the long months of electioneering, and to the polling places. The University of Michigan studies of the 1950s (Campbell et al., 1954, 1960) extended the survey method to include representative national samples. Some of these studies also kept track of media output during campaigns, whereas others followed the work of journalists assigned to cover the politicians. A few studies observed the performance of political parties and candidates—as well as their advertising agencies and political consultants. Research in Britain and Canada was only a step behind that in the United States, but most other Western countries did not follow until the 1970s and 1980s. By now many of the once new states are also conducting their own election studies.[1]

This global trend surely constitutes one of the major examples of continuity in social research, for it allows for analysis over time and, to a certain extent, across cultures. Yet, even though survey research is now a common feature of election studies, it is well to keep in mind how recently all of this has happened; 50 years is not a very long time. Nor does any unifying theory underlie these many studies; there is wide disagreement on how much "distance" is appropriate in making observations, that is, on whether election cam-

1

paigns are a time for activation and enactment of prior commitments to tradition, party, or class, or whether they are moments of actual choice.[2] The early Columbia studies focused on demographics such as religion and rural/urban residence, although they also considered the media and the interpersonal influence exerted within families and friendships. In contrast, the more psychologically minded Michigan studies focused on party identity, attitudes, and issue positions as more proximate predictors of the vote.[3] Noting the modest role that the Columbia findings attributed to the media, Jay Blumler and Denis McQuail (1969) proposed a more interactional approach to the reception of mediated information by different kinds of citizen-voters.

Most of these numerous studies can be characterized as ad hoc attempts to identify the factors that influenced voters in a particular election, and thus to "explain" the outcome of the contest. Some convergence is in evidence, more methodological than substantive, although divergence and differences still abound. Overall, there appears to be increased awareness of the need to assign relative weights to the roles of demography, party, issues, and media, or better to chart the paths that connect them. The early studies tended to divide up these sources of influences, and to specialize in one or another of them. Though it is still fashionable to bet on their relative importance, there seems to be an increased sense nowadays that serious election studies must comprehend all of them. Moreover, there is a consensus among many scholars that party identification is declining in importance in Western democracies in favor of voters' attraction to the perceived personalities of candidates, their stands on issues, their records of performance, and their associations with good and bad times.[4] It appears that more recent studies are trying to explain the presumed voter volatility that the pioneer studies failed to find.

The convergence on shared methods is even stronger on an international scope. Continuity and standardization of this degree have been the dream of the major research groups from the very first—though funding agencies have not always cooperated. The two Columbia studies are the pioneering examples: the same team of researchers conducted repeated interviews, face to face, with a sample of respondents in a particular city over the months of a presidential election campaign in 1940 and again in 1948. The Michigan studies—which later became the National Elections Studies—have persisted far longer. For every U.S. election since 1952, national samples of voters have been interviewed face to face once or more during the campaign, using cross-sectional surveys and panels, while experimenting with newer forms of data collection. An international consortium for the Comparative Study of Election Systems (CSES) has spun off from the Michigan initiative for sharing research design and data. Taking a different tack, the Canadian Election Studies have attempted to keep very close watch on their (much shorter) national campaigns by adapting a one-time Michigan experiment. Their method is to telephone a "rolling" cross section of voters daily such that representative subsamples are available day by day to study the "before" and "after" of the specific events that punctuate the campaign (e.g., a debate). The subsamples, of course, add up to the large samples needed to make the major over-time comparisons. This method is being used by the Annenberg School for Communication at the University of Pennsylvania under the leadership of Kathleen Hall Jamieson, in its study of the 2000 elections; its focus on the everyday workings of campaign events draws inspiration from the panel method and the media of influence that are so central to the Columbia studies.

In anticipation of the Annenberg study, the colloquium "What's a Good Election Study, and What Are Election Studies Good For?" was organized in the Fall of 1999. The invited speakers were a mix of longtime observers and practitioners of election studies. They were asked to look back on the half century of voting research, to look forward to the Annenberg study, and to consider how the new study might benefit from the experience of its predecessors. The audience for the colloquium, however—and one hopes the same holds true for the readership of this volume—was not at all limited to voting specialists. In fact, it was addressed to a larger community of social scientists who were invited to contemplate a major subdivision of their discipline from the vantage point of several areas of specialization (communication studies, in particular).

The colloquium—as reproduced in this volume—might have been a celebration; after all, looking back on half a century of cumulative academic research on election campaigns should be an occasion for justifiable pride. But that is just half the story. In fact, each of the speakers spoke with ambivalence about voting studies. Major achievements were reported, but everyone used the occasion to spell out not only what has gone right, but also what has gone wrong in election research to date. The rights and wrongs were evaluated in response to the two leading questions of the colloquium: (1) What's a good election study? and (2) What are election studies good for?

What's a Good Election Study?

There was an underlying consensus on the answer to the first question: a good election study is one that is conceptualized and contextualized as part of a political system. The chapters in this volume repeatedly assert that election studies are too often disconnected from the political system in which the actual decisionmaking and voting are embedded. This assertion implies that election studies go astray when they overlook the "before" and "after" of the election itself; that is, an election campaign is an element in a particular institutional structure of representative democracy, it is a parenthesis in the performance of government and the fluctuations of public opinion. It originates in the years *prior* to the election and feeds into the performance of government and the fluctuations of public opinion that follow from the election. This insistence on treating the parenthesis—the "time-out" of elections—as part of a system is of particular concern to the political scientists writing in this volume. It underlies the call for continuity in the design of election studies, and for comparative studies of how elections are structured and implemented in different institutional settings. Even the process of making up one's mind differs in a presidential system and a parliamentary system. Systems in which candidates and leaders are firmly anchored in political parties invite quite different kinds of cognitions than do systems in which candidates are only loosely tied to parties.

In light of the chapters assembled here, it is useful to think of election campaigns as sandwiched between the routine politics that precede and follow them. Thus, students of voting should situate their studies in the context of voters' understanding of their political systems. Juan Linz argues that it is important to distinguish among the legitimacy accorded to the system itself, its efficacy, and the performance of its incumbents. In pre-war Europe and in certain new states, Linz argues that citizens were/are ready to abandon democracy for alternative arrangements whenever the efficacy of government or the performance of incumbents was/is perceived as unacceptable. Under such circumstances, voters go to the polls ostensibly to choose among competing parties or candidates, but actually they are choosing among political systems. Even the desirability of having competing political parties was not well established in many of these states, and hence the legitimacy of democracy itself was or is in question.

In another invocation of history, Seymour Martin Lipset alludes to the continued importance of demographic variables when he refers to the persistence of certain patterns of religious and class voting that have long outlived their relevance. Richard Johnston's analysis of the Canadian election of 1993 demonstrates how the lurking issue of Quebec independence entered the campaign uninvited and probably decided the outcome. Asher Arian and Michal Shamir also invoke long-smoldering differences over identity in Israel—as expressed in attitudes toward territory and toward religious versus secular Jewishness—to explain recent Israeli elections. Thus does social structure affect elections and elections in turn illuminate social structure.

Or consider recent U.S. elections in which political loyalties are on the wane, and insurgent candidates may even dissociate themselves from their own parties or from their immediate predecessors. In asking the generic question of how voters "make up their minds in a presidential campaign," it seems foolhardy to overlook the more basic question of why the party system has apparently weakened in so many polities.[5]

Linz also asks about voters' attitudes toward political parties, and he shows the deep ambivalence within democratic systems and among voters over the balance between direct versus indirect democracy. These attitudes find expression in party versus candidate predominance, primary versus party nominations, and party discipline versus parliamentary responsiveness to constituency opinion. The study of voting behavior takes on new significance within such institutionally and culturally defined contexts.

The contextual framing of campaign research also encompasses the state of public opinion since the previous election. For example, what changes have taken place in voters' assessments of social and economic problems, what changes have taken place in party loyalty and in party images, and is the incumbent government in good standing? It is very important to gather such attitudinal information along with voting inclinations prior to the campaigns in order to assess the changes that occur during the campaign. One of the oft-heard gripes against voting research is that preelection vote intentions, or even the previous election itself, is as good at predicting outcomes as the last-minute surveys taken just prior to the election.[6]

The same framework applies to the relationship between what goes on inside the campaign and what happens afterward. If voting studies are limited to studying the contest, they ignore whether and under what conditions the results of the contest, and indeed the contest itself, affect the performance of the newly elected leadership. In parliamentary systems, the ostensible outcome of the voting may be altogether lost in the process of building a governing coalition (i.e., where no single party has achieved a clear majority of the vote). Alternatively, the election contest itself—the rivalries it makes salient, for example—may constrain the willingness of parties to join together in a coalition. Under what conditions, Larry Bartels asks, do election returns give leaders a "mandate" to enact certain policies? When do winning candidates or parties actually fulfill their campaign promises and under what conditions do they maintain, or surrender, the popularity they achieved during the campaign?

In short, the election process is never over. In this view, a good election study is one that contextualizes individual and aggregate voting as elements in political systems that have a past and a future, not just a present. It also explores the ways in which a particular set of institutional arrangements—the executive, legislature, political parties, and media—"call" elections and situate citizens within them. Furthermore, a good study takes account of the periodicity of elections and the laws governing elements such as voter registration and polling practices.[7] That an election begins long before the official opening of a campaign is not only an academic observation; it is an obvious fact of social life, certainly in the United States. The institutions of opinion polling, end-running candidates, primaries, and political talk shows all begin years before the election. Whether this dispersion over time enhances interest, increases deliberation, or empowers citizens are empirical questions that a good election study must answer. In this view, election research is one of a series of readings of the institutions and values of a society taken at a moment of high citizen activation.

If election campaigns deserve to be contextualized within political systems, the vote itself needs to be contextualized within the parentheses of a campaign. To focus only on the crystallization of voting choices or on the final distribution of actual votes is to ignore one of the important processes of democratic societies. Hypothetically, election campaigns are great learning experiences; they make visible the institutional organization of the executive and legislative branches; they teach issues; they give insight into the differences of attitudes and values that divide society; they give a glimpse of the leadership on television; they cause people to talk to each other; and they offer the experience of membership in community and polity. As soon as one asks, for example, whether on-line voting will change all this, the importance of studying other aspects of the campaign—not just votes and vote intentions—becomes obvious.[8]

From a methodological viewpoint, this means that a good election study must be all but continuous, well grounded not only in public opinion, but also in political institutions. Within the campaign itself, the need for a combination of continuous monitoring of cross sections and panels is widely accepted (though not by all). Proposals to begin this monitoring even earlier and to extend it even later may sound convincing, but would require an altogether different kind of research design and data gathering, which could prove to be very expensive. The decision of whether or not to invest in such expanded monitoring depends on what kind of information one is seeking. That leads to the question of why undertake election studies in the first place.

What Are Election Studies Good For?

Each of the chapters in this volume—as well as several colloquium presentations that do not appear here—enumerates one or more of the uses of election studies. From the foregoing discussion, one of the most important contributions is the comparative study (over time and across societies) of political systems. Several other uses will also be considered.

The most obvious "use" is the provision of real-time feedback to the players involved—politicians, voters, and media. Politicians, of course, need to know how well they are doing among their constituencies. To illustrate the strength (and independence) of public opinion, one need only think of the importance of approval ratings, which preoccupy the leadership, almost as if elections were being held monthly. Lipset points to the saved presidency of Bill Clinton; if not for the polls, Clinton would not have survived the impeachment proceedings following the Lewinsky affair. More routinely, parties and the political establishment consume every bit of information available from polls. In addition to surveys, focus group research has been given a prominent place in election studies as a way to evaluate the public image of candidates, to critique advertising campaigns, and to assess the problems and issues that campaigns should address.[9]

Feedback to the electorate is another of the functions of real-time election polling. But different kinds of voters want different kinds of information, whether from the media or from the polls. In this connection, Blumler and McQuail distinguish among voters who follow the campaign for its interest as a contest— horse race is the term often used—and those who actually use campaign information for guidance in making decisions. Still other voters use this information to reinforce their prior opinions or to store information for use in a political argument.

Knowledge of the distribution of vote intentions during the course of a campaign may well affect voters' decisionmaking, although this proposition still needs much work. One such idea is the bandwagon effect, whereby voters are attracted to what is presented as the winning side or, in its cognitive version, strategic voting, which enables people to calculate which candidate is best situated to defeat the candidate they oppose. Johnston supplies a closely related example from the Canadian elections of 1993. Toward the close of that campaign, the defection of Conservative Party voters to the Reform and Liberal Parties was apparently accelerated by media coverage of this trend. "What changed," says Johnston, "was not so much Reform's actual strength as voters awareness of it."

Society at large—as distinct from its members—has an interest in the effects of immediate reporting on public attitudes toward a campaign. For example, is negative campaigning inducing cynicism? Are voters signaling low turnout because they perceive little difference between the parties? In the colloquium, Kathy Frankovic, director of the *New York Times*/CBS Poll, discussed election news polls as news, and the voter's right to follow the progress of the campaign.

Of course, most academic polls are reluctant to intervene during the course of a campaign, and even if they wished to do so, says Bartels, they are too slow to provide feedback to voters and to politicians until long after the campaign is over. Some of the colloquium speakers regretted this slowness. Academics show interest in (mostly commercial) campaign polling only as an object for study and as a source of possible influence. Yet it need not be so demeaning for academic voting research to consider playing this reflexive role as well. But most speakers showed little interest in providing the public with information in real time; academics have different ideas about what election studies are good for.

One thing is clear: election studies are good for science. The early Columbia studies, for example, debunked the image of the good citizen who retires to the quiet of his or her study on election eve, weighs the pros and cons of each candidate, and saunters out the next morning to express a well-considered decision at the polling place. According to the Columbia studies, this kind of citizen is far less likely to be interested in politics, or to follow the campaign in the media, than the neighbor whose mind was made up long before the campaign began.

Political scientists want to learn things about specific elections: What were the issues? Was the election a realignment, that is, were incumbents unseated after a long period in office and, if so, why? They also want to know how voters behaved during the campaign: Were there many or few changes of opinion, even if the aggregate change may show no change at all? What was the predominant factor, issue voting, candidate voting, or party voting? Is the decline in party loyalty still continuing? What is the predictive power of demographic variables, or are these—along with party loyalty—also continuing to wane? Did the introduction of primary voting reduce attention to the nominating convention? Regarding voter attentiveness and learning, what is the best format for televised presidential debates? Does seeing the "other" side up close undermine the kind of party loyalty that was based on exposure primarily to one's favored party? On a larger scale, what are the effects of different forms of campaign financing? All of these questions are also relevant for any society that wishes to optimize the potential of election campaigns for citizen learning, for experiencing attachment to the nation, for reaffirming the legitimacy of the system, and for policing fairness (as in the monitoring of political ads, free time for candidates, and so on).

Another measure of the worth of election studies is their contribution to more theoretical issues in the social sciences. These interests lie not so much in the campaign itself as in the opportunity it provides to exploit the extensive (and expensive) observations of individual and institutional behavior at a heightened moment. For example, the Columbia studies viewed election campaigns as a process of massive decisionmaking by individuals, that is, the process of forming and changing opinions and the influence of mass and interpersonal influence. These studies did not quite find what they were looking for—there was relatively little change in the electorate during campaigns of the 1940s, a time when party loyalty and demographics were predominant. In the course of analysis, however, they produced findings of enduring interest on the political homogeneity of primary groups, on the behavior of citizens under cross-pressures, on opinion leadership, and on the paradox of who is most influenced by campaign communications. The latter problem is still evident in the work of John Zaller (Chapter 9) and Jay Blumler. As the role of parties continues to decline and the role of the media increases, campaigns provide a major vantage point for investigating not only the direct influence of media on opinion but also the indirect influence via phenomena such as media analysis of campaign events ("spin"), media representations of the distribution of opinion, media forecasts that may produce "bandwagon effects" and "spirals of silence," or strategic "horse-race" coverage that may produce cynicism toward the electoral process. The interaction between media and candidates is also of great interest to Zaller and to Meyrowitz (1994). Other questions include how television has changed the practice and strategies of politics and how presidential debates provide insight into these processes.[10]

Elections also provide opportune moments for observing the workings of "imagined communities." The experience of nationhood is being altered by both individualism and globalism, and events such as elections—but also other major events—provide an opportunity to assess the extent and ways in which political ritual bolsters national identity (Shils, 1962). Opposing such ritual theories are theories of "rational choice," which posit that voting, and political participation more generally, is of very marginal value to the sentiments and interests of individual citizens. Data on voter turnout and other forms of political involvement are of direct relevance to such theoretical debates. How, for example, do rational choice partisans explain the fact that turnout for national elections is higher than turnout for local elections? Or alternatively, how do ritual theorists respond to Lipset's and Berelson et al.'s (1954) observation that economic and other dissatisfactions sharply (and dangerously?) increase voter turnout.[11]

The workings of the public sphere are also more easily accessed during the course of a political campaign. Who talks to whom, and where? Do people talk to those with opposing views, or only to those with whom they feel comfortable? Has influence within the home become more multilateral than it used to be? Do people avoid political talk even during campaigns, as Noelle-Neumann (1993), Eliasoph (1998), and Schudson (1997) might suggest? How then do such conversations crystallize opinions? Are public opinion polls the only mechanisms for aggregating opinion and feeding it back to the political establishment? All of these are applications of voting studies to questions that are more general than the elections themselves. One hears too little about them from voting researchers.

The same rule holds for methodological developments in matters such as questionnaire construction, sampling, and scaling, and in the design of methods to sort out the relative influence of different factors. Merrill Shanks (Chapter 7) does so in the case of political issues, the continuing thrust of the Michigan tradition. In this volume Johnston makes a major methodological contribution to the problem of continuous monitoring of election campaigns.

It is interesting—and sobering—to note that some of the theoretical and methodological suggestions made in these pages coincide, quite independently, with some of Peter Rossi's suggestions of forty years ago in his classic article "Four Landmarks in Voting Research" (1959). On the basis of his review of the pioneering early studies, Rossi suggested (1) that future studies worry less about representative sampling and more about research designs that will allow for the testing of hypotheses (e.g., an adequate case base of "changers"); (2) that sociometric data be incorporated into survey research as a measure of the influence of interpersonal relations in a participatory democracy; (3) that the panel design be expanded to include observations between elections; (4) that comparative data be assembled from off-year and local elections; and (5) that comparative data be gathered from communities (and perhaps even societies) with different political structures.

Organization of the Volume

This book naturally falls into two parts. The first part begins with William McGuire's overview of half a century of voting studies. Famous for imposing order on scientific disarray, McGuire maps the continuities and discontinuities in the history of election research, and offers a critical assessment of their theoretical and methodological achievements, failings, and prospects. Larry Bartels and Juan

Linz broaden these assessments by their insistence on context, that is, that "good" election studies can be made more meaningful by connecting them more explicitly to their institutional settings. Linz, like Arian and Shamir, and Johnston, provides data from other political systems to contrast with U.S. studies and to argue, in effect, that systems should be treated as "variables" for the purpose of studying the effects of different political cultures and electoral arrangements on voting behavior.[12]

The papers in the second part offer new insights into the workings of the four major sources of influence that have underlain empirical voting research from the beginning: demographics, parties, issues, and media. In his sketch of the earliest studies, Seymour Martin Lipset identifies their theoretical and methodological leanings and elaborates on the relationships among background factors, political party affiliation, and voting, pointing to Lazarsfeld's "index of political predispositions" as the pioneering example. Arian and Shamir also examine deep-seated ideological voting patterns in Israeli elections.

Working in the Michigan tradition, Merrill Shanks discusses the conceptual and methodological complexities of voters responding to a candidate's or party's stand on an issue (and, if so, whether the voter is aware of this response), or whether the prior inclinations of voters lead her or him to project congenial ideas on liked candidates. Richard Johnston shows how latent issues may be triggered during the course of a campaign, and how keeping close watch on a campaign can reveal how such agenda setting (intended or not) may result in reinstating a familiar equilibrium or, on occasion, instituting change.

The final two chapters address the role of the media in election campaigns. Jay Blumler and Denis McQuail focus on how mediated information is used by different kinds of voters, whereas Zaller's paper argues from the supply side that different kinds of candidate coverage reflect the needs of journalists to assert their own worth and independence in the power struggle among voters, candidates, parties, and the media.

Notes

1. The introduction in Norris (1998) describes the spread of voting studies, mostly inspired by the Michigan model.

2. The "funnel" in which Michigan studies array these variables is discussed by Bartels (Chapter 2) and Shanks (Chapter 7).

3. Peter Rossi's early comparison of these pioneering studies is a classic, to which we will return below (Rossi, 1959).

4. See the papers collected in Norris (1998); for earlier statements about the shift from party and demographic loyalties, see Nie, Verba, and Petrocik (1976, chap. 19), Miller (1976), and Pomper (1976).

5. That voting studies should address the question of why party organizations and party loyalties have declined was proposed decades ago by Miller (1976). The notion that television might be responsible for moving politics "inside" and for humanizing the "other" side is an often-voiced but not easily studied assertion (Norris, 1998; Nie et al., 1976; Katz and Feldman, 1962). Altogether, the relationship between party decline and the rise of television is debatable as is the fact of party decline (Polsby, 1983; Polsby and Orren, 1987; Putnam, 2000).

6. In her colloquium talk, Kathleen Frankovic suggested that comparing absentee voters (who vote early) with voters who vote on election day is a promising approach to studying campaign effects.

7. See the chapters on Institutional Context and Political Participation in Norris (1998).

8. For an early statement of this point see Katz (1971) and Bartels (Chapter 2) and McGuire (Chapter 1) in this volume.

9. Popkin (1991) deals with focus groups in his book and in the paper presented at our colloquium.

10. See the series of studies of presidential debates edited by Kraus (1962, 1976). The first volume contains the paper by Katz and Feldman.

11. These ostensibly different theories can be reconciled. Rational choice should join functional theories in predicting that high dissatisfaction should increase voter turnout.

12. In private conversation, Richard Johnston pointed to the paradox of considering the nuances of institutional differences while at the same time calling for cross-cultural comparisons. The more one treats the idiosyncracies of context, the less easy it is to group and compare contexts.

References

Berelson, Bernard R., Paul F. Lazarsfeld, and William N. McPhee. 1954. *Voting: A Study of Opinion Formation in a Presidential Campaign*. Chicago: University of Chicago Press.

Blumler, Jay G., and Denis McQuail. 1969. *Television in Politics: Its Uses and Influence*. London: Faber & Faber.

Campbell, Angus, Gerald Gurin, and Warren E. Miller. 1954. *The Voter Decides*. New York: Row, Peterson.

Campbell, Angus, Philip E. Converse, Warren E. Miller, and Donald E. Stokes. 1960. *The American Voter*. New York: Wiley.

Dayan, Daniel, and Elihu Katz. 1992. *Media Events: The Live Broadcasting of History*. Cambridge, Mass.: Harvard University Press.

Eliasoph, Nina. 1998. *Avoiding Politics: How Americans Produce Apathy in Everyday Life*. Cambridge, England: Cambridge University Press.

Katz, Elihu. 1971. "Platforms and Windows: Reflections on the Role of Broadcasting in the Israel Elections." *Journalism Quarterly* 48: 304–314.

Katz, Elihu, and Jacob J. Feldman. 1962. "The Debates in the Light of Research: A Survey of Surveys." In *The Great Debates: Background, Perspective, Effects,* Sidney Kraus, ed., pp. 173–223. Bloomington: Indiana University Press.

Kraus, Sidney, ed. 1962. *The Great Debates: Background, Perspective, Effects.* Bloomington: Indiana University Press.

Kraus, Sidney, ed. 1979. *The Great Debates: Carter vs. Ford, 1976.* Bloomington: Indiana University Press.

Lazarsfeld, Paul F., Bernard R. Berelson, and Hazel Gaudet. 1948. *The People's Choice: How the Voter Makes Up His Mind in a Presidential Campaign,* 2nd ed. (1st ed., 1944). New York: Columbia University Press.

Meyrowitz, Joshua. 1994. "Visible and Invisible Candidates: A Case Study in 'Competing Logics' of Campaign Coverage." *Political Communication* 11(April-June): 145–164.

Miller, Warren E. 1976. "The Challenges of Election Research." In *American Electoral Behavior: Change and Stability,* Samuel A. Kirkpatrick, ed. Beverly Hills, Calif.: Sage.

Nie, Norman, Sidney Verba, and John R. Petrocik. 1976. *The Changing American Voter.* Cambridge, Mass.: Harvard University Press.

Noelle-Neumann, Elizabeth. 1993. *Spiral of Silence: Public Opinion, Our Social Skin.* Chicago: University of Chicago Press.

Norris, Pippa. 1998. *Elections and Voting Behavior.* Aldershot, England: Ashgate Publishing Co. and Dartmouth Publishing Co.

Polsby, Nelson W. 1983. *Consequences of Party Reform.* New York: Oxford University Press.

Polsby, Nelson W. and Gary R. Orren, eds., *Media and Momentum.* Chatham: Chatham House.

Putnam, Robert D. 2000. Bowling Alone: *The Collapse and Revival of American Community.* New York: Simon & Schuster.

Pomper, Gerald M. 1976. "Impacts on the Political System." In *American Electoral Behavior,* Samuel A. Kirkpatrick, ed. Beverly Hills, Calif.: Sage.

Popkin, Samuel. 1991. *The Reasoning Voter: Communication and Persuasion in Presidential Campaigns,* 2nd ed. Chicago: University of Chicago Press.

Rossi, Peter. 1959. "Four Landmarks in Voting Research." In *American Voting Behavior,* Eugene Burdick and Arthur J. Brodbeck, eds., pp. 5–24. Glencoe, Ill.: Free Press.

Schudson, Michael. 1997. "Why Conversation Is Not the Soul of Democracy." *Critical Studies in Mass Communication* 14(December 4): 297–309.

Shils, Edward. 1962. *Political Development in the New States.* The Hague: Mouton.

Zaller, John. 2001. *A Theory of Media Politics: How the Interests of Politicians, Journalists and Citizens Shape the News.* Chicago: University of Chicago Press.

1

AFTER A HALF CENTURY OF ELECTION STUDIES: WHENCE, WHERE, AND WHITHER?

WILLIAM J. MCGUIRE

Yale University

Here in the free world there is a saying, "If it ain't broke don't fix it," which by a slightly invalid logical transformation becomes, "If everyone asks how it can be fixed there may be something wrong with it." The basic question addressed in this volume, "What are election studies good for?" suggests that they may be good for nothing, or at least may leave much room for improvement. If election studies have not contributed all that has been hoped, in what ways have they been disappointing and how might they be improved?

The Nature of Our Present Discontents

Three shortcomings of election studies that bother students of the topic are epitomized by three popular T-shirt captions that one sees in souvenir shops. The first caption is the world-weary "Been there, done that." The initial studies of the U.S. presidential elections by the Columbia University sociology team were exciting, both the Erie County (Sandusky) study of the 1940 Roosevelt versus Wilkie election (Lazarsfeld et al., 1944) and the Elmira study of the 1948 Truman versus Dewey election (Berelson et al., 1954). However, in subsequent decades as the University of Michigan's Survey Research

Center and other teams published research on subsequent U.S. presidential elections, their studies appeared progressively more repeti-
tious, making only small advances such as the tripartite analysis of
voting determinants into party identification, issue stands, and candidate attractiveness. Current proposals for new studies are wont to
elicit a "been there, done that" disenchantment.

A second cautionary T-shirt caption, "That was then. This is
now," reminds us that election realities have been constantly
changing since those 1940s founding studies so that findings
quickly become irrelevant or obsolescent. Successive waves of researchers must play a new ball game but they always seem to be
preparing to study the last election. There results little cumulative
knowledge, with earlier studies quickly becoming of little relevance
beyond historical interest. Future studies need to be completely re-
cast if they are to be relevant to the new conditions. As one astute
political philosopher put it: The times they are a-changing. When
the founding studies of the 1940s elections were conducted, there
was little television and few state primaries, national nominating
conventions played a major role, campaigning was done from the
back of railroad trains, and voters had strong attachments to parties. In the 1940s, elections were studied as interesting in themselves; now elections serve as opportunities for basic research investigating theoretical and methods topics such as agenda setting,
question wording, and negative campaigning; or, at the other extreme, for their practical "how to" prescriptions for devising winning campaigns.

Disappointment with election studies is poignantly captured by a
third T-shirt caption, "My mom went to London and all she
brought me back is this lousy T-shirt." Some interesting findings
have emerged from the half century of election studies, but their
yield is disappointing considering that highly talented researchers
are involved, that they have sufficient time, experience, and organization to plan their studies systematically, and that the studies are
funded generously by social science standards. Illustrative of the
modest yield is that the most thoroughly studied topic in the election studies, the effect of television and other mass media on voting
participation and partisanship, has demonstrated only marginally
small impacts. In general, even obvious hypotheses have often not
been confirmed and few surprising relations have emerged from

elections studies considering how much effort has been put into them for the past half century.

Historical Overview of Election Studies

Studies of the 1940 and 1948 elections by the Columbia school (Lazarsfeld et al., 1944; Berelson et al., 1954) constitute the heroic age of election research, when pioneers carried out demanding tasks that might not have been attempted had the tasks' difficulty been appreciated at the outset. The questions asked were seldom surprising and the answers seldom convincing but (like the dog walking on its hind legs) readers should be impressed that these pioneer studies got done at all. Illustrative of the early findings was the Lazarsfeld Index of Political Predisposition (IPP). From independent variables like the citizens' demographics (class, religion, residence) and conflicts (social or ideological), effects were predicted on mediating variables such as campaign exposure and cross-pressures, and thence on dependent variables like participation in the election and partisanship as regards which candidate received the vote. For example, cross-pressured voters' partisanship—ranging from monolithic support of one party, through conflicted support, to monolithic support for the other party—has a nonmonotonic U-shaped relation to participation as measured by early decision or probability of voting. Foreshadowing the following half century of research findings (or nonfindings), these pioneers found surprisingly little evidence that the presidential mass media campaigns (for all their sound and fury, then as now) had appreciable effects on the choice of candidate. Lipset (Chapter 4 in this volume) discusses this Columbia/Lazarsfeld election research in more detail.

In the half century since those founding studies additional relations have been discovered but they seem less impressive, perhaps due to frustration of rising expectations. Starting with the first Eisenhower versus Stevenson contest in 1952 and continuing through the 1992 Clinton versus Bush election, teams of researchers at the University of Michigan's Survey Research Center were dependably studying each quadrennial U.S. presidential election (e.g., Campbell et al., 1954; Miller and Shanks, 1996). The concentration of social science resources and publications on these full-scale election studies probably peaked in the years around 1970, although good volumes on the genre continue to appear (Weisberg and Box-Steffensmeier, 1999). The timeline of this enthusiasm can be traced in various works. Regarding the successive editions of the *Handbook of Social Psychology,* the proportion of space devoted to election studies went up from the 1935 to the 1954 and again to the 1968 editions, and then dropped in the 1985 and still further in the 1998 edition. McGuire (1993) describes the history of the field of political psychology as consisting of three twenty-year waves, each wave with its preferred topics, theoretical explanations, and methods: (1) a political personality era in the 1940s and 1950s; (2) a political attitudes and voting behavior era in the 1960s and 1970s using survey research (the era when these election studies dominated the political psychology field); and (3) a 1980s and 1990s era when election studies were replaced on center stage by a growing interest in political cognition and ideology.

Although election studies may no longer be the dominant focus of political psychology research, they still elicit healthy interest, increasingly taking the form not of full-scale studies of individual U.S. presidential elections but of testing minitheories by secondary analysis of archival data on presidential, congressional, or primary elections (Zaller, 1992; Mutz et al., 1996; McGuire, 1998). If a fine and representative example of the heroic age in the 1940s is Lazarsfeld's research on the Index of Political Predispositions, a similarly fine and representative example of current election research now, a half century later, is Zaller's (1992, 1996) Exposure Gap/Crosscutting Model. Both Lazarsfeld et al. (1944) and Zaller (1996) grant that there is only weak empirical evidence that campaigns have massive effects in changing voters' preferences among candidates. Lazarsfeld was resigned to the "law" of minimal effect: campaigns may not directly convert many (except perhaps a few opinion leaders), but media campaigns do encourage the already committed to keep the faith and turn out to vote. Zaller (1996), with more powerful analytic tools and a greater bank of archival data, theorizes more strongly that in special conditions campaigns can convert sizable numbers of voters to switch between challengers and incumbents.

A history of election studies should at least touch on the history of communication research, because they were born contemporaneously in the 1940s and their subject matters overlap considerably (e.g., their central shared topic is how the mass media affect voting behavior). Despite this high potential for interchange, the two lines of inquiry developed surprisingly independently. Lazarsfeld and Elihu Katz in the United States and Hilde Himmelweit in Great Britain were rare exceptions in making substantial contributions to both fields. Most of the communication researchers (e.g., Schramm, Shannon, Lewin, Hovland, Rogers, and N. Maccoby) did not get involved in election studies, and most of the election researchers (e.g., A. Campbell, Lipset, P. E. Converse, W. E. Miller, and Nie) were from disciplines other than communications and did not engage heavily in other areas of communication research. In recent years, however, there has been more collaboration between the two disciplines. A number of useful volumes on the history of communication research have recently appeared (Rogers, 1994; Dennis and Wartella, 1996; Schramm, 1997).

Change of Direction During the Fifty Years of Election Studies

Changes in election studies during the half century since their 1940s launch have been modest to a fault (as reflected in the "Been there, done that" complaint), but there have been some changes in direction that are worth mentioning because they are probably selective improvements and may indicate future directions (projecting past trends being one of the less objectionable ways to forecast future innovations). How election studies have evolved since the classic 1940s research will be described in terms of their changes on five dimensions in order of increasing importance: (1) geographic changes in centers of scholarship; (2) changes in the disciplinary affiliations of the researchers; (3) changes in publication modes; (4) changes in preferred variables; and (5) changes in general strategies for studying elections. Lipset (in Chapter 4 of this volume) also describes historical changes in election studies.

Changes in Geographic Centers

Full-scale empirical election studies were begun at Columbia University in New York in the 1940s by a team and in a setting that grew into the Bureau of Applied Social Research, consisting of Paul Lazarsfeld and his talented collaborators. That such a social science flourishing began at that time and in New York City is not surprising, considering the concentration of social movements and talent in the city during the depression, and the jump-start given by the influx of Central European intellectual refugees from National Socialism, including Lazarsfeld.

Interest and effort soon spread to many centers across the United States and some in Europe, especially concentrated in the "Big Ten" great state universities in the U.S. Midwest. In the next decade leadership passed to the University of Michigan at Ann Arbor, its numero uno status sustained by its excellent Survey Research Center. While many other social science research innovations thrived in the Far West, at least in California, election studies were slower to flourish there, it being difficult to take seriously the politics practiced there, three thousand miles from the ocean. Other research teams with similar orientations have routinely published scholarly volumes on each U.S. presidential election since 1976 (Pomper, 1997) or 1980 (Abrahamson et al., 1998), the latter including studies of congressional elections as well.

Changes in Disciplines

The disciplines from which students of elections came were also changing. During the heroic age of the 1940s, sociologists predominated in part because of the historical accident that founding father Paul Lazarsfeld, although a methodologist with a doctorate in mathematics, was appointed to Columbia University's Sociology Department along with Robert Merton, so the two would preserve the methodology/theory balance in the department. Political scientists might seem to be the natural cadre for conducting election studies but in the 1940s and 1950s their primary efforts were focused on political personality research (McGuire, 1993) on both the macro (national character) and micro (psychobiography) levels (Runyon, 1993). In recent decades those with political science and communication backgrounds are becoming more predominant in the field (Iyengar and McGuire, 1993; Miller and Shanks, 1996; Mutz et al., 1996).

Changes in Modes of Publication

During the 1940s and 1950s, election studies were done by teams who attempted to provide an inclusive picture of an individual presidential election, covering each of the traditional topics, and so the results were appropriately published as book volumes. Recently reports are more likely to come out as journal articles or chapters in edited books reporting results on specific issues, often across multiple elections. While the Columbia University Bureau of Applied Social Research published almost as many books as articles, the later Michigan Institute for Social Research published five times as many articles as books (J. M. Converse, 1987). The shift to article publication may be symptomatic of a discipline's analytical maturing. The "one election, one book" tradition continues to fill a need, however, and has been kept up in several series that review each quadrennial election (Pomper, 1997; Abrahamson et al., 1998).

This change in publication packaging is probably due to two factors. Firstly, the earlier studies tended to be relatively atheoretical, their main intellectual contributions being descriptive tours of the horizon of an individual election, rounding up in successive chapters the usual topics as they played out in that election. Secondly, it has become more affordable for the individual researcher to conduct theory-oriented hypothesis-testing research suitable for journal article publication by using the increasing availability of standardized data deposited in social data archives (e.g., content analysis of mass media political campaigns, voting statistics not only from a national sample of voters in presidential elections but also on numerous congressional elections and even primaries, and information on demographics for each election district, sometimes with time-series data that lend themselves to causal models). These archives make it affordable for individual researchers to do secondary analyses to test hypotheses that can be reported expeditiously in journal articles and so reach a wider audience of basic researchers who work on topics other than elections.

Changes in Popular Variables

Newly emerging practical concerns and theoretical issues have shifted the popularity of variables, including independent variables (e.g., from demographics to media exposure), dependent variables (e.g., from voting participation to issue salience), and mediating explanatory variables (e.g., from cross-pressures to political involvement). The final sections of this chapter will return to further shifts in favorite variables likely to dominate future election studies.

Changes in General Strategies for Studying Elections

Over a half-dozen general strategies for studying elections have enjoyed popularity, either throughout the half century of voting research or at least for a briefer interval. Their succession does not represent progressive evolutionary replacement of poorer by superior methods; rather, the several strategies occupy different niches, each reemerging when especially suitable for some new research enthusiasm. All of these strategies have promise for certain purposes in future election studies. The utilization of one or another approach has often been determined by accidental availability, particularly in the early, poorly funded studies. For example, Lazarsfeld adapted his study of the 1940 election to take advantage of funds available for a commercial study of potential refrigerator buyers, moonlighting to collect election data by asking the fridge interviewees additional political questions.

The Panel Study Approach.   The strategy of choice in the pioneering Columbia studies of elections and political influence (Lazarsfeld et al., 1944; Berelson et al., 1954; Katz and Lazarsfeld, 1955) was survey research using a demanding repeated-wave panel design, which provided some chance of identifying if, when, and why individuals changed their voting intentions during the presidential campaign. These time-series measurements of each individual imposed a high sampling cost that panel researchers partially mitigated by using, not a nationwide sample, but a sample within a single, nondescript community chosen for its undistinguished typicality or accidental availability (e.g., Erie County, Ohio; Elmira, New York; Decatur, Illinois), even at the cost of requiring hazardous generalization of parochially found relations to the nation as a whole. Compromises had to be made for economy (e.g., using self-nominations to measure who influenced whom). Reassuringly, these compromises have usually yielded findings robust enough to replicate in subsequent studies employing more representative samples, better measures, and improved techniques.

The Nationwide Sample Approach.   The second wave of election studies, dominated by the University of Michigan (e.g., Campbell et al., 1954, 1960, 1966, studying the 1952–1960 presidential elections and exploiting the resources and sophistication of the Survey Research Center), used an alternative national sampling strategy that facilitated geographic generalizability, but at the cost of losing the repeated-measures information on individual voters provided by the panel study. Better funded, these later studies could use repeated-measure subpanels and could oversample groups of special interest (e.g., ethnic minorities). Diffusion of telephone subscriptions even to economically impoverished people in the second half of the twentieth century made possible the use of random-digit telephone dialing rather than face-to-face interviews by little old ladies and gents in tennis shoes. This advance avoided intolerable sample distortion, making nationwide sampling of interviewees economically feasible.

Approaches Using Secondary Analysis of Data in Social Archives. A third strategy emerged in the 1960s as the usefulness of social data archives became sufficiently recognized to elicit the establishment and funding of interuniversity consortia to organize the effort. Among the first data to be archived and made available in standardized form were those central to election studies, including measures of dependent variables like voting behaviors and independent variables like demographics and media content and exposure. Organizing such data by census tracts or electoral precincts made possible macro analyses using the tracts as units of sampling, thus supplementing the conventional micro analyses based on individual voters. As these social data archives accumulate more time-series data, increasingly sophisticated multivariable causal analyses become feasible. For example, the National Election Study makes conveniently available good data not only on U.S. presidential elections but also on 100 to 150 congressional election districts going back 40 years. This archival resource has increased the feasibility of the secondary analysis strategy for studying elections, in conjunction with causal, structural equation modeling of longitudinal archived political data (Nie et al., 1976; Miller and Shanks, 1996). The latter allows one to test a large set of hypotheses that assume alternative causal pathways, and to use data on naturally covarying variables.

Correlational Approaches Using Convenience Samples. Election researchers using the three strategies just described all made laborious if not always successful sampling efforts to obtain relations that were generalizable to the national (or other specified) population; or at least they called attention to their failure to do so. Social psychologists, whose routine use of convenience sampling has resulted in their discipline sometimes being called "the study of the college sophomore," often use a fourth general strategy: studying hypothesized relations by intercorrelating chronic scores on the variables obtained by the students in a conveniently available class. An example is testing the "people positivity" hypothesis that evaluations of political leaders are more polarized than evaluations of political parties, that is, leaders are more liked or disliked than are the parties that they lead (see Chapter 3 in this volume and Sears, 1983).

To test this hypothesis a researcher might have students in a college classroom rate their liking for prominent party leaders and for the parties they lead. Although these college students may not be typical of the general population regarding their scores on one or the other variables, generalization is still valid if the sampled group is representative of the population regarding the relation between the variables. It is dangerous to assume such representativeness, as is shown by the finding that the people positivity prediction is confirmed in the United States, where party ties tend to be weak, but tends to reverse (with liking more polarized for parties than for leaders) in countries like Sweden and the Netherlands, where parties are more ideologically distinct and evoke more affect than do individual politicians (Granberg and Holmberg, 1990). Johnston (Chapter 6 in this volume) discusses further how relations among political variables can differ between countries, even those as similar as Canada and the United States.

Variable-Manipulation (Laboratory) Approaches. A fifth general strategy is to study political hypotheses by manipulational studies that call for selecting a sample and then randomly assigns its members to levels on the independent variable (not by measuring their chronic level on that variable as in the "correlational" strategy, but rather by random assignment to conditions that determine their levels on the independent variable). This manipulational strategy is more artificial than the correlational (chronic, natural level) strategy but it lessens confounding and provides more information about the causal direction of any obtained relation between the variables. The manipulational (acute level) strategy tends to be used in laboratory situations, but in principle it can be used in the field as well. For example, there tends to be a positive relation between the dominant attitudes and interests of the members of a community and the attitudes and interests covered in that community's mass media. The causal direction that accounts for this correlation could go in either or both directions, either in an "agenda-setting" direction such that media emphasis on issues establishes their salience for the community members, or in the opposite causal direction, such that the media adopts the interests or attitudes of their subscribing publics.

To resolve the causal-direction ambiguity, Iyengar and Kinder (1987) conducted a field study that manipulated among different groups of the public how much media coverage they received of various issues; they found an effect in the agenda-setting direction. Masters and Sullivan (1993) report a laboratory manipulational study of nonverbal behavior in cognitive and affective political information processing. Such manipulational strategies, after being relatively neglected in the first half century of political research, will probably become a more popular (although still secondary) approach in coming election studies because of their power to control by randomization and to clarify causal directions that other research strategies tend to leave ambiguous.

Macro Approaches Using Groups as Units of Sampling. In contrast to the preceding micro approaches, all of which use the individual person as the unit to be measured, this sixth general approach uses groups (e.g., nations or census tracts) as the units observed and measured on the variables. Such macro approaches are likely to be used increasingly in political studies as national and regional social data archives become fuller and better organized. The third general approach in our list here, secondary analysis, also uses archival data but uses it on the micro level with the individual voter serving as the unit of sampling. The macro strategy uses archival social data on larger units, typically looking for cross-national differences that reveal the relation between political variables. For example, Lipset (1960) measured Latin American nations regarding how the degree of crosscutting of their subgroup differences related to how democratic their political systems are; Almond and Verba (1963) measured how national differences on a variety of social variables affected voting rate and other political participation scores.

"Media Event" Approaches. Dayan and Katz (1992) developed a seventh general strategy that will probably receive more usage in future electoral studies. This approach postulates that even if the general public have become satiated and disenchanted with ordinary events depicted on the mass media and are no longer much affected by the usual range of media contents, there are occasional surprising or even expected sensational actual occurrences or fictional entertainment shows that have sizable impacts, even on a generally jaundiced public. The availability of time-series social statistics (e.g., crime levels, suicide rates) and social survey data in archives is making this strategy more cost-effective. For example, Phillips (1982, 1983) studied how broadcasts of violent events like heavyweight champion prize fights affect crime rates in the public, and how the suicide of a character on a popular daytime television serial affects national suicide rates; however, these analyses can be treacherous (Kessler and Stipp, 1984).

How popular television fictional miniseries (like *Roots* or *The Holocaust*) or factual news stories (like "Sadat in Jerusalem") have affected political attitudes has also been studied. The effects may be indirect: for example, showing *The Holocaust* miniseries on West German television may not have moved the public to oppose a statute of limitations on war crimes, but worry that it might so affect the public may have influenced Bundestag members to refrain from legislating such a limitation. Regarding U.S. presidential campaigns, the best-studied predictable media events have been the "Great Debates" between the major party presidential candidates, which since the 1960 (Kennedy versus Nixon) election have been televised in almost all subsequent quadrennial elections (Kraus, 1999; Jamieson and Birdsell, 1987). It is harder to study the effects of less predictable media events such as an unexpected scandal involving one of the candidates or how the incumbent responds to a sudden crisis (e.g., terrorist hostage takings). In studying the effects of media events (especially unexpected ones), it may be useful to examine the news media's procedures for covering such crises or to set up a standby "disaster" panel of researchers experienced in methods and theorizing about such occurrences. These experts would be ready to spring into theoretical and empirical action when a media event occurs. There are other general strategic approaches that could be used in election studies, for example, theory-guided meta-analyses of past studies.

Why Study Elections?
What Is Voting Research Good For?

Considering that for over a half century talented researchers have conducted a vast number of election studies (particularly on the quadrennial U.S. presidential elections), we can hope and expect that there have been substantial yields, some planned and others fortuitous, some enhancing our understanding of elections in themselves and others using elections to clarify and explain some broader characteristics of persons or society, some being applied research designed to guide societal practices, and some being basic research to clarify theoretical issues arising in liberal arts disciplines. Both applied and basic research (especially the latter) provide guidance on a general, abstract level; in addition, election studies have yielded more concrete "how-to" information that provides guidance for fine-tuning current election campaigns or for designing future ones. Each of these three types of contributions (abstract practice relevant, abstract theory relevant, and concrete how-to) deserve at least brief illustration here.

Contributions to Applied Issues:
Elections as Intrinsically Interesting

The founding midcentury election studies by the Columbia University team, focused on voting in the 1940 and 1948 U.S. presidential contests, were presented as applied contributions. Lazarsfeld and his colleagues regarded presidential campaigns and the elections in which they culminated as social occurrences of sufficient importance and interest such that a better understanding of them was an end in itself that justified the research, and not just a useful context in which to study some basic theoretical issues, although some basic issues were elucidated in these early studies (e.g., decisionmaking and the role of interpersonal and intrapersonal cross-pressures on the citizen's level of political participation). The young Lazarsfeld had spent a great amount of time and effort in the 1930s and 1940s in Austria and the United States raising research funds, and the funds that trickled in came mainly (except for some Rockefeller Foundation grants) from commercial firms to support applied research relevant to marketing their goods and services. Hence, when Lazarsfeld set up an organization at Columbia to administer and broaden the

Radio/Election research (Lazarsfeld and Stanton, 1941, 1944, 1949) he was insistent for tactical reasons to call it the Bureau of Applied Social Research, despite the strong preferences of some colleagues to omit the "Applied" and despite Lazarsfeld's being personally less interested in applied than in theoretical and methodological issues.

Considering that by midcentury America had become a "super-power," that the U.S. president played an increasingly decisive role in laying down and executing U.S. policy, and that the peculiar election process by which presidents are selected is not well understood, it is not surprising that presidential elections were believed to have sufficient practical interest to justify close study. Other social influence processes, like advertising and mass media consumption, which are of far less practical and theoretical interest than presidential elections, receive far more research attention. The U.S. presidential election remains an event of world importance, still mystifying and consequential enough to justify a high level of research. Learning how advertising works and when and why it is particularly effective are questions of practical importance even when the ads studied are designed only to sell soap. When studying political advertising to elect U.S. presidents, the importance of understanding the process of persuasive communication is multiplied by the importance of the subject matter being studied.

Contributions to the Clarification of Basic Theoretical Issues

Election studies have also served as a useful tool in basic research. A wide variety of theoretical issues about the person and society can be investigated conveniently and meaningfully in the context of election studies. Voting studies have a good track record for yielding theoretical advances on basic processes as varied as communication effects, the nature of social influence, person perception, group processes, and the structure of ideology. They have also made notable advances on diverse methodological issues such as sampling, attitude scaling, questionnaire construction, interviewer effects, causal analysis, and mathematical models. Examples of such basic research contributions are described in this volume. Basic research yields are likely to accelerate because those engaged in election studies are becoming more aware of these possibilities and more sophisticated in exploiting them.

An example of a basic research advance is the question of positive/negative asymmetry, which has received renewed attention since the "framing" concept proposed in Tversky and Kahneman's (1981) prospect theory, the Peeters et al. (1992) work on positivity biases, and the McGuire and McGuire (1992) investigation of cognitive versus affective positivity. The traditional "retrospective voting" theory, which states that in good economic times incumbents do well in elections and in hard times voters tend to throw the rascals out, provides an opportunity to study positivity asymmetries by testing whether there is a negativity bias such that bad times contribute to incumbents' ouster more than good times help their reelection (Ansolabehere and Iyengar, 1995). In this volume, Shanks (Chapter 7), Lipset (Chapter 4), and Linz (Chapter 3) all discuss this retrospective voting, economic determinism theorizing. Future election studies can also test whether positivity asymmetries interact with the cosmopolitan–local issue (i.e., the extent to which negativity bias in retrospective voting is more pronounced for personally experienced economic distress like loss of one's own job or for national economic trends like a stock market crash or a widespread economic depression). Another such issue is whether the election outcome is more affected by the economy's absolute level or direction of change. The positive/negative asymmetry question can be further pursued by examining the effects of positive versus negative political advertising, for example, the impact on voting participation and partisanship of praising one's own side versus criticizing the opposition (Lemert et al., 1999).

Organizational problems need to be solved if the basic research potential of election studies is to be fully exploited. The substantive and methodological issues that could be efficiently advanced come from a wide range of social science disciplines (e.g., political science, psychology, sociology, and communication) and from diverse subdisciplines in each. The varied basic researchers whose topics could be studied in election research are seldom familiar with this type of work and will tend to be shy about asking relative strangers who conduct election studies to modify their procedures (e.g., by adding dependent-variable measures or independent-variable manipulations to the design) in order to make the election study more pertinent to specified basic research issues. Hence, election researchers might usefully take the initiative in proposing collaboration. If election studies are to test hypotheses with basic theoretical relevance, we must also shift our focus from relatively exciting but rare presidential elections to the more numerous congressional and state and local elections, thus allowing replication, estimates of residual (error) variance, and effect size.

Election Study Contributions of a "How-To" Type

Some election research is blatantly partisan, done on a commercial basis to collect proprietary information that provides specific ad hoc guidance to one faction in an ongoing or anticipated election. Most of this commercial research, whose uses have been discussed by Kathleen Frankovic (2000), involves attitude surveys. However, additional techniques are or could be used, such as having focus groups select among political ads in rough copy, using audience data to decide on optimal media mix, doing surveys to get guidance on selecting a running mate, determining what issues to stress (and even, if one can bear it, which side to take on them), and choosing geographic areas or demographic sectors on which to focus.

Ivory tower scholars may wonder if such partisan election studies are uses or misuses of social science research. Such uses in a market economy can be justified as doing one's job (and even boasted about and admired when well done) for all one's worry that it may be unfair when one side (usually the incumbent) has far more campaign funds to buy such expertise and information, or that it results in candidates' incurring obligations to big contributors, or in candidates' devoting too much time to fund-raising, or to concentrating on winning the office to the neglect of what to do in office, or to giving disproportionate influence to some sectors of society (e.g., the gun industry or superstar entertainers). Other objections are that these almost daily reports of poll results by contestants and the media add to the perception of elections as sporting events and can distort the outcome by promoting bandwagon effects (although these may be partially balanced by underdog sympathy effects). Frankovic has pointed out as a possible public benefit in current alienated society that the publication of polls enhances the interest and knowledge of the lonely voter.

Inevitably, a small research cadre of political consultants has arisen who offer to use social science research (as well as their creative genius) to help candidates win elections. Entry to this election guru profession still seems to be gained by on-the-job apprenticeship, but it is likely that soon many universities will offer advanced degrees, perhaps as a specialty in MBA marketing programs, that will provide credentials to those wishing to enter the election-research profession with more qualification than "Do polls; will travel" (Adams, 1999; Newman, 1999; Perlmutter, 1999).

"How-to" guidance for winning elections also comes as unintended practical fallout from basic research by academics who typically have some ambivalence about turning out such consumer goods. Some basic researchers are surprised and annoyed to discover that practitioners have used a first- or second-hand acquaintance with their abstract findings to distill rigid rules of thumb (e.g., maxims like "people don't vote for candidates but against candidates"; "better ignore a charge than answer it"; and "negative campaigning reduces turnout and so helps incumbents"), rules that the researcher thinks should be qualified by many contextual interaction variables. Those who are annoyed when their research is used to sell soap tend to be even more perturbed when it is used to sell politicians, especially ones whom the researcher dislikes. Such partisan applications of election studies have become more tolerated as elections in America have become increasingly viewed as a national sport (Farley, 1938; McGinness, 1969), so that it is permissible and even praiseworthy to work for the home team or the team that pays one's salary (Sabato, 1981). In such a climate, having one's research used by the wrong side may come to be seen as better than its not being used at all. Some blame the sports style in which the media covers the campaign (in terms of who is ahead rather than who should be ahead) for promoting both the public's and the candidates' sense of politics as a game in which the objective is to win the office without necessarily knowing what to do with the victory (success being counted sweetest by those who ne'er succeed).

Promising Independent Variables for Use in Election Studies

The conceptual space of a research domain such as election studies can be mapped out in terms of the process and product, that is, the methods used and the substantive content produced. The content consists of the relations among relevant variables, including independent, mediational, interactional, and dependent, the mediational typically used to explain the relation that allows prediction from the independent to the dependent variable. Variables in each of these categories can be reviewed either descriptively or prescriptively, that is, either descriptively by discussing variables whose relations have been most frequently investigated in past election studies or prescriptively by listing the neglected variables whose relations deserve investigation in future studies. I shall review each of the variable types in turn, for each type first listing the variables frequently studied in past research and then listing neglected but promising variables, those understudied in past elections compared to their potential yield and so most deserving of inclusion in future studies.

In considering the independent variables that best predict political cognitions, attitudes, and behaviors, I shall review nine categories, starting with those most studied and ending with the independent variables undeservingly neglected: (1) voters' demographics; (2) voters' mass media exposure; (3) their reference groups; (4) voter predilection variables; (5) candidates' personal characteristics; (6) campaign material tailored to the individual voter; (7) content analyses of campaign materials; (8) current historical conditions; and (9) art and rituals. Here space allows only cryptic description of the most popular independent variables in each of the nine categories.

Voter Demographics as Independent Variables

From the earliest to the most recent election studies voter demographics (sex, age, class, geography, ethnicity, etc.) have been routinely measured and evaluated even when the study's theorizing does not predict their relation to participation (voting rate) or partisanship (party or candidate preference). Demographics are relevant to all three types of contributions (practical applications, basic research, and how-to) and have several assets that contribute to their popularity. Firstly, characteristics like age and sex are powerful individual difference variables that tend to account for a lot of the variance on a wide range of humanly and socially relevant variables including voting behavior, even when not explicitly predicted to do so. Secondly, demographic characteristics tend to be easily and reliably measured (e.g., the voter's sex can be measured with almost perfect reliability and validity in a few seconds, either by self-report or by observer rating). Thirdly, finding relations between demographics and voting (e.g., between voter's sex and preferred presidential candidate) usually has practical implications for how to run an election campaign.

Regarding more analytical, basic research criteria, demographics have the serious limitation of being ambiguous. Sex or ethnicity tends to be embedded in a complex of other variables, any one of which could account for the gross relation that shows up between the demographic and political variables. If ethnicity is found to be related to voting turnout, is it due to differences between ethnic groups in culture, socioeconomic status, preferred language, education level, genetic endowment, access to polling places, or ingroup or outgroup pressures? Getting direct measures of these possible mediators and doing covariance analysis can reduce such ambiguities. Demographic variables are (and should be) generally included in the experimental design of election studies because of their low measurement cost and high relational yield, but the theoretical interpretation of their relation to voting behaviors should be recognized as ambiguous until resolved by more complex experimental designs and analyses.

Concerning the practical utility in guiding the design of specific election campaigns, demographic relations are more valuable. For example, finding a pronounced sex difference in preference for opposing candidates, whatever its theoretical meaning, has useful implications for focusing the campaign's get-out-the-vote effort, for publicizing endorsements from the displeased sex, and for emphasizing their issues. Basic researchers will want to follow up by further probing, perhaps by use of both reactive and open-ended questions to identify reasons for the sex difference (e.g., are men and women concerned about different issues, or do they have different preferences on given issues, or do they have different perceptions of candidates' positions or character?).

Mass Media as Independent Variables

The mass media campaigns mounted by the opposing candidates are of particular interest to basic and applied researchers and practitioners because interesting media variables likely to affect the election outcome are easy to manipulate. Indeed, the media campaigns are probably regarded as the most important single factor in affecting the election outcome (or at least second only to which candidates are nominated). Much of the major party campaign is currently presented via the mass media, including paid advertisements, news reports, and public service programs such as interviews and debates.

The Columbia University founding studies of presidential elections in the 1940s were carried out before the pervasive entry of television but even these early studies were much concerned with effects of the then-dominant media, radio and newspapers. With the diffusion of television sets in the following decades, students of elections have directed an even greater proportion of their efforts into studying the purported impact of the mass media, perhaps disproportionately studying television. Indeed, candidate selection may itself be largely determined by the potential nominees' perceived television personality and ability.

The most surprising finding of the last half century of election research is that the demonstrated effects of media exposure on election outcomes have been so modest. So much campaigning is done on television that one would expect more impact to have been found. McGuire (1986) proposed dozens of excuses that would allow one to keep the faith in pervasive massive media effects despite the weakness of the empirical results. Five categories of such excuses include: methods excuses (e.g., poor measures of variables and relations, poor control of extraneous variables); excuses regarding prevailing conditions (e.g., media clutter, mutual cancellation); fallback excuses that massive effects do occur but only in highly susceptible subgroups (e.g., children, opinion leaders); or only under special conditions (e.g., new modes of communicating, media events); or occur as indirect effects (e.g., two-step flow, agenda setting).

One wonders if even this plethora of excuses justifies keeping the faith in massive media effects considering that in the dozen best-studied areas of purported effects, both intended (e.g., commercial ads, public service announcements) and unintended effects (e.g., media violence, social stereotypes), massive effects have seldom been found (McGuire, 1986). True Believers in the media might argue that social scientists generally have difficulty detecting societal effects, but in this area often the best-done studies yield the slightest effect (although the advent of meta-analysis may have yielded a social science method so sensitive that no relation is so small that it will fail to be significantly confirmed). Effects of television (and perhaps of other media) have been found, sometimes even at conventionally accepted levels of significance, but usually with very modest effect sizes. McQuail and Blumler (Chapter 8 in this volume) discuss more fully the disappointing yield of the mass communication research and how it might be improved. Future election studies should not depend on the assumption that somehow routine methods will eventually serve to demonstrate massive effects. Perhaps there should be a retreat to a more conservative position (e.g., that election campaigns do not in general produce massive effects but can be seen in certain special conditions such as primaries but not elections, for challengers but not incumbents) or a focus on special groups of voters (e.g., those with high need cognition or the naive), but past efforts even along these lines have found only modest effects. Perhaps indirect effects can be picked up by use of neglected methods, for example, tapping sociometric networks to show influence flow, or using open-ended probes to tap what issues are spontaneously salient in the voters' decisionmaking processes, or refining the exposure independent-variable measure by a content analysis of the campaign material, as described in Zaller (1996). More effort might be put into studying media other than television (e.g., direct mail) or into neglected aspects of the television content (e.g., the effects of "objective" news programs rather than of explicitly partisan political ads).

Reference and Membership Groups as Independent Variables

The early election studies gave considerable attention to the effects on voting of a third class of independent variables, the citizens' membership and reference groups. Despite early findings of sizable effects of groups, subsequent studies have paid less attention to these interpersonal variables, possibly because of a suspicion that many of the voters' traditional groups (e.g., the family, labor unions) are becoming marginalized in society. The early studies focused primarily on the family, nuclear and extended, of origin and of procreation, and secondarily on friends and coworkers. High parent-offspring and husband-wife correlations in voting behavior have been found, but there is ambiguity regarding the extent to which this represents reciprocal indoctrination (social influence by discussion within the household) or the exposure of all members of a given family to similar pressures. This ambiguity of meaning (plus researchers' suspicion that society is growing more anomic, especially regarding the traditional family) may account for loss of interest in these group variables. However, the magnitude of the relations usually found suggests that more work should be put into conceptualizing and evaluating how such personal relationships and interactions affect voting behavior, taking into account historical changes in the relative importance in society of various reference and membership groups, particularly a shift from family to peer influence in the crucial political-generation years of adolescence (Mannheim, 1952).

The classic studies examined voting effects of other groups beyond the family, for example, friendship groups and coworkers. Solidarity might be decreasing over recent decades within the family but it may be increasing within age-peer groupings both directly through face-to-face contact and indirectly via a strong and homogeneous youth culture. Election researchers may be so out of touch with this culture that it would be appropriate in future studies to use cross-cultural anthropological methods such as participant observation and informant interviewing to comprehend each wave of youth culture. Some ambiguity in the causal mechanisms underlying group voting homogeneity might be resolved by measuring and analyzing relations involving directly measured mediators, interaction variables, and partial definitions (e.g., differences in worker homogeneity among occupation groups, such as those in public versus private employment, and union members versus nonmembers). The founding 1940s studies extracted theoretically relevant information by tenaciously probing such relations.

Voter Characteristics as Independent Variables

Voting behavior may be affected by a fourth class of independent variables, namely, the voters' personal characteristics other than demographics (e.g., ability level, personality, values, cognitive styles, and lifestyle, each of which can be touched on only fleetingly here). Ability level can be measured economically in children by using chronological age as an index of mental age, but adult studies call for more effortful ability measures such as the participant's score on a test of information regarding the campaign. Voting is now allowed in the United States and many other countries when a citizen reaches age 18. A voter's maturity, knowledge, and sophistication are likely to continue growing through the twenties at least, so election studies should make special efforts to study first voters and should consider oversampling those in the 18 to 30 age range to pick up trends at ages when political sophistication and interest may be changing rapidly. Indeed, future studies might usefully include in the sample adolescents as young as 12 to trace early political socialization; sampling problems would arise but could be mitigated and the gain in socialization information might be worth the cost (Niemi, 1999). Of course, chronological age is related to numerous variables that are likely to affect voting behavior, so that obtained age relations will be ambiguous unless appropriate experimental designs and analyses are used (e.g., covariance analysis of mediational effects, interaction effects, and structural equation multiple-path models).

Personality variables have been relatively neglected in election studies probably because they are expensive to measure in surveys, because election campaigns must affect all types of voters, and because theorizing about personality and politics has not flourished since the 1940s and 1950s (McGuire, 1993). Interest has been shown in some personality variables such as anomia, authoritarianism, hostility, and sense of efficacy, provoking the cynical report that respondents, asked whether the declining voter turnout in recent elections is due to ignorance or apathy, may reply "I don't know and I don't care." The current rage in personality theory is for the "Big Five" personality variables (neuroticism, extroversion, etc.). Future election researchers with resources sufficient to use 10 minutes of respondent time for self-report measures of these personality variables, at least in a subsample of respondents, could obtain a cost-effective analysis of voters' five-dimensional personality space (preferably with subvariable scores). These measures could then be analyzed to answer some interesting theoretical issues or at least for hypothesis-generating explorations.

Voting behavior is also likely to be affected by citizens' values such as needs for achievement versus power versus affiliation in the Murray/McClelland/Reisman tradition, or valuing freedom versus equality in the Rokeach tradition. Lipset (Chapter 4 in this volume) discusses the role of religious and other values in affecting voting behavior. Cognitive styles like internal versus external perceived locus of control, need for cognition, category width, and risk aversion are appealing because they have accumulated interesting bodies of research, allow efficient measurement, and have theoretical relevance to voting behavior. Some qualitative researchers are interested in how stages in the life cycle and one's "political generation" affect voting. Still another category of personal variables that deserve inclusion in the experimental design of election studies are typologies, which are currently popular in advertising/marketing research on psychographics, lifestyle analysis, and market segmentation. This research has identified interesting typologies for partitioning the

American public that deserve further investigation in election studies. Worth more study is the sorting of voters on multiple characteristics at one time (e.g., the 480 categories of voters evoked early interest [Pool et al., 1965], but follow-up interest has been greater in fiction [Burdick, 1964] than in fact).

Some of the subcategories I have used here have mutually hazy borders, such as distinguishing between personality characteristics and values; also the higher-order categorizations of some of these variables are ambiguous (e.g., is "ethnicity" best classified as a demographic, group membership, or personal characteristic?). Such questions do not demand answers in the present undertaking because my basic aim is not to classify independent variables into neat, mutually exclusive cubbyholes but rather to construct a thought-generating structure to serve as a diversifying mechanism for suggesting a wide variety of promising hypotheses and theories. At this stage of study overlapping classification and redundancy are affordable and self-correcting.

Independent Variables Concerning Candidate Characteristics

So far I have been discussing how characteristics of the citizen affect his or her voting behavior. Now I shall consider how characteristics of the candidate affect voting, a topic relatively neglected in past election studies, in part because they focused almost exclusively on U.S. presidential contests that involve only two or three consequential candidates that are chosen by procedures that do not allow much variance on candidate characteristics. A small amount of work has been done on the effects of candidates' nonverbal behavior and self-presentation modes (Noelle-Neumann, 1980; Masters and Sullivan, 1993). Other work involves predicted interactions between candidate and voter characteristics (e.g., are voters in the ethnic or sexual minority and in low-power statuses more likely to vote for candidates of their own ethnicity or sex than are voters in the majority or high-power status?). As election research expands further to hundreds of congressional and state and local elections, each with multiple candidates, analyses of the effects of variations in candidate characteristics will become more powerful and open up new lines of inquiry on this interesting but neglected independent-variable category of candidate characteristics. Another way of studying these effects is to do historical analyses of which characteristics have contributed to effective leadership of the U.S. presidents and others over a wide period (Simonton, 1987, 1994; Barber, 1992).

Personalized Communications as Independent Variables

The membership/reference group category of independent variables described above as affecting voting (e.g., homogeneity of family, friends, and coworkers in voting preferences) probably operates by a number of mechanisms, one of which is face-to-face tailored arguments by which one family member exercises political influence on another member during one-on-one discussion. Arguments tailored to the individual voter can occur not only in face-to-face discussions but also via indirect channels that are increasingly used, such as posted mail or e-mail advertising. It is becoming easier to analyze address lists so that mailings can focus on issues relevant to the concerns of each segment of recipients. A political development of recent decades has been the efficient direct-mail solicitation of campaign contributions using ingeniously compiled mailing lists. Many studies appear in advertising and marketing journals on how to design direct-mail solicitations to evoke maximum response (e.g., color of envelope and various types of personalization), although their yield has been reduced by the lack of theoretical relevance.

Direct mail's growing political use (especially for fund-raising in primary contests) and e-mail's potential usefulness invite their inclusion in any large-scale multimedia election study to the extent that they appear effective and have theoretical relevance. Any study of the 2000 C.E. campaign might well experiment with personalized communication made possible by tailored e-mail messages and computerized lists of addresses (some originally selected for commercial rather than political purposes). Evaluation will tend to lag behind manipulation, but a well-funded year 2000 election study can contribute by systematically manipulating and evaluating within a subsample of voters these electronically personalized political messages. Quite possibly any effects found in the near future will wear out as the novelty of the medium declines.

Another personalized face-to-face political influence channel that deserves more systematic study is use of fund-raising dinners and invitations or fund-raising ceremonies in the White House and other venues to extract the substantial sums of money that candidates feel are necessary for winning elections, a preoccupation that seems to have reached new heights in the Clinton era. Candidates increasingly flaunt early fund-raising totals to intimidate rivals from entering the contest, just as a dominant male baboon might use other displays to chase off potential challengers.

Campaign Content Characteristics as Independent Variables

Archives are being assembled, kept up to date, and made available to researchers, particularly by university and interuniversity consortia. These archives store in a standard format samples of campaign materials used in each presidential campaign, for example, political ads, particularly for television, political reports in the nightly television news, videos of the presidential debates, policy statements, and nomination and acceptance speeches of the candidates (Kaid et al., 1996; Kaid and Bystrom, 1998). Some of this archived material is available already scored on several independent variables regarding substance and style of the competing campaigns; successive users may add scores on additional variables of theoretical or applied interest.

To exploit such archived campaign material the researcher must creatively identify relevant variables, develop a content-analysis system to score on these variables a sample of each candidate's messages through the campaign, and train intelligent and motivated assistants (say, college-student research aides). These analyses can then be used to score campaign communications for the substantive and stylistic characteristics hypothesized to affect voting behavior. Devising content-analysis systems is a demanding art, craft, and science. Smith (1992) assembled a handbook that describes in usable detail a number of systems already available for analyzing the thematic content of communications, some of which (e.g., cognitive complexity) have been shown to be politically relevant. Using content-analysis systems even after they are tediously devised is an additional labor-intensive process.

Historical Developments During
the Campaign as Independent Variables

Every election campaign is carried on during a specific period of history when there occur events, unique but fitting into theoretical categories, sometimes foreseeable but often unexpected (e.g., an international crisis or a personal scandal), that are likely to affect voting as main effects or in interaction with other campaign variables. Some observers have suggested that historic shifts in the political zeitgeist occur at thirty-year intervals (see Chapter 4 in this volume). Especially important are momentous events that become collective memories (Pillemer, 1998). If an election study includes frequent pollings that provide baseline data, then suitable analytic procedures can be applied even retrospectively (e.g., Phillips, 1983). One expedient is for the election research community to assemble a watch-and-wait emergency team (modeled after "disaster panels" of the crises decades) made up of people familiar with studying crisis interventions, interested in political processes, and ready and able to respond immediately when critical events occur. Such panels might suggest questions to be added to ongoing surveys or the need to oversample critical subpopulations likely to be especially affected by the event as ways of monitoring the effects of the historical occurrence.

More foreseeable historical developments should also be monitored during the campaign and analyzed to evaluate their impacts on preferences and participation. Especially cost-effective are politically relevant variables on which detailed time-series data are routinely provided (e.g., closely followed economic indices such as various stock market, inflation, and unemployment levels). Time-series measures of such economic indices, in parallel with periodic poll data on voting intentions and preference, when broken down into contrasting geographic units, will allow the testing of, say, the "retrospective voting" hypothesis, which states that the electorate returns (versus ousts) incumbents as a positive function of economic improvement (versus deterioration). Additional analyses could then determine if improvement and deterioration have symmetrically equal effects or have a negativity bias, and if the economic hardship must be personal or whether there is a cosmopolitan effect such that national economic downturn suffices. Cluster analysis may show if some segments of the electorate (e.g., those at specifiable life stages) are particularly susceptible to certain economic developments.

To study the effects of such historical events the election researcher might assemble retrospectively, or ongoing from the early primaries until after election day, a social data archive including time-series data obtained at frequent intervals on a variety of historical independent variables theorized to affect voting behavior, such as economic indices (daily Dow Jones Industrial indices, monthly unemployment and cost-of-living estimates, etc.), periodic crime statistics, and even weather reports. These might be usefully measured both absolutely and regarding the direction and rate of change since last report. Such a time-series archive could also include weekly or monthly data on politically relevant subjective states that are already being collected for other purposes (e.g., judgment that one is better off than last year, intention to make major purchases, fear of crime, satisfaction with the president, Congress, etc.). One could then test how these background historical variables affect political variables (e.g., salience of issues, intent to vote, candidate preferences). Whether a given time series would be included in the archives is a cost/benefit judgment: Is the cost of obtaining valid data (and these data are often conveniently available) outweighed by the variable's promise for testing theory-relevant hypotheses? In Chapter 2, Bartels discusses in greater detail how the specific historical context of a given election can give more meaning to the individual election.

Analyzing such archival time-series data could be facilitated by dividing it into two stages. Firstly, there should be some reduction of the data in the matrix of historical independent variables versus successive time periods, in the cells of which matrix would be the scores on the row time period of the column independent-variable index. Factor analysis might reduce the twenty to forty such historical independent variables to five or ten orthogonal dimensions, including the political variables of interest. These dimensions could then be interpreted by variables' loadings and would include most of the information in all twenty to forty initial historical variables. Secondly, the reduced data matrix, now containing time-series data on the five or ten factors underlying the twenty to forty historical variables measured over numerous time intervals, would be subjected to causal analysis, probably using structural equation models. These could be either exploratory or preferably test among alternative models of the causal pathways connecting historical antecedents and political effects. These analyses could also explore the different directions and different time lags at which the causality operates.

Ceremonial, Ritual Independent Variables

Quite neglected in electoral studies (and in the study of most other social science dependent variables) is how rituals, the ceremonial aspects of social life, affect voting. Election campaigns involve a series of rituals beginning with the candidates' denial of interest and then their struggle for and acceptance of the nomination, ending with the election night victory or concession speech. Subsequent rituals include postelection preparations for taking office and preparing for the next campaign for the same or higher office. In this series of traditional ceremonies the candidate makes ritually ordained responses with subtle peculiarities of his or her own that constitute the candidate's idiosyncratic political style. An early research step is to identify and factor out as baseline the standard series of ritualized responses shared by most candidates and then identify each given candidate's deviations from the common pattern of his or her personal style.

The rituals that make up much of the campaigns of the U.S. presidential candidates have persisted, though with considerable modifications, over the last fifty years. The "man who . . ." nominating speeches at the convention and the candidates' own nomination acceptance and victory speeches have prescribed content and style ("I wish to thank also . . . "). There is the basic campaigning "barnstorming" trip on which the candidate waves from a motorcade moving rapidly through a normally busy street, with stops several times a day to give edited versions of "the" ritual speech (with slight variations to enhance local relevance); in earlier years these were delivered from the back of a train, but now they are given at airports or photo opportunities. The now ubiquitous 30-second television and radio spots have largely replaced the long political speech. Press conferences, appearances on talk shows, and highly orchestrated debates between candidates are staged. Debate performance attracts considerable "who won/who lost" evaluation from the public and the pros. Parades, fireworks, and ritual symbols (buttons, colors, campaign songs, etc.) are less common than at midcentury, but posters remain a campaign mainstay and are constant in their "smiling heads" iconography. The fund-raising "rubber chicken" dinners for the faithful, with a brief feel-good speech by the candidate and handshaking and photo opportunities for rich entertainers and corporate executives (although less often similarly rich athletic celebrities) are receiving increased use.

Once such rituals and their usages have been inventoried, it is still difficult to evaluate their impact. Presidential debates are a familiar example and have been closely watched since the 1960 Kennedy–Nixon election. They may provide a model for studying the impacts of some of the other ritual events (Jamieson and Birdsell,

1987; Kraus, 1999). Studies of the 2000 C.E. U.S. presidential election should include preliminary work in the form of general theorizing and a descriptive inventory of such ritual processes, even if it must be left for later studies to do careful nomothetic evaluations of how these processes affect voting and other political responses.

Promising Dependent and Mediating Variables for Use in Election Studies

The preceding sections describe and categorize a long list of independent variables of election campaigns that future research might investigate regarding their theoretical- and practical-relevant relations to voting behavior. Here I turn from independent variables to dependent variables that are particularly deserving of being included in future election studies as important campaign effects. These dependent-variable effects that election campaigns are designed to produce include political actions, political cognitions, and political affects, three categories that will be discussed in turn.

Political Actions as Dependent Variables

The ultimate payoff dependent variables in any election study are actions such as contributing, proselytizing, volunteering, and most obviously voting. Voting behavior includes participation as well as partisanship; indeed, campaigns may have more impact on participation (turnout, whether citizens cast their votes) than on partisanship (which candidate the citizens vote for). Both participation and partisanship will inevitably and deservedly continue to be measured as major dependent variables in future election studies, but here I shall describe some innovations that are called for.

Studying Neglected Elections. Voting behavior is a high-priority dependent variable, but the question arises, voting in which elections? In the first half century of U.S. voting research, federal elections, and particularly presidential elections, captivated attention to the relative neglect of voting in state and local elections. Obviously national elections are more glamorous but some hypotheses can be better tested within local elections or as interactions between local and national elections. Also, there are more replication possibilities on the state and local levels, and replication allows more powerful hypothesis testing. Relatively more attention should be given to subnational executive (gubernatorial and mayoral) and legislative (state assemblies and city councils) elections and especially to referenda (Beyle, 1997), which are increasingly appearing on subnational ballots and are of considerable theoretical and practical interest. An initial step in this direction might be to assemble a study group of election researchers and students of state and local government to develop hypotheses that would be better tested on state and local levels and hypotheses about relations that are predicted to be different between national and local elections. The group could then propose theory-relevant slates of states and localities on which to focus in future studies, beginning by augmenting the already valuable archived data on past elections. Another committee might focus on the prevalence of referenda and come up with hypotheses about their theoretical and practical significance.

The overconcentration of research on national to the neglect of state and local elections is aggravated by the overconcentration on presidential to the neglect of congressional elections. The study of House and Senate elections, in which many seats are at stake, allows replication that is not possible with the single presidential election (although the high probability of incumbents winning congressional elections reduces their use in hypothesis testing). A recent U.S. trend that calls for explanation in the year 2000 and subsequent elections is the tendency for yoked voting in the form of favoring opposed parties in the executive and legislative branches of the U.S. federal government. In twenty-seven of the first thirty biennial elections in the twentieth century, American voters did the expected thing of leaving the Congress and the presidency under control of the same party. However, since 1970 this familiar and plausible pattern has reversed, with the electorate frequently sending the candidate of one party to the White House while giving at least one house of Congress to the opposite party. In ten of the fifteen biennial elections since 1970, voters gave the presidency and one or both houses of Congress to opposite parties. Furthermore, the process is speeding up: in seven of the eight most recent biennial elections, at least one house of Congress was left in control of the party in opposition to the president. Future election studies should investigate theoretical explanations of this strange reversal. Is it another symptom of distrust of government such that voters want to hobble government by leaving opposed parties in control of the executive and legislative branches so that the power of each cancels the other? Is this emerging pattern also exhibited in state and local elections?

Another rebalancing of focus on political actions, even more radical than studying neglected types of elections and the campaigns leading up to them, is to study neglected postelection political actions. We have just argued that U.S. presidential elections may have been (over)abundantly studied, but this preoccupation stops on election night, even though there follows (especially when the victorious presidential candidate is not the incumbent) a hyperactive, crucial two-month transitional phase between November and January of setting up a new administration. This interim period has not received the close study it deserves: the personnel selected, the operating modes adopted, and the policies to which the administration commits itself may be more determined during these several transitional months than in any other several months of campaigning and incumbency. In national elections outside the United States (e.g., in the United Kingdom and other parliamentary systems) this transitional period between parliaments may be even more crucial. In studies of the U.S. 2000 C.E. presidential election there might be a research team focusing on this postelectional period. This team should include not only the communications theorists, social psychologists, and political behaviorists who would study the election campaign, but also organizational behaviorists, students of management, and administrative scientists who are knowledgeable in person/institution processes.

Better Scaling of Dependent Variables.   Dependent variables, even more than independent variables, need to be measured on a "continuous" (multilevel) scale because this allows testing relations to which dichotomously measured variables are not sensitive and allows the use of more powerful inferential statistics for testing hypotheses. Unfortunately, the less sensitive dichotomous scales tend to be used for measuring voting behavior, participation usually being measured on a vote/no-vote scale and partisanship on voting for candidate A versus B (or, more accurately, for incumbent versus challenger). In the future, election researchers should try harder to develop multilevel scales, perhaps by measuring time of decision to vote (or to vote for candidate A) or perhaps by obtaining voter's self-report of confidence in that decision or of that decision's stability during the campaign.

Studying Political Actions Beyond Voting. Election studies should broaden their spectrum of action dependent variables beyond the usual two dependent variables, voting participation and partisanship, to other theoretically or practically important political actions, such as making financial contributions, signing petitions, displaying political posters, joining political groups, registering self and others to vote, attending rallies, proselytizing for one's candidates, phoning call-in shows, making public endorsements, volunteering time or skills, and participating in demonstrations or in heckling the opposition. These other action-dependent variables can cross-validate voting actions and may be more suitable for continuous scaling, and some (e.g., making campaign contributions) may be more practically and theoretically important than voting itself. It would be useful to combine these multiple political action measures into a composite scale or to use multivariate analysis to identify several orthogonal or oblique action factors.

Political Actions as Mediating Variables. Many political action variables deserve to be included in the experimental design of future election studies because they have the logical status of mediating variables as well as of dependent variables. Examples are exposure to the campaign on the mass media, discussing the campaign with friends, and responding to other compliance-gaining tactics such as signing petitions (Cialdini, 1993). Such actions can serve as mediating variables in a causal chain, being the dependent variable in one hypothesis and the independent variable in the next. For example, exposure to the television campaign is a mediator that serves as a dependent variable in one hypothesis (say, that being personally affected by the issues increases media exposure) and then serve as the independent variable in the next hypothesis in the causal chain (say, that increasing media exposure increases the likelihood of voting for incumbent rather than challenger). Subsequent sophisticated election studies can then use the method of strong inference, introducing multiple theorized mediating variables into the experimental design by creatively inferring the operation of alternative mediators, measuring the participants' levels on the mediators, and then using covariance analyses to evaluate the mediators' power to account for the predicted relation between independent and dependent variables, in this way testing among alternative theoretical explanations for that relation.

Changes in Voting Intentions During the Off Years. In the preceding section it was suggested that past neglect makes it inviting for future election studies to focus on less studied kinds of elections (e.g., on state and local rather than federal, on legislative rather than executive, on within-party primaries rather than among-party elections, on referenda rather than candidates). A more radical, oxymoronic suggestion is that election research, rather than studying election years, should study nonelection years. That is, researchers should theorize about and collect data about issue salience and positions, voting intentions, and other political inclinations and actions during the two years prior to the presidential or congressional vote. It is likely that the longer it is before the next election (and to a lesser extent after the previous one), the more fluid will be citizens' thoughts, feelings, and actions regarding the candidates, parties, and issues. Past election studies have tended to start just before or even after the primaries, missing the earlier period when the potential voters and the political system may be most responsive to theory-relevant independent variables. An earlier start may provide more powerful tests of the hypothesized relations.

Political Cognitions as Dependent Variables

Since the Hellenic period students of the person have found it useful to distinguish among thoughts (cognitions, beliefs), feelings (affects, emotions), and actions (conations, behaviors, responses) as the three basic types of human manifestations. Particularly since the eighteenth century, when Christian von Wolff used the three to reorganize and reprofessionalize philosophy by reinstating it in the academy, and when Immanuel Kant used them in his three *Critiques*, students of the person have found this tripartite division attractive (Hilgard, 1980). As applied to election studies this division suggests that any inclusive analysis of the effects of political campaigns should measure their impacts on the thoughts, feelings, and actions of the electorate. The preceding section reviewed effects on political actions (including voting and other modes of participation). The present section turns from impacts on political actions to impacts on political cognitions.

Political Information as a Cognitive Variable. Probably the most studied and rewarding cognitive variable is political knowledge (the amount and especially accuracy of information) about the candidates, parties, and issues in the campaign being studied and about the society's abiding political institutions. Across studies political knowledge has served a variety of logical functions, not only as an independent or dependent variable, but also as a mediational or interactional variable. As a mediational variable knowledge can serve as a dependent variable in one hypothesis (e.g., in the hypothesis that political knowledge is a positive function of the amount of exposure to the political campaign via face-to-face discussion or mass media depiction) and in another hypothesis it might serve as an independent variable (e.g., the hypothesis that knowledge is a predictor of political commitment and so positively related to stability of voting intention over the campaign). When used as an interaction variable, political knowledge is hypothesized to affect how another independent variable is related to a dependent variable (e.g., as in the hypothesis that political knowledge increases the likelihood of voting in citizens who support the incumbent and decreases voting likelihood in those supporting the challenger). This knowledge (information) variable should be a high priority for inclusion in future election studies because it has a good track record for entering into a variety of confirmed hypotheses as an effect in its own right, as well as a theorized mediator or interaction variable that helps explain hypothesized relations.

Tests Versus Self-rating Measures of Cognitive Variables. The obvious measure of a cognitive variable like political knowledge is an information test, but a less costly self-rating measure is often substituted. An information test uses questions about the candidates, issues, parties, or (less often) the society's political institutions and is administered in a multiple-choice format or (easier to construct but harder to score) in an open-ended format. Information tests have the drawbacks of being difficult to construct and expensive to administer. Even a dozen-item information test (worrisomely brief considering that reliability increases as the square root of the number of items) administered to each of a couple of thousand respondents in a national survey would be formidably expensive. Another drawback of the information test is that the correct information content will differ from election to election in a given year and especially across years, which makes it hard to compare levels and relations across elections.

Such drawbacks have led to use in some election studies of a simple self-report measure of knowledge (e.g., "On a seven-point scale how well informed are you about the current election?"). This type of self-rating measure can be obtained in 10 seconds rather than the several minutes needed for the dozen-item information test and can be used in identical format from election to election. A priori, there seems reason to worry about the face validity of such self-ratings (e.g., because they may be affected by social desirability artifacts), but in studies using both an information test and a self-rating to measure political knowledge the two have correlated positively and have related similarly to third variables. For other variables besides political knowledge, quick-and-dirty self-ratings have also yielded results similar to those derived from ponderous objective-test measures. So future election studies in which participant time availability and other resources are limited may use self-ratings in lieu of (or in addition to) an onerous objective test, rather than not measuring the variable at all, even though one makes the substitution with fear and trembling.

Self-ratings may be the only feasible way we have of measuring some political cognition variables (e.g., amount of time spent following the campaign on the media, or discussing it face-to-face, or intention to vote, or confidence in one's choices). In the future, more objective and overtly observable indices such as physiological or nonverbal behavior may become available.

Ideology as Dependent Variables.   Neglected domains of political cognitions other than information may be worth considering in future studies, particularly political ideology, that is, the content, structure, and functioning of systems into which political thoughts are organized (McGuire and McGuire, 1991). Several lines of evidence raise doubts about the extent to which members of the public have organized ideologies: political preferences tend to be fickle within and between elections; knowledge is sparse even on crucial issues and is only slightly related to preferences or self-interest; stands on closely related specific issues are little related to one another and stands on a general issue are little related to stands on its specifics; and minor changes in wordings or even orderings of questions often produce large differences in responses.

Although such findings have led some students of politics (P. E. Converse, 1970; Abelson, 1972) to doubt the existence of ideology, others have kept the faith in, or at least an open mind about, the pervasiveness of ideologies and many excuses have been offered (McGuire, 1989) that might explain away the weakness of the obtained empirical evidence for organized ideology. Some excuses are methodological, attributing the lack of empirical support to methods shortcomings (e.g., poor measures of individual attitudes and especially of relations between attitudes; poor control over extraneous variables; and the obscuring effects of "non-attitudes"). Other excuses are fallback positions that admit ideologies may usually be generally weak but are stronger in certain subpopulations. For example, they are stronger in European countries, where politics are more party based and parties differ more on issues than in the United States where candidates' personalities are purportedly more important. Some researchers believe that ideologies exist, if not in the masses, at least in the classes; or that ideologies are becoming stronger than they used to be; or that they are strong in "one-issue" voters or in certain personality types such as high need-cognition.

A more radical excuse is that people have ideological systems but that these systems are organized, not on the usual suspects such as liberalism–conservatism or individualism–collectivism, but on exotic dimensions such as Jungian animus–anima or on Lévi-Straussian polarities such as raw–cooked and nature–culture. Another radical excuse is that ideologies are organized but the alignment of their dimensions is not as commonly believed; for example, the possibility that liberalism and conservatism are orthogonal dimensions (Kerlinger, 1984) rather than a single bipolar dimension as usually assumed, so that liberals and conservatives differ not by holding opposite beliefs on the same issues but by caring about and holding beliefs on different issues. These controversies about the nature and even the existence of ideology discourage study of its relations, but its past neglect and its high theoretical relevance to basic research make political ideology appealing as a dependent and mediating variable in future election studies provided they use sophisticated conceptualization and ingenious methods.

Open-Ended Measures of Cognitive Variables.   One promising method for studying ideology and other cognitive variables like salience, which has been relatively neglected in election studies but deserves more use, is measuring the cognitive variables by open-ended responses. Most election studies use reactive measures of

their variables in that the researcher decides what aspects of a political stimulus (e.g., a candidate, party, issue) are to be measured,
and the respondent is reduced to reacting to this researcher-chosen
dimension by indicating where the stimulus falls on it. This reactive method yields no information on how often if ever the respondent spontaneously thinks of where the stimulus lies along that dimension; this results in the loss of information about the salience
of the rated characteristics, that is, about its accessibility in the respondent's own cognitive arena (McGuire and McGuire, 1992).
Future election studies should make more use of open-ended, free-
association measures (e.g., having the respondent do free or re-
stricted associations, such as "List desirable characteristics that
candidate X lacks") as a way to collect information on the relative
salience of various dimensions of the candidate, party, or issues, to
discover serendipitous new information, and to test a priori the-
ory-derived hypotheses. The National Election Studies already
make available open-ended responses to some questions (Smith et
al., 1999).

Political Affect as Dependent Variables

The two previous sections described high-priority political action
variables and political cognition variables, both of which act as dependent (and mediational) variables. This final section turns to high-
priority political affect variables. Affective variables are usually measured by subjective self-report questionnaire measures and
occasionally by more objective observational measures of affects.

Reactive Self-report Measures of Political Affect.   Reactive paper-
and-pencil self-report measures have been the overwhelmingly popular choice for measuring political affect (i.e., liking for candidates,
parties, and issues) and will probably maintain their popularity.
Promising improvements in these measures include analyzing the
neutral ("don't care") responses to detect "non-attitudes," determining how many response categories should be used, whether and how
they are to be labeled, how to word questions, and how to order
them. Election researchers should be familiar with such advances or
should consult experienced survey researchers. Recent advances in
paper-and-pencil self-report measures of attitude strength (confi-

dence, stability, extremity, etc.) should be incorporated in future election studies (Petty and Krosnick, 1995).

Physiological and Nonverbal Indices of Affect.   Another line of current advance in measuring affect variables involves observing overt physical responses from which affect can be inferred through a somewhat tenuous chain of conjectures. Particularly promising are physiological indices and nonverbal-behavioral indices of political affect. The use of myocardial measures of multiple muscle patterns of response (Cacioppo and Petty, 1983) and the use of EEG indices (Alwitt, 1985) are particularly promising. The use of nonverbal behaviors, both visual and vocalic, to measure political affect is also advancing (Masters and Sullivan, 1993).

Most of these physiological and nonverbal behavior indices of political affect are demanding in money, technology, and skill. For example, it is often necessary to measure participants one-by-one, with multiple researchers observing each subject, using expensive equipment that may have to be calibrated individually for each participant. Technicians of considerable skill must be trained to write computer programs and obtain and interpret measures, and the signal-to-noise ratio must be enhanced. At present even well-funded election studies can afford such political-affect indices only for demonstration purposes on a small subsample of the respondents in a survey study. For the next several years, election studies are more likely to contribute to rather than gain from basic research on physiological and nonverbal indices, but there will be gains in both directions. Thus election studies can be producers as well as consumers of basic research.

Conclusion

The past fifty-year era of election studies started vigorously with the Columbia University investigations of the 1940 and 1948 U.S. presidential elections. Progress has been steady during this half century despite the conservative use of established methods. Still, a number of approaches have emerged that have contributed to basic theorizing about the person and society, to practical guidance on applied issues, and to "how-to" insights into winning elections. Progress will accelerate only to the extent that future election studies are guided by a priori theorizing to include in their experimental designs specified independent, dependent, mediational, and interactional variables that have been neglected in previous studies.

References

Abelson, R. P. 1972. "Are Attitudes Necessary?" In *Attitudes, Conflicts, and Social Change*, B. T. King and E. McGinnies, eds., pp. 19–32. New York: Academic Press.

Abrahamson, P. R., J. H. Aldrich, and D. W. Rhode, eds. 1998. *Change and Continuity in the 1996 and 1998 Elections*. Washington, D.C.: Congressional Quarterly Press.

Adams, K. H. 1999. *Progressive Politics and the Training of America's Persuaders*. Mahwah, N.J.: Erlbaum.

Almond, G., and S. Verba. 1963. *The Civic Culture*. Princeton: Princeton University Press.

Alwitt, L. F. 1985. "EEG Activity Reflects the Content of Commercials." In *Psychological Processes and Advertising Effects*, L. F. Alwitt and A. A. Mitchell, eds., pp. 201–207. Hillsdale, N.J.: Erlbaum.

Ansolabehere, S., and S. Iyengar. 1995. *Going Negative: How Political Advertisements Shrink and Polarize the Electorate*. New York: Free Press.

Barber, J. D. 1992. *The Presidential Character: Predicting Performance in the White House*, 4th ed. Englewood Cliffs, N.J.: Prentice-Hall.

Berelson, B., P. F. Lazarsfeld, and W. N. McPhee. 1954. *Voting*. Chicago: University of Chicago Press.

Beyle, T. 1997. "The State Elections of '66." In *Toward the Millennium: The Election of 1997*, L. Sabato, ed., pp. 189–203. Boston: Allyn & Bacon.

Burdick, E. 1964. *The 480*. New York: McGraw-Hill.

Cacioppo, J. T., and R. E. Petty, eds. 1983. *Social Psychophysiology: A Source Book*. New York: Guilford Press.

Campbell, A., P. E. Converse, W. E. Miller, and D. E. Stokes. 1960. *The American Voter*. New York: Wiley.

Campbell, A., P. E. Converse, and D. E. Stokes. 1966. *Elections and the Political Order*. New York: Wiley.

Campbell, A., G. Gurin, and W. E. Miller. 1954. *The Voter Decides*. Evanston, Ill.: Row, Peterson.

Cialdini, R. B. 1993. *Influence: Science and Practice*. New York: Harper Collins.

Converse, J. M. 1987. *Survey Research in the United States: Roots and Emergence, 1890–1960*. Berkeley: University of California Press.

Converse, P. E. 1970. "Attitudes and Non-attitudes: Continuation of a Dialogue." In *The Qualitative Analysis of Social Problems*, E. R. Tufte, ed., pp. 168–189. Reading, Mass.: Addison-Wesley.

Dayan, D., and E. Katz. 1992. *Media Events: The Live Broadcasting of History*. Cambridge, Mass.: Harvard University Press.

Dennis, E., and E. Wartella. 1996. *American Communication Research — The Remembered History*. Mahwah, N.J.: Erlbaum.

Farley, J. A. 1938. *Behind the Ballots*. New York: Harcourt, Brace.

Frankovic, K. A. 2000. "Election Polls." *Media Studies Journal* 14: 104–109.

Granberg, D., and S. Holmberg. 1990. "The Person Positivity and Principle Actor Hypothesis." *Journal of Applied Social Psychology* 20: 1879–1901.

Hilgard, E. R. 1980. "The Trilogy of Mind: Cognition, Affection, and Conation." *Journal of the History of the Behavioral Sciences* 16: 107–117.

Iyengar, S., and D. R. Kinder. 1987. *News That Matters*. Chicago: University of Chicago Press.

Iyengar, S., and W. J. McGuire, eds. 1993. *Explorations in Political Psychology*. Durham, N.C.: Duke University Press.

Jamieson, K. H., and D. S. Birdsell. 1987. *Presidential Debates: The Challenge of Creating an Informal Public*. New York: Oxford University Press.

Kaid, L. L., and D. Bystrom, eds. 1998. *The Electronic Election: Perspectives on the 1996 Campaign Communication*. Mahwah, N.J.: Erlbaum.

Kaid, L. L., K. J. M. Haynes, and C. E. Rand. 1996. *A Catalog and Guide to the Archival Collections*. Norman: Political Communications Center, University of Oklahoma.

Katz, E., and P. F. Lazarsfeld. 1955. *Personal Influence*. Glencoe, Ill.: Free Press.

Kerlinger, F. N. 1984. *Liberalism and Conservatism: The Nature and Structure of Social Attitude*, 2nd ed. Hillsdale, N.J.: Erlbaum.

Kessler, R., and H. Stipp. 1984. "The Impact of Fictional Television Suicide Stories on U.S. Fatalities: A Replication." *American Journal of Sociology* 90: 151–167.

Kraus, S. 1999. *Televised Presidential Debates and Public Policy*. Mahwah, N.J.: Erlbaum.

Lazarsfeld, P. F. 1940. *Radio and the Printed Page*. New York: Duell, Sloan, and Pearce.

Lazarsfeld, P. F., and F. N. Stanton, eds. 1941, 1944, 1949. *Radio Research, 1941; Radio Research, 1942–43; Communication Research, 1948–49*. New York: Harper.

Lazarsfeld, P. F., B. Berelson, and H. Gaudet. 1944. *The People's Choice*. New York: Columbia University Press.

Lemert, J. B., W. Wanta, and T-T. Lee. 1999. "Party Identification and Negative Advertising in a U.S. Senate Election." *Journal of Communication* 49: 123–134.

Lipset, S. M. 1960. *Political Man*. New York: Doubleday.

Mannheim, K. 1952. *The Problem Generations. Essays of the Sociology of Knowledge*, pp. 276–320. Oxford: Oxford University Press (originally published in 1923).

Masters, R. D., and D. G. Sullivan. 1993. "Nonverbal Behavior and Leadership." In *Explorations in Political Psychology*, S. Iyengar and W. J. McGuire, eds., pp. 150–182. Durham, N.C.: Duke University Press.

McGinness, J. 1969. *The Selling of the President 1968*. New York: Simon & Schuster.

McGuire, W. J. 1986. "The Myth of Massive Media Impact: Savagings and Salvagings." In *Public Communication and Behavior*, G. Comstock, ed., Vol. 1 , pp. 173–257. New York: Academic Press.

McGuire, W. J. 1989. "The Structure of Individual Attitudes and Attitude Systems." In *Attitude Structure and Function*, A. R. Pratkanis, S. J. Breckler, and A. G. Greenwald, eds., pp.37–69. Hillsdale, N.J.: Erlbaum.

McGuire, W. J. 1993. "The Poly–Psy Relationship: Three Phases of a Long Affair." In *Explorations in Political Psychology*, S. Iyengar and W. J. McGuire, eds., pp. 9–35. Durham, N.C.: Duke University Press.

McGuire, W. J. 1998. Book review of *Political Persuasion and Attitude Change*, by D. C. Mutz et al. *Public Opinion Quarterly* 62: 279–282.

McGuire, W. J., and C. V. McGuire. 1991. "The Content, Structure, and Operation of Thought Systems." In *Advances in Social Cognition*, R. S. Wyer, Jr., and T. K. Srull, eds., Vol. IV, pp. 1–78. Hillsdale, N.J.: Erlbaum.

McGuire, W. J., and C. V. McGuire. 1992. "Cognitive-versus-Affective Positivity Asymmetries in Thought Systems." *European Journal of Social Psychology* 22: 571–591.

Miller, W. E., and J. M. Shanks. 1996. *The New American Voter: Conflict and Consensus in American Presidential Elections*. Cambridge, Mass.: Harvard University Press.

Mutz, D. C., P. M. Sniderman, and R. A. Brody, eds. 1996. *Political Persuasion and Attitude Change*. Ann Arbor: University of Michigan Press.

Newman, B. I., ed. 1999. *Handbook of Political Marketing*. Thousand Oaks, Calif.: Sage.

Nie, N. H., S. Verba, and J. R. Petrocik. 1976. *The Changing American Voter*. Cambridge, Mass.: Harvard University Press.

Niemi, R. G., ed. 1999. "Special Issue on Political Socialization." *Political Psychology* 20: 471–592.

Noelle-Neumann, E. 1980. *The Spiral of Silence*. Chicago: University of Chicago Press.

Peeters, G., J. Czapiski, and M. Lewicka. 1992. "Positive–Negative Asymmetry in Affect and Evolution." *European Journal of Social Psychology* 22: issues 5 and 6.

Perlmutter, D. D., ed. 1999. *The Manship School Guide to Political Communication*. Baton Rouge: Louisiana State University Press.

Petty, R. E., and J. A. Krosnick. 1995. *Attitude Strength: Antecedents and Consequences*. Mahwah, N.J.: Erlbaum.

Phillips, D. P. 1982. "The Impact of Fictional Television Stories on U.S. Adult Fatalities: New Evidence on the Effect of the Mass Media on Violence." *American Journal of Sociology* 87: 1340–1359.

Phillips, D. P. 1983. "The Found Experiment: A New Technique for Assessing the Impact of Mass Media Violence on Real-World Aggressive Behavior." In *Public Communication and Behavior*, G. Comstock, ed., Vol. 2, pp. 260–307. Orlando, Fla.: Academic Press.

Pillemer, D. B. 1998. *Momentous Events, Vivid Memories*. Cambridge, Mass.: Harvard University Press.

Pomper, G. M., ed. 1997. *The Election of 1996: Reports and Interpretations*. Chatham, N.J.: Chatham House.

Pool, I. deS., R. P. Abelson, and S. L. Popkin. 1965. *Candidates, Issues, and Strategies: A Computer Simulation of the 1960 and 1964 Presidential Elections*. Cambridge, Mass.: MIT Press.

Rogers, E. M. 1994. *A History of Communication Study: A Biographical Approach*. New York: Free Press.

Runyon, W. M. 1993. "Psychohistory and Political Psychology: A Comparative Analysis." In *Explorations in Political Psychology*, S. Iyengar and W. J. McGuire, eds., pp. 36–63. Durham, N.C.: Duke University Press.

Sabato, L. J. 1981. *The Rise of Political Consultants: New Ways of Winning Elections*. New York: Basic Books.

Schramm, W. 1997. *The Beginnings of Communication Study in America: A Personal Memoir*, S. H. Chaffee and E. M. Rogers, eds. Thousand Oaks, Calif.: Sage.

Sears, D. O. 1983. "The Person-Positivity Bias." *Journal of Personality and Social Psychology* 44: 233–250.

Simonton, D. K. 1987. *Why Presidents Succeed: A Political Psychology of Leadership*. New Haven: Yale University Press.

Simonton, D. K. 1994. *Greatness: Who Makes History and Why*. New York: Guilford.

Smith, C. E., P. M. Radcliffe, and J. H. Kessel. 1999. "The Partisan Choice: Bill Clinton or Bob Dole?" In *Reelection 1996: How Americans Voted*, H. F. Weisberg and J. M. Box-Steffensmeier, eds. New York: Chatham House.

Smith, C. P., ed. 1992. *Motivation and Personality: Handbook of the Thematic Content Analysis*. New York: Cambridge University Press.

Tversky, A., and D. Kahneman. 1981. "The Framing of Decisions and the Psychology of Choice." *Science* 211: 453–458.

Weisberg, H. F., and J. M. Box-Steffensmeier, eds. 1999. *Reelection 1996: How Americans Voted*. New York: Chatham House.

Zaller. J. 1992. *The Nature and Origins of Mass Opinion*. New York: Cambridge University Press.

Zaller, J. 1996. "The Myth of Massive Media Impact Revived: New Support for a Discredited Idea." In *Political Persuasion and Attitude Change*, D. C. Mutz, P. M. Sniderman, and R. A. Brody, eds., pp. 17–78. Ann Arbor: University of Michigan Press.

2

AN AGENDA FOR
VOTING RESEARCH[1]

LARRY M. BARTELS

Princeton University

As a beginning graduate student in the late 1970s, I can still recall hearing my fellow students refer to voting research as "intellectual masturbation." What they meant, I suppose, is that the manifest attractions of the field—rich data, sophisticated analyses, and even occasional theoretical elegance—could not compensate for a certain sterility stemming from the apparent lack of connection between studies of voting behavior and broader political or theoretical concerns. Although they probably didn't know it, these student critics were echoing complaints that have had a good deal of currency since the early days of election studies. For example, Key and Munger (1959, 297) argued that

> the isolation of the electorate from the total governing process and its subjection to microscopic analysis tends to make electoral study a nonpolitical endeavor. That isolation tends, perhaps not of necessity but because of the blinders on perception associated with the method, to divorce the subjects of microscopic examination from their place in the larger political situation. Hence, all the studies of so-called "political behavior" do not add impressively to our comprehension of the awesome process by which the community or nation makes decisions at the ballot box.

It seems clear to me that Key and Munger's complaint was overstated even in their own day. For example, one need only compare the Columbia University research team's account of Harry Truman's comeback in 1948 (Berelson et al. 1954, chap. 12) with contemporaneous journalistic accounts to realize that "studies of so-called 'political behavior'" had already added impressively to our comprehension of American politics—not only of the electorate in microscopic isolation, but also of collective "decisions at the ballot box" and their political meaning. The subsequent research presented in *The American Voter* (Campbell et al. 1960), *Elections and the Political Order* (Campbell et al. 1966), and other major works, including Key's own subsequent study of *The Responsible Electorate* (1966), provided further examples of how data from election surveys could be made to shed valuable light on "the larger political situation."

At the same time, however, Key and Munger in their day (and my graduate student colleagues in theirs) clearly identified what is still the key intellectual challenge facing scholars of voting behavior— how to connect detailed analysis of individual responses in election surveys to broader political issues. It would be fruitless to deny that a good deal of voting research consists of dreary minutiae utterly devoid of any broader political significance—"normal science" in the worst sense of that ambiguous phrase. The fact that "the blinders on perception associated with the method" have sometimes been overcome should not be taken as a justification for less inspired work, but as a spur to further creativity.

Obviously, creativity cannot be called up at will, and the directions it may take cannot usually be planned or predicted. Nevertheless, the successes of such past masters as Converse, Key, Lazarsfeld, Miller, and Stokes, and of subsequent scholars who have followed in their footsteps, seem to me to suggest several promising avenues for further progress in harnessing the study of voting behavior to broader ends. My aim here is to highlight some of those promising avenues of research; by doing so, I hope as well to highlight the political significance of the scholarly agenda they would advance.

My suggestions fall into three general categories. First, I advocate more attention to the *political meaning* of specific elections, both as a contribution to political science and as a contribution to public understanding of "decisions at the ballot box." Second, I advocate more attention to the *impact* of elections on the broader political system, including representation, policymaking, and public attitudes toward politics, government, and the national community. Third, I advocate more attention to the effects of *historical and contextual variation* arising from the behavior of political elites, the technology of political communication, economic and social circumstances, and other factors. I believe these three areas of study offer significant promise for the further development of voting research as an indispensable part of a broader and more important intellectual enterprise, namely, understanding the role of ordinary citizens in modern democratic politics.

Interpreting Elections

In the first fifteen years following the publication of *The American Voter*, the University of Michigan team produced a series of quasi-official summary analyses of successive presidential elections (Converse et al. 1961, 1965; Converse 1966; Converse et al. 1969; Miller et al. 1976). While the focus of each of these analyses was dictated in part by theoretical concerns, each also provided an authoritative statement about the political meaning of a given election. For example, Converse et al. (1961) provided both a theoretical and a political characterization of 1960 as a "reinstating" election, while Miller et al. (1976) emphasized "ideological polarization within the Democratic ranks" as a prime explanation for the resounding defeat of the majority party in 1972.

It seems very unlikely, given the evolving sociology of the political science profession, that any single analysis of a current election could be as authoritative as the Michigan analyses of the 1960s were in their day. The proliferation of scholars and scholarly agendas in the field of voting research, the vastly expanded efforts of journalists, commercial pollsters, and political pundits, and the increasingly ponderous pace of academic data analysis and publication have all conspired to make "the story of the election" a less compelling target of scholarly investigation.[2]

Despite these difficulties, it seems to me that academic voting research can and should make a much greater contribution to public understanding of contemporary election outcomes. One excellent model of how that might be done is provided by Stanley Kelley's book *Interpreting Elections*. Kelley (1983) employed detailed coding of responses to open-ended questions in National Election Studies (NES) surveys to account for the outcomes of presidential elections from 1952 through 1976. In addition to using the balance of positive and negative comments about the competing parties and candidates to ascertain the electorate's relative enthusiasm for the winner in each election, Kelley used the substance of those comments to identify the *reasons* for that candidate's victory. For example, he characterized the 1972 election as "a close landslide" in which "the issues central to the New Deal party system remained highly salient and strongly biased toward the Democrats," while many Nixon voters supported their man with considerable antipathy, and on the basis of factors that "were largely nonpartisan in their implications for the future" (Kelley 1983, 125).

In addition to offering his own interpretations of specific elections, Kelley provided an insightful critique of the interpretations offered by journalists and political pundits. Focusing particularly on interpretations of Ronald Reagan's "mandate" in the immediate wake of the 1980 election, Kelley complained that "the press's interpretation of the 1980 election was at its weakest in sorting out the effects of particular issues on the outcome," that it "lacked historical perspective," that it exaggerated "the one-sidedness of Reagan's victory," and that "once the election was over the press folded its tents too quickly" (Kelley 1983, 222–223). It seems rather likely that similar complaints could be directed toward press interpretations of most elections, and that academic voting research along the lines of Kelley's own analyses could help to counteract those faults.[3]

A series of analyses by Miller and Shanks (1982, 1996; Shanks and Miller 1990, 1991) provides a rather different but equally compelling example of how systematic voting research might shed useful light on the bases and meaning of specific election outcomes. Building on the notion of a "funnel of causality" in *The American Voter*, Miller and Shanks arrayed a wide variety of potentially relevant variables in a recursive statistical model of voting behavior leading from stable social and economic characteristics through partisan and policy predispositions, current policy preferences and perceptions, impressions of the candidates, and prospective evaluations to the eventual vote choice. Building as well on Stokes's (1966) analysis of "Some Dynamic Elements of Contests for the Presidency," they attempted at each step in their analysis to isolate both the direct and indirect effects of each explanatory variable on *individual voting behavior* and the net impact of those effects on *the aggregate election outcome*. Thus, for example, the aggregate impact of party identification would be seen to depend both on the effect of partisanship on individual vote choices (directly and indirectly, through partisan biases in perceptions of current and future performance, candidates, and issues) and on the distribution of partisanship in the electorate (since an exactly even balance of Republican and Democrat loyalties, however powerful, would have no *net* impact on the election outcome).

As with Kelley's analyses of open-ended survey responses, the results of Miller and Shanks's multistage statistical analyses sometimes confirm and sometimes challenge, but invariably refine, conventional interpretations of specific election outcomes. In 1980, for example, they concluded that negative evaluations of Carter's performance in office contributed almost seven percentage points to Reagan's vote total, while ideology and policy preferences added another eight percentage points. Thus, their analysis provided concrete evidence for both of the prevailing interpretations of the 1980 election outcome—one emphasizing the repudiation of an unpopular incumbent and the other positing a "policy mandate" for his conservative challenger. At the same time, they noted that Reagan's policy advantage primarily reflected the impact of abstract ideology and desires for a change in the *direction* of government policy, whereas relative proximity to the two candidates' specific issues positions actually *reduced* Reagan's vote margin. They concluded that Reagan assumed office with considerable public support "for a conservative change in the *direction* of federal policy—changes which are consistent with the direction, if not the magnitude, of the new policies he has been implementing" (Miller and Shanks 1982, 354).

Political assessments of this sort would obviously be more valuable if they could be made in the immediate aftermath of an election rather than months or years after the fact. Still, as Kelley (1983, 223–224) argued, "Coverage of an election can reasonably be thought of as a branch of investigative journalism, the products of which can appear at any stage of the investigation. To the objection that presidential elections interest no one a few months after they are over, one can cite the sales of T. H. White's books, which surely show that new material on an election, or old facts in a new light, interests readers."

Of course, scholars of voting behavior are unlikely to reach the bestseller list, or even the news columns, with recursive regression models or clever manipulations of open-ended survey responses. Nevertheless, they can and should perform an important public service by providing careful, detailed, and politically informed analyses of specific election outcomes for anyone willing (or, in the case of students, compelled) to pay attention. Even in a political culture

dominated by pundits and political entrepreneurs, good analysis
may sometimes drive out bad conventional wisdom.

The Impact of Elections

Interpreting election outcomes should be an important aspect of the
agenda for voting research; but we should also give more concerted
attention to public opinion, voting behavior, and election outcomes
as *explanatory* variables. Writing in 1960, the authors of *The American Voter* complained that, "Almost no research has had as its primary objective the description of influence relations connecting the
electoral process with other decision processes of American government" (Campbell et al. 1960, 540). Forty years after those words
were written, they still pinpoint one of the most significant failings
of the scholarly literature on voting behavior.

This failing surely reflects, in significant part, "the blinders on perception associated with the method" (to return to Key and Munger's
related complaint). The primary focus of the NES surveys on attitudinal *antecedents* of the vote, and the traditional NES survey design
in which interviews are completed as soon as possible after election
day, have contributed to the illusion that *our sort* of politics ends at
the conclusion of every even-numbered year. To explain what happens next, we turn to our colleagues studying the presidency, Congress, interest groups, and public policy—who in their turn often
seem to give little thought to the electoral process except insofar as it
occasionally produces new faces inside the Washington beltway.
This traditional division of labor is in some sense quite efficient, but
also intellectually constraining.[4]

The problem is to figure out how data from election surveys can
fruitfully be combined with data on "other decision processes of
American government" to shed light on the political consequences
of electoral politics. So far, most work in this vein has focused on
roll-call voting by members of Congress, following in the footsteps
of Miller and Stokes's (1963) pathbreaking study of "Constituency
Influence in Congress." This ingenious study combined systematic
data on the preferences and perceptions of congressional candidates
with parallel data on the views of ordinary voters in their districts to
trace the responsiveness of political elites to both real and imagined
constituency opinions in a variety of policy areas. It spawned a great
deal of subsequent research, some of which improved on Miller and

Stokes's data and methods, but none of which departed significantly from the conceptual framework they set out (e.g., Achen 1978; Erikson 1978; Converse and Pierce 1986).

The basic problem with this conceptual framework, in my view, is that it is better suited to exploit cross-sectional survey designs than to answer substantive questions about political representation. What we usually want to know is not whether relatively liberal politicians represent relatively liberal constituencies, or even whether an increase in the liberalism of a district will produce a more liberal representative, but how collective policy outcomes change in response to changes in public preferences and voting behavior. Often that will require more than a simple adding up of separate effects in discrete districts. Though the Miller-Stokes framework may sometimes be stretched to fit (e.g., Bartels 1991), it is really not the right tool for the job.

Stimson and his colleagues (1995) have provided a powerful alternative framework in their research on "Dynamic Representation." Using highly aggregated survey data gathered over a period of thirty-five years, they showed that governmental institutions do respond significantly to changes in what Stimson (1999) referred to as "policy mood," both through electoral turnover and through "rational anticipation" of changing public preferences by incumbent politicians (Stimson et al. 1995, 560). This finding seems to come a good deal closer than Miller and Stokes's to the heart of what we mean by political representation. At the same time, however, it raises a variety of important second-order questions about the specific role of campaigns and elections in producing policy responsiveness.

For example, to what extent does an effective postelection policy mandate depend on the preconditions for "issue-oriented political behavior" posited forty years ago by the authors of *The American Voter*—issue cognition, intensity of feeling, and recognition of party differences (Campbell et al. 1960, 170)? To what extent is the fulfillment of these preconditions within the power of the candidates and political parties, and under what conditions will they give voters what Barry Goldwater once called "a choice, not an echo" (Page 1978; Franklin 1991)? How specifically, and how successfully, can political elites set the terms upon which campaigns are fought and elections decided (Johnston et al. 1992; Petrocik 1996)? These questions and others like them should have a prominent place on any agenda for voting research. Addressing them will require creative analysis of detailed survey data, but also of much more wide-ranging data on the strategies of parties and candidates, the rhetoric of campaigns, and the subsequent workings of governmental institutions.

In pursuing this enterprise, it will be essential to bear in mind that the impact of elections on the behavior of political elites will often be subtle and indirect. In *Public Opinion and American Democracy,* Key emphasized the political significance of "latent opinion," that is, the public preferences and beliefs that politicians *expect* to confront in future elections, after today's policies have had their effects and tomorrow's political opponents have had their say. To the extent that elections are read as signals of future propensities rather than as direct policy mandates, the task of specifying which aspects of electoral behavior "governments find it prudent to heed," and why, becomes "singularly slippery," as Key himself (1961, 262) acknowledged. Notwithstanding some fruitful applications of the notion of "latent opinion" by Arnold (1990) and Zaller (1994, 1998a), the methodological difficulties inherent in pinning down this "singularly slippery" concept have discouraged scholars of public opinion and voting behavior from giving it the prominence it clearly deserves.

On the other hand, an appreciation of the importance of "latent opinion" may also reinforce and extend the significance of more conventional analyses of directly observable public opinion and electoral behavior. For example, from this perspective the demonstrated importance of "retrospective voting" on the basis of an incumbent party's political and economic record (Key 1966; Fiorina 1981) matters not only in its own right, but also because politicians are likely to recognize that importance and act accordingly—as shown in Jacobson and Kernell's (1983) analysis of strategic behavior by potential congressional challengers or Tufte's (1978) analysis of political influences on economic policymaking. These works and others in the same vein have helped to break down artificial boundaries between the study of voting behavior and the study of elite politics and policymaking; however, much more can and should be done to explore what might be called the "latent impact" of voting behavior.

If scholarly research on the connection between elections and public policy is still at a rudimentary stage, research on the broader impact of elections on American political culture is even less advanced. Although we have occasionally given lip service to the notion that campaigns and elections are the primary rituals of modern democracy, we have done remarkably little to specify what that means, or why it matters. Again, survey data from election studies should be one important resource for analysts attempting to trace the impact of campaigns and elections on popular attitudes and orientations toward politics and government.

One useful indication of how such research might proceed, and what it might turn up, is provided by Rahn and her colleagues, who used data from the 1996 NES survey to compare levels of social trust, trust in government, and external political efficacy before and after the election (Rahn et al. 1999). They found that all three of these forms of "social capital" (Coleman 1990) increased between the preelection interviews in September and October and the postelection interviews in November and December, and that these increases were related to the campaign-related attitudes and behavior of individual citizens and to the mobilizing efforts of political elites. "If we can improve our elections to make them more social-capital enhancing," Rahn et al. (1999) concluded, "by, for example, increasing mobilization by the political parties and enticing quality candidates to run, such efforts may redound to civil society with higher levels of political efficacy, more trust in government, and greater social solidarity."

Historical and Contextual Variation

Having railed against "the blinders on perception associated with the [survey] method" in the passage I quoted earlier, Key and Munger (1959, 298) went on to suggest that

> Some of the difficulties of theory and analysis will be solved in due course, doubtless in a serendipitous manner, as the number of studies multiplies. New types of election situations will be analyzed; provisional generalizations will be modified to account for new situations; and the process will be repeated. By the observation of a greater variety of types of situations it may be possible to tie the study of electoral behavior more directly to the workings of the state. Such a linkage might enable us to talk with a bit more information about the conditions under which an electorate can most effectively perform its decision-making role in the governing process.

The accumulation of data from a series of two dozen National Election Studies covering half a century has gone a considerable way toward redeeming Key and Munger's hope that observing "a greater variety of types of situations" would help to overcome some of the "difficulties of theory and analysis" facing voting researchers. To some extent, this progress has come about in exactly the "serendipitous manner" they foresaw—by clever analysts testing "provisional generalizations" against the "new situations" thrown up by political history.

The fruitful role of historical variation in both solving and generating theoretical problems is nicely illustrated by the revisionist and counterrevisionist literatures stemming from the application of the "Michigan model" to voting data from the 1960s and early 1970s. Ironically, if not surprisingly, the first explicit effort in this direction was by one of the core members of the Michigan team—Stokes's (1966) analysis of "Some Dynamic Elements of Contests for the Presidency." Beginning from the premise that the "number of presidential campaigns since the advent of survey studies of voting [was] now large enough to be pressed hard for evidence about the sources of electoral change," Stokes focused systematic attention on "the importance of changes in the issues and leaders which the electorate is asked to appraise" (Stokes 1966, 19).

Subsequent work by Pomper (1972), Nie et al. (1976), and many others similarly exploited historical variation in the sets of candidates, issues, and political contexts brought forth by successive elections to test broad propositions about stability and change in the behavior of "the American voter." Notwithstanding the various theoretical and methodological controversies and confusions that attend any such scholarly effort, and regardless of the outcome of the substantive debate, the result was in one important sense a triumph for the Michigan studies as an ongoing enterprise. The continuity of what would eventually become the NES time series had begun to bear significant scientific dividends.

In these relatively early works, longitudinal data were often used simply to trace how variables or relationships of interest changed over time. Though some explanation for these changes might be offered (e.g., changes in the electoral impact of issues might be attributed to sharper contrasts between the policy views of the two parties' candidates in 1964 and 1972 than in 1956), the aim of such analyses was often essentially descriptive, with specific elections or historical eras treated as "proper nouns" (in much the same way that specific political systems are often treated as "proper nouns" in cross-national comparative research) rather than as instances of more general, theoretically significant political contexts.

More recently, longitudinal data have increasingly been used more systematically to supply variation in theoretically relevant explanatory factors. The analytical power of this approach is evident, for example, in Markus's (1988) work on economic voting. Whereas scholars of economic voting for years had relied either on aggregate-level data on economic conditions and election outcomes (e.g., Kramer 1971; Tufte 1978) or on individual-level data on economic circumstances and vote choices in single elections (e.g., Kinder and Kiewiet 1979; Fiorina 1981), Markus pooled NES data from eight presidential election years with varying economic conditions ranging from recession in 1980 to economic boom in 1964. The result was the first credible effort to distinguish the effects of national economic conditions and personal economic perceptions—and also the first credible effort to reconcile apparent disparities between previous findings based on aggregate-level and individual-level evidence (Kramer 1983). Markus concluded that national economic conditions had a substantial "sociotropic" impact "even with perceived personal economic circumstances held constant," and that personal economic circumstances were "moderately influential" in determining individual votes but "relatively unimportant" at the aggregate level "for the simple reason that the proportion of individuals feeling personally 'worse off' has not fluctuated very much from election to election during the period under study" (Markus 1988, 151).

Markus's study cleverly exploited natural variation across election years in national economic conditions. Other scholars working in the same vein have similarly exploited natural variation in the content and tone of campaign advertising and media coverage (Finkel and Geer 1998; Bartels 2000), the ideological extremism of the candidates (Zaller 1998b), and other potentially important contextual factors. Still, it seems to me that we have only begun to explore the range of possibilities for contextual analysis presented by a data set that now includes two dozen distinct national elections spanning a period of fifty years.

Many more possibilities are suggested by other aspects of contextual variation within or across election surveys. Voters in different congressional districts evaluate different incumbents with varying constituency service efforts, voting records, and exposure to scandals (Cain et al. 1987; Powell 1989; Jacobson and Dimock 1994). Voters in different presidential primaries have different sets of viable candidates to consider (Bartels 1988; Abramson et al. 1992). Respondents interviewed at different points in a given election season have been exposed to varying amounts and kinds of campaign communication (Markus 1982; Kinder and Sanders 1996, chap. 9; Jacobson 1997). In each of these cases, contextual variation provides crucial leverage for connecting individual voting behavior to the broader workings of the political system.

For other purposes, the most valuable aspect of the cumulative NES data set is its sheer size, which makes it possible to isolate relatively large numbers of respondents with particularly interesting political characteristics, or in particularly interesting political circumstances. For example, Gay (1997) pooled data from seven NES surveys conducted between 1980 and 1992 to analyze the political attitudes and perceptions of about 600 constituents of African-American members of Congress. Obviously, given the racial composition of Congress in this period, no single national survey would have included enough constituents of black representatives to allow for reliable description of their attitudes, much less to make meaningful distinctions between black and white constituents, more or less confrontational representatives, and so on.

Possibilities for fruitful contextual analysis have occasionally been enriched by conscious efforts to *create* or *magnify* theoretically interesting contextual variation through innovative study designs. For example, NES has experimented periodically with African-American oversamples (in 1964, 1968, and 1970), state- or district-based samples (in the 1978 and 1980 NES surveys and, on a larger scale, in the 1988–90–92 Senate Election Study), primary campaign surveys (in 1980, 1984, and 1988), and timed release of independent subsamples at various points in the general election campaign (beginning in 1992). All of these may be thought of as attempts to facilitate contextual analysis by interviewing respondents whose geographical, institutional, temporal, or social locations differed in significant, measurable ways.

Of course, meaningful contextual analysis will often require a good deal of additional investment in gathering relevant contextual data. For example, much of the best work based on the 1988–1992 NES Senate Studies has involved detailed coding of campaign themes, media coverage, incumbents' activities in the Senate and in their districts, and the like. This work has helped to shed valuable light on the connection between elite politics and electoral behavior. Thus, for example, Franklin (1991) examined the ways in which reelection campaigns sharpened (or failed to sharpen) constituents' recognition of their Senators' policy views. He found that the impact of campaigns in this sense was strongly dependent on the campaign strategies of incumbents and challengers: incumbents who emphasized issues significantly reduced the variance of voters' perceptions of their positions, especially when they focused on a small number of issue themes, whereas challengers who emphasized issues significantly increased the variance of voters' perceptions of the incumbents' ideologies (presumably by contradicting the incumbents' own ideological appeals with negative advertising). Franklin (1991, 1209) concluded that "the dominant elements in determining the clarity of candidate perception rest with the candidates themselves."

In Franklin's analysis, elite behavior was measured at the level of states, with all of the survey respondents in a given state treated as if they were reacting to a single, homogeneous campaign. More recently, advances in measurement have made it possible to investigate even more specific campaign effects. For example, Goldstein (1997) merged data on the magnitude and content of presidential candidates' television ad buys in each of the nation's seventy-five largest media markets in each week of the 1996 campaign with data from the 1996 NES survey on the location, media exposure, and political behavior of prospective voters. By treating the intensity of the presidential campaign in each media market as a contextual variable, Goldstein was able to examine the effect of campaign advertising on turnout and vote choice in considerably more detail than would otherwise have been possible. NES has attempted to facilitate analyses of this sort by providing detailed information on respondents' locations and on their potential exposure to campaign communications (e.g., by measuring entertainment television viewing and access to cable television). As a result, any aspect of political context that can be keyed to geographical location at the census tract, zip code, county, or other level can be associated with individual survey respondents, and thus connected with a wealth of data on individual political attitudes and behavior.[5]

Meanwhile, NES has pushed the frontier of contextual analysis in still another direction by collaborating with parallel national election study teams in more than fifty other countries to produce an ambitious Comparative Study of Electoral Systems (CSES). An international planning committee developed a ten-minute module of common questions for inclusion in each country's national election survey, as well as a common battery of contextual variables identifying parties, candidates, electoral rules, and government structures. As of early 1999, the CSES module had been administered in twenty-one countries; the first wave of data, including survey data and contextual data from eleven of these countries, had just been publicly released; and international planning had begun for a second round of CSES covering the period 2000–2004.

The intellectual, organizational, and political challenges involved in mounting a cooperative data collection enlisting dozens of scholars from every part of the globe are obviously formidable. That it has been done at all is enormously impressive. If the resulting data set continues to expand in breadth and scope as envisioned by the architects of the project —and if comparable energy and intelligence can be brought to bear on the fascinating question of how best to *analyze* these remarkably rich data—then CSES may come to be recognized as a new landmark in the integration of election studies into the broad mainstream of contemporary political science.

The Future of Election Studies

The field of voting research, perhaps more than any other field of political science, has been shaped by the availability of data. The extraordinary energy, intellectual vision, and generosity of Warren Miller and his colleagues in what has come to be called the National Election Studies project have provided scholars of voting behavior with easy access to data of unparalleled scope and quality—and with an influential model for a variety of independent data-gathering efforts. The wealth of data in the field has in turn helped to attract an unusually large and active community of scholars. The American Political Science Association's organized section on Elections, Public Opinion, and Voting Behavior is one of the largest in the profession with over 600 members. Most of the section's members—and many other political scientists, and social scientists more generally—rely in significant part on election surveys to pursue their various research agendas. The cumulative bibliography maintained by the NES project staff, though probably far from complete, lists almost 3000 scholarly works that have used NES data. When data from the 1998 NES survey were released in March 1999, over fifty scholars downloaded the data from the NES Web site within the first *six hours*. These facts underline the crucial role of data in stimulating and facilitating contemporary voting research.

Despite these indicators of a thriving research community organized in significant part around election surveys, the scientific utility of further data-gathering efforts in this vein, and of further NES surveys in particular, has been a matter of periodic professional controversy. In part that controversy reflects simple but powerful resource constraints: NES is the most prominent example of "big science" in a discipline that has mostly had to make do with much smaller, less expensive research enterprises.[6] However, qualms about the role of election surveys in the field go deeper than that. In some critics' assessments, the rich vein mined by Lazarsfeld, Converse, Miller, Stokes, and Key has simply run out, with too little in the way of new findings and new ideas to justify significant further investment in election surveys.

Critics of election studies have tended to focus on the limitations of survey data in conventional cross-sectional analyses, and on the declining marginal value of gathering additional survey data in each new election cycle simply to replicate previous analyses. However, those criticisms seem to me to overlook the extent to which the growing scope and sophistication of election studies have actually contributed to transcending the stereotypical limitations of voting research. Although new data have sometimes been used to replicate (or overturn) previous findings, they have also been employed in much more creative and powerful ways.

Consider, for example, the uses to which scholars have put the growing historical archive of NES data. The scientific value of the NES time series was showcased in a special panel at the 1998 meeting of the American Political Science Association organized to mark the 50th anniversary of the NES project. Given the challenge of demonstrating how longitudinal data could be used to illuminate the nature and implications of political change over a half century of American political history, several of the leading figures in the field—Edward Carmines, Gary Jacobson, Donald Kinder, Warren Miller, John Petrocik, and John Zaller—explored topics as diverse as the evolution of racial attitudes, the changing role of congressional candidates, the social and cultural bases of shifting party coalitions, and the relative sensitivity of different voters to changing political conditions. In a very literal sense, this work (and much more like it, and much more still to be done) would be impossible to carry out without access to the NES time series.

The growing prevalence of historical analyses of voting behavior is just one example of how more and better data have opened up new avenues for research in the field. The growing scope and sophistication of election studies have also reopened avenues for research in areas where the best scholars of previous generations struggled mightily—and only partially successfully — against the limitations of the data available to them. Three pioneering efforts to extend the range of conventional election studies and the data presently available to pursue them will illustrate this point.

When Donald Stokes, fresh from having coauthored *The American Voter*, turned to the study of "elections as total social or political events" (Stokes 1962, 689), he was compelled to rely on highly aggregated historical election returns with all of their limitations. In contrast, Stokes's successors today have ready access to richly detailed data on individual attitudes, perceptions, and behavior in a dozen presidential elections, and thus to unprecedented leverage on the interplay between changing patterns of individual electoral behavior and their systemic causes and consequences.

When Miller and Stokes (1963) merged survey data with elite interviews to examine constituency influence in Congress, they relied on a survey sample with an average of about 15 respondents in each of 116 congressional districts in a single year (and a rather inefficient sample at that, since it was primarily designed for other purposes). Scholars interested in revisiting the issues of representation explored by Miller and Stokes can now draw on a purpose-built sample with an average of 180 respondents in each of the 50 states in the 1988–90–92 NES Senate Study, or on much larger samples (albeit with much less detailed data) from a variety of commercial or media polls (Erikson et al. 1993).

When the various principals in the Michigan studies turned their attention to electoral attitudes and behavior outside the United States, they proceeded by engaging in bilateral collaborations with individual scholars in Norway (Campbell and Valen 1961), France (Converse and Dupeux 1962; Converse and Pierce 1986), and Britain (Butler and Stokes 1969). Scholars with similar interests today can draw on much broader and more ambitious cross-national data collections, including the Comparative Study of Electoral Systems, the Euro-Barometer series (Lewis-Beck 1988; Inglehart 1990), and the World Values surveys (Inglehart 1997).

In these instances, among many others, more and better data have made it possible not only to replicate and extend prior findings, but to pursue fundamentally new lines of research. How does the salience of specific issues in the voting booth vary with historical circumstances and candidates' campaign strategies? How do legislators weigh the policy preferences of different constituents, and when do constituents' preferences trump those of presidents, parties, interest groups, and campaign contributors? How do the institutional features of different electoral systems condition the relationship between citizens' preferences and subsequent policy?

All of these are clearly important questions. But they are especially important from the viewpoint I have adopted here — that political context and political consequences belong at the forefront of the contemporary agenda for voting research. Indeed, from that viewpoint many of the most important questions in the field of voting research can only be effectively addressed with consistent survey data spanning a wide variety of political, historical, or institutional contexts. By providing those data, and the energy and imagination necessary to exploit them, contemporary voting researchers have brought their work into closer and more productive contact with other aspects of politics and political science. Perhaps ironically, the most important path to progress in transcending the stereotypical limitations of conventional survey-based voting research has been to employ even more survey data, albeit in new ways and (often) in combination with other kinds of data.

Having been a user of data from election surveys for some twenty years (and a collaborator in their production for a significant fraction of that time), I see little evidence of diminishing scientific returns, and much reason to hope that election surveys will continue to play a prominent role in voting research. If they do, new generations of scholars will no doubt continue to pursue the questions raised here, and many others besides. If they do not, those of us who strive to comprehend "the awesome process by which the community or nation makes decisions at the ballot box" will find our resources for doing so much diminished.

Notes

1. A somewhat different version of this chapter was presented as the third annual Miller–Converse Lecture at the University of Michigan's Center for Political Studies, April 13, 1999. I am grateful for the reactions of friends and colleagues on that occasion, as well as those of two anonymous

reviewers. Given my official role as chair of the Board of Overseers of the National Election Studies (NES) project at the time the lecture was delivered, it is more than usually incumbent upon me to stress that the views presented here are offered in my capacity as an independent scholar, and should not be attributed to the Board of Overseers, NES, the University of Michigan, or anyone else.

2. It is remarkable to recall that the first Michigan interpretation of the 1960 election appeared in the *American Political Science Review* in June 1961—before the publication of the first book in Theodore White's *Making of the President* series. By contrast, *Newsweek* magazine's comprehensive report on the 1996 election (Thomas 1997) appeared in print the week after the votes were counted (and in book form within several weeks). The first scholarly analysis comparable in scope to the Michigan election reports of the 1960s was published in October 1998 (Alvarez and Nagler 1998).

3. Krasno (1998) applied Kelley's method to the 1994 congressional election—another instance in which politicians and pundits offered sweeping interpretations of the winning party's "mandate." He found that "the Republicans' victory was a narrow one" by comparison with other recent midterm elections, but that "ideology . . . came up more often and strongly favored the Republicans" and that "Republicans were also preferred on a wide variety of other issues, including a handful formerly 'owned' by the Democrats." He concluded that the GOP had "some claim on a conservative mandate," but that "there was no conservative tide that swept beyond, or far beyond, the slim majority who supported Republican candidates" (Krasno 1998, 232).

4. It may be worth noting that a parallel division of labor often simplifies and constrains the work of political reporters. As David Broder of the *Washington Post* once put it (with a telltale mixture of pride and chagrin), "I've often said to our White House reporters, 'My job is to deliver these turkeys; after they're in office, they're your responsibility'" (quoted by Fallows 1996, 252).

5. To safeguard the confidentiality of respondents, NES does not publicly release geographical information below the county or congressional district level. However, by arrangement with the NES staff (and subject to some procedural restrictions), scholars may separately construct lower-level contextual variables and then have them merged with the survey data.

6. Although quite small by the standards of "big science" projects in other fields, NES is quite large by the standards of academic political science projects. For example, the US$1 million or so per year currently being devoted to NES by the National Science Foundation represents about 0.03

percent of the total NSF budget, but about 18 percent of the NSF budget for political science. Moreover, unlike other political science projects, NES has received substantial NSF support for three decades, including continuing support since 1978 as a "national social science resource." In a discipline as vibrant and diverse as contemporary political science, it seems likely that any project absorbing such a large fraction of such a small budget over such a long period of time would be subject to significant scrutiny and occasional resentment. NES has already absorbed a substantial budget cut in the current (1998–2001) funding cycle by reducing sample sizes, relying increasingly on telephone interviewing, curtailing pilot studies and other development work, and trimming project staff. Meanwhile, the National Science Foundation has embarked on a general reexamination of "infrastructure" funding priorities in the social sciences and has solicited proposals for new infrastructure projects to compete with the current "big three" survey projects—the Panel Study of Income Dynamics in economics, NES in political science, and the General Social Survey in sociology. As of this writing, it is unclear whether any or all of these long-standing projects will continue to be supported by NSF.

References

Abramson, Paul R., John H. Aldrich, Phil Paolino, and David W. Rohde. 1992. "'Sophisticated' Voting in the 1988 Presidential Primaries." *American Political Science Review* **86**: 55–69.

Achen, Christopher H. 1978. "Measuring Representation." *American Journal of Political Science* **22**: 475–510.

Alvarez, R. Michael, and Jonathan Nagler. 1998. "Economics, Entitlements, and Social Issues: Voter Choice in the 1996 Presidential Election." *American Journal of Political Science* **42**: 1349–1363.

Arnold, R. Douglas. 1990. *The Logic of Congressional Action.* New Haven: Yale University Press.

Bartels, Larry M. 1988. *Presidential Primaries and the Dynamics of Public Choice.* Princeton: Princeton University Press.

Bartels, Larry M. 1991. "Constituency Opinion and Congressional Policy Making: The Reagan Defense Buildup." *American Political Science Review* **85**: 457–474.

Bartels, Larry M. 2000. "Campaign Quality: Standards for Evaluation, Benchmarks for Reform." In *Campaign Reform: Insights and Evidence,* Larry M. Bartels and Lynn Vavreck, eds. Ann Arbor: University of Michigan Press.

Berelson, Bernard R., Paul F. Lazarsfeld, and William N. McPhee. 1954. *Voting: A Study of Opinion Formation in a Presidential Campaign.* Chicago: University of Chicago Press.

Butler, David, and Donald Stokes. 1969. *Political Change in Britain: Forces Shaping Electoral Choice.* New York: St. Martin's Press.

Cain, Bruce, John Ferejohn, and Morris P. Fiorina. 1987. *The Personal Vote: Constituency Service and Electoral Independence.* Cambridge, Mass.: Harvard University Press.

Campbell, Angus, and Henry Valen. 1961. "Party Identification in Norway and the United States." *Public Opinion Quarterly* 25: 505–525.

Campbell, Angus, Philip E. Converse, Warren E. Miller, and Donald E. Stokes. 1960. *The American Voter.* New York: John Wiley & Sons.

Campbell, Angus, Philip E. Converse, Warren E. Miller, and Donald E. Stokes. 1966. *Elections and the Political Order.* New York: John Wiley & Sons.

Coleman, James S. 1990. *Foundations of Social Theory.* Cambridge, Mass.: Belknap Press/Harvard University Press.

Converse, Philip E. 1966. "Religion and Politics: The 1960 Election." In *Elections and the Political Order,* Angus Campbell et al., eds. New York: John Wiley & Sons.

Converse, Philip E., and Georges Dupeux. 1962. "Politicization of the Electorate in France and the United States." *Public Opinion Quarterly* 26: 1–23.

Converse, Philip E., and Roy Pierce. 1986. *Political Representation in France.* Cambridge, Mass.: Harvard University Press.

Converse, Philip E., Angus Campbell, Warren E. Miller, and Donald E. Stokes. 1961. "Stability and Change in 1960: A Reinstating Election." *American Political Science Review* 55: 269–280.

Converse, Philip E., Aage R. Clausen, and Warren E. Miller. 1965. "Electoral Myth and Reality: The 1964 Election." *American Political Science Review* 59: 321–336.

Converse, Philip E., Warren E. Miller, Jerold G. Rusk, and Arthur C. Wolfe. 1969. "Continuity and Change in American Politics: Parties and Issues in the 1968 Election." *American Political Science Review* 63: 1083–1105.

Erikson, Robert S. 1978. "Constituency Opinion and Congressional Behavior: A Reexamination of the Miller–Stokes Representation Data." *American Journal of Political Science* 22: 511–535.

Erikson, Robert S., Gerald C. Wright, and John P. McIver. 1993. *Statehouse Democracy: Public Opinion and Policy in the American States.* New York: Cambridge University Press.

Fallows, James. 1996. *Breaking the News: How the Media Undermine American Democracy.* New York: Vintage Books.

Finkel, Steven E., and John G. Geer. 1998. "Spot Check: Casting Doubt on the Demobilizing Effect of Attack Advertising." *American Journal of Political Science* 42: 573–595.

Fiorina, Morris P. 1981. *Retrospective Voting in American National Elections.* New Haven: Yale University Press.

Franklin, Charles H. 1991. "Eschewing Obfuscation? Campaigns and the Perception of U.S. Senate Incumbents." *American Political Science Review* 85: 1193–1214.

Gay, Claudine. 1997. *Taking Charge: Black Electoral Success and the Redefinition of American Politics.* Ph.D. dissertation, Department of Government, Harvard University, Cambridge, Mass.

Goldstein, Kenneth M. 1997. Political Advertising and Political Persuasion in the 1996 Presidential Campaign. Unpublished paper prepared for presentation at the annual meeting of the American Political Science Association, Washington, D.C.

Inglehart, Ronald. 1990. *Culture Shift in Advanced Industrial Society*. Princeton: Princeton University Press.

Inglehart, Ronald. 1997. *Modernization and Postmodernization: Cultural, Economic, and Political Change in 43 Societies*. Princeton: Princeton University Press.

Jacobson, Gary C. 1997. Measuring Campaign Spending Effects in U.S. House Elections. Unpublished paper presented at the conference Capturing Campaign Effects, University of British Columbia, Vancouver, Canada.

Jacobson, Gary C., and Michael A. Dimock. 1994. "Checking Out: The Effects of Bank Overdrafts on the 1992 House Elections." *American Journal of Political Science* 38: 601–624.

Jacobson, Gary C., and Samuel Kernell. 1983. *Strategy and Choice in Congressional Elections*, 2nd ed. New Haven: Yale University Press.

Johnston, Richard, André Blais, Henry E. Brady, and Jean Crête. 1992. *Letting the People Decide: Dynamics of a Canadian Election*. Montreal: McGill-Queen's University Press.

Kelley, Stanley, Jr. 1983. *Interpreting Elections*. Princeton: Princeton University Press.

Key, V. O., Jr. 1961. *Public Opinion and American Democracy*. New York: Knopf.

Key, V.O., Jr., with the assistance of Milton C. Cummings, Jr. 1966. *The Responsible Electorate: Rationality in Presidential Voting, 1936–1960*. New York: Vintage Books.

Key, V. O., Jr., and Frank Munger. 1959. "Social Determinism and Electoral Decision: The Case of Indiana." In *American Voting Behavior*, Eugene Burdick and Arthur J. Brodbeck, eds. Glencoe, Ill.: Free Press.

Kinder, Donald R., and Roderick D. Kiewiet. 1979. "Economic Discontent and Political Behavior: The Role of Personal Grievances and Collective Economic Judgments in Congressional Voting." *American Journal of Political Science* 23: 495–527.

Kinder, Donald R., and Lynn M. Sanders. 1996. *Divided by Color: Racial Politics and Democratic Ideals*. Chicago: University of Chicago Press.

Kramer, Gerald H. 1971. "Short-Term Fluctuations in U.S. Voting Behavior, 1896–1964." *American Political Science Review* 65: 131–143.

Kramer, Gerald H. 1983. "The Ecological Fallacy Revisited: Aggregate- versus Individual-Level Findings on Economics and Elections, and Sociotropic Voting." *American Political Science Review* 77: 92–111.

Krasno, Jonathan S. 1998. "Interpreting the 1994 Elections." In *Politicians and Party Politics*, John G. Geer, ed. Baltimore: Johns Hopkins University Press.

Lewis-Beck, Michael S. 1988. *Economics and Elections: The Major Western Democracies*. Ann Arbor: University of Michigan Press.

Markus, Gregory B. 1982. "Political Attitudes During an Election Year: A Report on the 1980 NES Panel Study." *American Political Science Review* 76: 538–560.

Markus, Gregory B. 1988. "The Impact of Personal and National Economic Conditions on the Presidential Vote: A Pooled Cross-Sectional Analysis." *American Journal of Political Science* 32: 137–154.

Miller, Arthur H., Warren E. Miller, Alden S. Raine, and Thad A. Brown. 1976. "A Majority Party in Disarray." *American Political Science Review* 70: 753–778.

Miller, Warren E., and J. Merrill Shanks. 1982. "Policy Directions and Presidential Leadership: Alternative Interpretations of the 1980 Presidential Election." *British Journal of Political Science* 12: 299–356.

Miller, Warren E., and J. Merrill Shanks. 1996. *The New American Voter*. Cambridge, Mass.: Harvard University Press.

Miller, Warren E., and Donald E. Stokes. 1963. "Constituency Influence in Congress." *American Political Science Review* 57: 45–56.

Nie, Norman H., Sidney Verba, and John R. Petrocik. 1976. *The Changing American Voter*. Cambridge, Mass.: Harvard University Press.

Page, Benjamin I. 1978. *Choices and Echoes in Presidential Elections: Rational Man and Electoral Democracy*. Chicago: University of Chicago Press.

Petrocik, John R. 1996. "Issue Ownership in Presidential Elections, with a 1980 Case Study." *American Journal of Political Science* 40: 825–850.

Pomper, Gerald M. 1972. "From Confusion to Clarity: Issues and American Voters, 1956–1968." *American Political Science Review* 66: 415–428.

Powell, Lynda. 1989. "Analyzing Misinformation: Perceptions of Congressional Candidates' Ideologies." *American Journal of Political Science* 33: 272–293.

Rahn, Wendy M., John Brehm, and Neil Carlson. 1999. "National Elections as Institutions for Generating Social Capital." In *Civic Engagement in American Democracy*, Theda Skocpol and Morris P. Fiorina, eds. Washington, D.C.: Brookings Institution Press.

Shanks, J. Merrill, and Warren E. Miller. 1990. "Policy Direction and Performance Evaluation: Complementary Explanations of the Reagan Elections." *British Journal of Political Science* 20: 143–235.

Shanks, J. Merrill, and Warren E. Miller. 1991. "Partisanship, Policy, and Performance: The Reagan Legacy in the 1988 Election." *British Journal of Political Science* 21: 129–197.

Stimson, James A. 1999. *Public Opinion in America: Moods, Cycles, and Swings*, 2nd ed. Boulder, CO: Westview Press.

Stimson, James A., Michael B. MacKuen, and Robert S. Erikson. 1995. "Dynamic Representation." *American Political Science Review* 89: 543–565.

Stokes, Donald E. 1962. "Party Loyalty and the Likelihood of Deviating Elections." *Journal of Politics* 24: 689–702.

Stokes, Donald E. 1966. "Some Dynamic Elements of Contests for the Presidency." *American Political Science Review* 60: 19–28.

Thomas, Evan. 1997. *Back from the Dead: How Clinton Survived the Republican Revolution*. New York: Grove/Atlantic.

Tufte, Edward R. 1978. *Political Control of the Economy*. Princeton: Princeton University Press.

Zaller, John. 1994. "Strategic Politicians, Public Opinion, and the Gulf Crisis." In *Taken By Storm: The Media, Public Opinion, and U.S. Foreign Policy in the Gulf*

War, W. Lance Bennett and David L. Paletz, eds. Chicago: University of Chicago Press.

Zaller, John. 1998a. Coming to Grips with V. O. Key's Concept of Latent Opinion. Unpublished paper presented at a symposium in honor of Philip Converse, Boston.

Zaller, John. 1998b. "Know-Nothing" Voters in U.S. Presidential Elections, 1948 to 1996. Unpublished paper presented at the annual meeting of the American Political Science Association.

3

Some Thoughts on Democracy and Public Opinion Research

JUAN LINZ

Yale University

In 1950, Paul Lazarsfeld wrote a paper entitled "The Obligations of the 1950 Pollster to the 1984 Historian." I think we should pay attention to his injunction. In fact, looking back at my research over the years, including my dissertation on the 1953 Konrad Adenauer election, the Spanish youth survey (the first national sample survey in Spain) in 1960, the study of Spanish entrepreneurs in 1959–1961, and the many surveys I did during the Spanish transition to democracy, it is obvious that today the main value of those studies is for the historian. Thus, one criterion in planning research should be how much our work will help the historian twenty-five or fifty years later to understand what happened in the past. In my work on the breakdown of democracies in the 1920s and 1930s, the rise of totalitarianism, and the origins of the Spanish Civil War, I always wished for the wealth of public opinion research that we have for a small number of countries since the late 1940s. Unfortunately, technological changes are making much of the data collected in the era of the IBM punched card inaccessible to contemporary researchers. Indeed, I worry about the future accessibility of some of the data being collected today in light of the inevitable changes that will occur in computer coding and storage.

A further problem arises from the fact that much of the work of students of public opinion is focused on specific political events, mainly elections and candidates. Those studies are invaluable but do not answer some of the questions that I, as a political scientist, feel are most pressing. I would like for contemporary research to explore basic questions about emerging democratic political institutions, to contribute to a truly comparative political science after the third wave of democratization (to use the expression of Samuel Huntington), and to address the even more challenging questions raised by him on the "clash of civilizations." Unfortunately, with some outstanding exceptions, little worldwide comparative survey research is being conducted.

We hear constantly about crises in new democracies based on reports of presidents losing public support. The focus on incumbents and candidates leads to a neglect of the study of citizen responses to the institutions of democratic politics. We have some evidence from surveys that people make a clear distinction between their identification with democratic institutions and their critical attitude toward those holding office. As I will show later, people can judge very negatively the performance of key institutions of democratic politics, but largely agree on the need for those institutions. They may have very negative opinions about the work of their parliament, but reject the idea that there should be no parliament. Worldwide, there is a low opinion of political parties, but parties are still considered an essential element of a political democracy. My impression is that this is something new, that in the ideological climate of the 1920s and 1930s, and even in some countries until the 1970s or after 1989, people who were dissatisfied with the performance of political leaders quickly turned to the rejection of democratic institutions. The alternatives offered by communism, fascism, conservative corporativism, and military populist saviors were favored against the decadent or decrepit democratic institutions.

We have few data and systematic surveys to document this radical historical change. Why and to what extent are democratic political institutions legitimate for the people independently of their performance and of the many crises afflicting many societies? Also, as Claus Offe and others have highlighted, the demise of the totalitarian and authoritarian myths in many countries and the passing of time since the transition to democracy make it more imperative to legitimize democratic institutions in and by themselves rather than by comparisons with the terrible institutions that preceded them. The memory of the failures of the past is not sufficient to support present institutions. Also, we need a much more systematic comparative study of alternative types of democratic politics. The advantages and disadvantages for the institutionalization of democracy, of presidential, semipresidential, and parliamentary democracies, and of unitary and federal democracies are topics on which I have long been working, but on which public opinion research does not provide much information. We need to know much more about how people perceive the role of political parties and politicians in a democracy, not of specific parties or individual politicians, but of all parties and all politicians. We need to explain why people who vote for parties and candidates may also hold negative opinions about them, not only of those they do not support, which would be reasonable. This chapter illustrates how these widespread attitudes reflect fundamental ambivalence about what people expect from the democratic political process and institutions. Until now, those attitudes that we can document to some extent have not led to a questioning of the institutions of democracy.

The historical change described here is well documented by Larry Diamond (1999): in 1974, only 39 of 145 countries (26.9%) were political democracies, whereas in 1997, 117 out of 191 countries (61.3%) claimed to be democracies, or at least held relatively free elections that presumably legitimated the authority of those governing through formally democratic processes. We should not be too optimistic about these numbers, however, since Freedom House ratings of political rights and civil liberties show that of the 76 formal democracies in 1990, 66 (85.5%) could be called free states or liberal democracies, and of the 117 formal democracies in 1997, only 81 (69.2%) could be considered free states or liberal democracies (Diamond, 1999, pp. 24–64). The comparison between the 85% of formal democracies that were also free liberal democracies in 1990 and the 69% in 1997 justifies the title of a 1994 Nobel Institute Symposium on "Democracy's Victory and Crisis" (Hadenius, 1997).

Decades ago, most observers were conscious that democracies with adjectives—popular democracies, basic democracies, organic democracies, and tutelary democracies—were all covers designed by the holders of power to claim democratic legitimacy for nondemocratic regimes. There is a tendency to label political regimes as defective democracies, illiberal democracies, ethnocratic democracies, electoral democracies, delegated democracies, and semidemocracies, among other terms (Collier and Levitsky, 1997; Collier and Adcock,

1999; Merkel, 1999). It is best not to succumb to the misnaming of such undemocratic political systems and to remain hopeful that regimes so labeled will sooner or later become truly representative democracies. A clear distinction must be maintained between democratic political systems based on free competitive elections in a society based on the rule of law, respect for a constitution, and freedom for all citizens and those other types of polity. It is essential that power not be retained by undemocratic or violent means nor any significant group attempt to gain it by nondemocratic means like a putsch or violent takeover.

I believe a strong dichotomy exists between democratic governments and nondemocratic regimes and would like to see the latter labeled as one form or another of authoritarianism. This is not to deny that there are degrees of freedom, liberalization, and democratic enclaves that suggest a continuum between democratic and nondemocratic institutions in many countries, and that some of those forms are more desirable than others. But social science and political science researchers should be clear that undemocratic systems do not deserve to be called democracies. We also need to be careful in distinguishing the distortion of democratic institutions, that is, their manipulation and abuse for nondemocratic purposes, from the problems that may arise in democratic governments. These problems can be quite significant in many countries: deficits in the administration of those societies, the performance of the police and the judiciary, and above all inequities in the social structure, which presumably the practice of democracy should change. But we must also understand that these problems cannot be changed even by the more committed democratic governments in the short or even the medium run. There are many democratic societies with serious flaws just as there may be a few nondemocratic societies in which people experience some positive changes. Systematic and comparative public opinion research across countries could clarify these dimensions which often are being confused.

A main theme in this chapter is the need for such cross-national systematic and comparative studies of democracies. We have some reasonably good comparative economic indicators for many countries of the world. We even have, under the auspices of the World Bank, some systematic data on social welfare. But with the exception of some regional studies, like the Eurobarometer of the European Union, the research of Richard Rose and his collaborators in the New Democracies Barometer for post-Communist Eastern Europe, the work of the Latinobarometer of Marta Lagos and her collaborators, and a few questions in the World Values Survey directed by Ronald Inglehart, we have no full-scale comparative international survey on democratic institutions, the nondemocratic patterns in many parts of the world presumed to be ruled democratically, and the performance of democratic institutions.

One of the great gaps in public opinion research is that it has been centered since the late 1940s on the limited number of old and stable democracies. Only slowly have some of the new democracies like those of Southern Europe been incorporated into the comparative framework. Basic works on democratic politics, like those of Arendt Lijphart (1984), have been limited to the twenty-five stable democracies of Western Europe and the English-speaking Commonwealth of Canada and the United States. In his most recent book, Lijphart (1999) has expanded his scope, but we still need to deal with a larger number of democracies and failed transitions to democracy. As I will point out later with a few examples, we also need to incorporate the United States into a broader comparative framework, something that is not that easy.

In the old democracies, those consolidated before April 1974, the students of public opinion did not need to focus that much on the institutions. They could do their excellent work on parties and elections and the current public opinion issues, without having to ask themselves some of the questions we now have to raise in dealing with the consolidation of new democracies and the failures of the democratization process. Formerly, the world in which we were dealing was composed mostly of nation-states, or what I have called state-nations, in which the legitimacy of the state was not questioned (Linz, 1993; Linz and Stepan, 1996). Following the breakup of the former Soviet Union and Yugoslavia, multinational, multilingual, and multireligious societies are now more common and the legitimacy of some of these states is questioned. There are also multinational and multilingual societies in which federal democratic institutions, as in Canada, Belgium, and Spain, have tried to accommodate multiple national identities.

In a world of change, one of the most important tasks for public opinion research is to document and explain basic changes over time. This requires the formulation of basic questions and their use in surveys over prolonged periods. This does not seem to be as easy as it should be because we are always looking for questions that, at each point in time, appear to be most relevant, ignoring those on which apparently considerable consensus has been formed and which are not particularly interesting for the clients of our research. Also, we are continually tempted to improve our questions, for who does not honestly think that he or she can ask a better question than his predecessors? To change even a few words in a question would seem to be justified, but this eliminates the valid comparison on the basis of long-term time series. Only the repetition of the same question over a long period of time allows us to describe and understand change. A few examples from recent research will illustrate these points.

Legitimacy and Efficacy in New Democracies

While not everybody agrees, the concept of legitimacy, originally formulated by Max Weber, occupies a central place in the study of political institutions. Put very simply: Do people think that these political institutions are the best to govern the country in which they live; that they are better than the alternatives; and that they deserve obedience, and in the case of those entrusted with their defense, even the use of force to protect them? Obviously, in no society have all the people agreed to grant legitimacy to those who are ruling. Only in a democracy can citizens freely express that belief in the right to vote. Independently of that belief, people might be more or less confident that the institutions are able to solve the problems that their society faces, a dimension that I have called efficacy (1976, 1985). There is, moreover, a third dimension: the opinion about the performance, that is, about the actual functioning of the institutions, their problem solving capacity, even if in principle they are considered capable of solving them. The second and particularly the third dimension lead to considerable and sometimes even drastic fluctuations. People are not stupid and perceive when the institutions are not capable of solving their problems, and they are even more aware of the failing of those in power in solving the problems. Indeed, democracy is based on the assumption that those elected are given power for a limited time to deal with certain problems, but also that if they fail to do so, the voters in the next election will be able to substitute another team in the hope that it will do better (Linz, 1998). In this way, democracy gives some breathing space to the system and hope for change over a period of some eight years. That is why democracies survive a period of economic downturn better than many authoritarian regimes.

Early in the Spanish democratic transition I formulated a question asking people if they agreed with the following statement: "Democracy is the best system for a country like ours." This question has been asked by DATA, a private survey research organization, and the Spanish Centro de Investigaciones Sociológicas (CIS) over the years since 1978. The answer has been remarkably stable, starting with 77% agreeing in 1978, continuing at about 74%, and in several surveys surpassing 80%. The same pattern can be found in other countries where the same question has been asked.

In 1980 the CIS formulated another question regarding the following three statements: "Democracy is preferable to any other form of government; in some circumstances an authoritarian regime, a dictatorship, may be preferable to democracy; to people like me it is indifferent to have one or another system." This question has been incorporated into the Latinobarometer. Table 3.1 shows, with the exception of the first survey in which the number of negative answers was strangely high, the democratic response was over 70% and rising (row 1), while the second alternative, the authoritarian statement, never went beyond 12% (row 2), and the indifference response generally was below 10% (row 3). The long time series for Southern Europe, a few Latin American countries, and the period 1991–1995 for some post-Communist countries show considerable stability on this indicator and in several cases a positive change toward democracy. The data, summarized in a table by Larry Diamond (1999) using this and other indicators, show considerable differences between countries in Southern Europe, Latin America, and Eastern Europe (using different indicators). In Latin America, Uruguay is equal to Southern Europe with 80% choosing the democratic alternative, while Brazil is continuously low; the Eastern European countries range widely, with Belarus, Ukraine, and Russia narrowly giving majority support and using some indicators below 50%. All three countries are significantly below the average for Central and Eastern post-Communist Europe (Diamond, 1999, pp. 176–177). It is clear that commitment to democratic institutions is not universal but is very stable in some countries.

As Montero, Gunther, and Torcal (1997) have shown, the perceptions of system efficacy have always been below those of the legiti-

TABLE 3.1 Legitimacy of Democracy in Spain, 1980–1996

	1980	1984	1985	1987	1988	1989	1990	1991	1992	1993	1994	1995	1996
1	49	69	70	71	72	68	80	76	73	81	73	79	81
2	10	11	10	12	10	10	7	10	12	7	8	9	8
3	8	11	9	11	10	10	8	8	10	7	10	8	7
4	33	9	11	6	8	12	5	6	5	4	9	4	4
(N)	(3457)	(2490)	(2498)	(2490)	(2488)	(3371)	(2382)	(2494)	(2497)	(2500)	(2491)	(2478)	(2481)

SOURCE: Data from the CIS Data Bank (Montero, et al., 1997, p. 128).

TABLE 3.2   "Legitimacy" and "Efficacy" of Democracy in Spain, 1978, 1980, and 1998

		Legitimacy		
		+	–	Totals
	+	73 (1978)	4 (1978)	77 (1978)
		47 (1980)	3 (1980)	50 (1980)
		66 (1998)	3 (1998)	69 (1998)
Efficacy				
	–	11 (1978)	12 (1978)	23 (1978)
		31 (1980)	19 (1980)	50 (1980)
		22 (1998)	10 (1998)	32 (1998)
Total		84 (1978)	16 (1978)	
		78 (1980)	22 (1980)	
		88 (1998)	13 (1998)	

NOTES: Surveys were conducted by DATA. The year 1980 reflects the "desencanto" or "disenchantment" with the transition generated by the high point of ETA terrorism. This crisis led to the resignation of Prime Minister Suárez and the putsch attempt on February 23, 1981. However, a survey in March 1981 reflects a rise of legitimacy to 81%. The table does not include those not answering or "don't know" responses on each of the questions, which were less than 15% on each of the surveys. The number of interviews in 1978 was 5898 and in 1998 it was 3921.

macy of democratic institutions. They also show how indicators of efficacy have fluctuated widely over the years and that those fluctuations have had only limited impact on the legitimacy of democratic institutions. However, my analysis of the surveys by DATA in Table 3.2 shows that a drop of 27% in the perception of the "efficacy" in the year 1980 following the year of the *desencanto* (or disillusionment) of 1978 led only to a small 6% drop in the positive responses to the "legitimacy" question, from 84% in 1978 to 78% in 1980, certainly not a major change. In turn, an increase in "efficacy" from 50% in 1980 to 69% in 1998 has reduced the percentage not believing in the desirability of democracy from a high of 22% to 13%, less than the 16% in 1978 when the "efficacy" perception was somewhat higher (77%).

The data from the Latinobarometer, which allow one to combine an indicator of legitimacy and one of efficacy, show that there are quite different patterns in the different countries; in some, there is considerable legitimacy together with the perception of low efficacy. In others, like Chile, efficacy might be considerably higher than in several countries, but legitimacy is not as high as we would expect if there were a direct relationship between efficacy and legitimacy.

The data from public opinion surveys in the last twenty-five years allow us to answer questions that I raised in my book *The Breakdown of Democratic Regimes* about the interaction between legitimacy and efficacy (1976, pp. 16–23). At that time, I assumed that low efficacy and incapacity to solve problems contributed quite directly to an erosion of legitimacy. Later, some of the comparative work on the impact of the world depression in different countries, particularly the high unemployment in the Netherlands and Norway, led me to question that relationship. In fact, I am inclined to consider that legitimacy protected the political system in the established and consolidated democracies against the impact of the great depression, whereas lack of legitimacy for significant segments on the political right and left in Weimar Germany contributed to the enormous political impact of the depression and the breakdown of democracy.

However, without comparative public opinion data we cannot test the different impacts of the crisis of efficacy on legitimacy during the interwar years and the protective consequences of having a legitimate political system with which to weather the crisis. If we were to continue having good time series like those we now have on Spain and some Southern European countries, and perhaps in the near future for Latin America, we could explore more carefully the interaction between efficacy and legitimacy. That is, we could examine the relationships among the belief in the capacity of democratic institutions to handle problems efficaciously, the actual performance of those institutions (the question of how well is democracy working in your country), and the legitimacy of those institutions. Since I believe that legitimacy is central to problems in the breakdown of democracy, comparative long-term time-series research by students of public opinion could help us understand the fundamental problems of the stability of regimes and democracy. In the work I have done with Alfred Stepan on the problems of democratic transition and consolidation, we have made use of the limited public opinion data available to answer some of those questions.

The "Legitimacy" and "Efficacy" of Capitalism

The other major social and economic change in the last few decades has been the unquestioned acceptance and wide success of capitalist private property and free market economies. Even social democratic leaders have clearly embraced the free market, forgetting the adjective "social" that was added to market economy in the 1950s in the Adenauer era. Economic neoliberalism is even invoked in the transformation of the Chinese economy under Communist post-totalitarian rule. Yet it is more than the economic success of capitalism in Western Europe, Southern Europe, and the newly industrialized countries in Asia that strikes the observer, but also the change in ideological climate. The success of entrepreneurial capitalism and the free market has been widely accepted; they introduced wealth and economic development, albeit together with social tensions and in some cases economic inequities. Indeed, Schumpeter, in his classic *Capitalism, Socialism and Democracy* (1942), argued strongly against those who theorize about the vanishing opportunities for capitalism and its structural crisis. The same Schumpeter wrote about the growing hostility in the social atmosphere of capitalism and answered his question—Can capitalism survive?—with a negative. He cautions us that this was a probabilistic statement of what would happen given present trends if they continued and no other factors intruded.

Schumpeter's argument was that capitalism inevitably produced an atmosphere of almost universal hostility within all social orders, that the social changes led to a loss of moral legitimacy that, in spite of its economic success, would lead in the end to its demise. In his address "The March into Socialism" in 1949, he insisted, with some reservations, on the migrations of people's economic affairs from the private into the public sphere, defining socialism as "that organization of society in which the means of production are controlled and the decisions on how and what to produce and who is to get what, are made by public authority instead of privately owned and privately managed firms." In this last lecture, he argued that "the scheme of values of capitalistic society, though casually related to its economic success, is losing its hold not only upon the public mind but also upon the capitalist stratum itself" (Schumpeter, 1950, p. 418).

Fifty years later it would seem that Friedrich Hayek's *Road to Freedom* and the thinking of a group of "economists meeting at

some Swiss mountain resort," to which Schumpeter referred somewhat sarcastically, have won out. We really do not know exactly
how and why, or even when, the dismal failure of real socialism revealed in the years of stagnation of the Brezhnev era and the fall of
the Berlin Wall helped to bring this about. This is one case where we
would need much more public opinion research about the attitudes
toward the economic system over a long period of time in different
countries. The data on attitudes toward the economic situation, the
indicators of the business cycle, the hopes and fears about employment, and the expectations about the economy are not sufficient to
answer the question raised by Schumpeter about the legitimacy of
the capitalist system independently of its performance.

In my own work (1985) I formulated a question parallel to the
that about the democratic system. I asked people to agree or disagree with two statements: (1) "the capitalist economy of private initiative is the best economic system for a country like ours" and (2)
"the capitalist economy of private initiative allows the economic
problems we Spaniards have to face to be solved." A similar question was asked by the Institute for Demoskopie in Germany, but
while similar ones can be found in survey research in Eastern Europe, it is not easy to make systematic comparisons. The same questions I asked in 1983 were repeated in 1986 and 1999 in Spanish national surveys. For simplicity's sake, I will limit myself in Table 3.3
to the responses to the two statements, ignoring those with no opinion (which in 1983 were 13.2% of the 3592 interviewed and in
1986 were 15.4% of the 1230 interviewed).

A few facts stand out: at no time did the capitalist economic system in Spain enjoy a legitimacy comparable to that of political
democracy. This fact belies the belief that the success of economic
systems is the basis on which the new democracies can legitimate
themselves, as we now know from the data about Eastern Europe
and particularly the former Soviet Union outside of the Baltic countries. Again, the perception of the capacity to handle the problems
that people confronted and the efficacy of the system was lower than
its legitimacy.

Now let us turn to the change between 1983 and 1998. Among
those with an opinion in 1983, 48.9% considered the system "the
best for our country." By 1986, after the election of a socialist government by a majority in 1982, the proportion was 56.0%, and by
1998 it was 61.0%. This represents a change of 12.1% over some

TABLE 3.3   "Legitimacy" and "Efficacy" of Capitalism in Spain, 1983, 1986, and 1998

| | | 1983 Legitimacy | | |
		+	–	Total
Efficacy	+	30.9	4.1	35.0
	–	18.0	46.9	64.9
	Total	48.9	51.0	100% (3359)

| | | 1986 Legitimacy | | |
		+	–	Total
Efficacy	+	34.7	4.8	39.5
	–	20.7	39.8	60.5
	Total	55.4	44.6	100% (1015)

| | | 1998 Legitimacy | | |
		+	–	Total
Efficacy	+	44.2	4.9	49.0
	–	16.9	34.1	51.0
	Total	61.0	39.0	100% (3752)

NOTES: Surveys were conducted by DATA. Respondents with no opinion or no answer on any of the four questions have not been included in the table. They represent about 15% in each of the surveys. The indicator for legitimacy is agreement or disagreement with the statement: "The capitalist economy of private initiative is the best economic system for a country like ours." The indicator for efficacy is the agreement or disagreement with the statement: "The capitalist economy of private initiative allows the economic problems we Spaniards have to face to be solved."

twelve years. Certainly the efficacy of the system perceived by people had something to do with its increased legitimacy, with 35% answering positively in 1983, 41.2% in 1986, and 49.0% in 1998, that is, a difference in efficacy of 14% between 1983 and 1998. These data do not confirm the expectations of Schumpeter in 1942. Too bad we do not have comparable data for the early 1940s and 1950s in Europe and at this time. The pollsters failed the historian!

The recent shift is reflected in responses to the following question: "There is a lot of discussion about the manner in which enterprises should be managed, which of the following opinions is closer to yours? (1) "The owners should direct their enterprises or appoint the managers." This was the option of 22.7% in 1983, and 33.7% in 1998. "(2) The owners and the workers should participate in the appointment of managers." In 1983, 49.3% agreed, and in 1998, 45.1% did so. This was a form of codetermination response. "(3) The ownership of enterprises should be of the state and it should appoint the managers." In 1983, 6.4% agreed, and in 1998, it was 4.2%. "(4) The ownership of enterprises should be of the workers and they should elect the managers." For this last statement, 14.3% agreed in 1983, and 6.8% in 1998, with no answer given by 7.2% and 10.2% for the respective years. The most striking finding is how the self-management model, inspired by the Yugoslavs' experience and included by many parties in their programs in 1977, has withered away and how private property has become accepted. This question, asked in my "Mentalities Study" in 1983, has been incorporated into the European and later the World Values studies.

Democratic Institutions: The Critique of Parties

We can make few comparisons of the responses of citizens to different systems. This is partly because different countries with longtime consolidated democratic institutions—whether parliamentary monarchy or republic, presidentialism, semipresidentialism or parliamentarism, or unitary or federal states—are largely taken for granted and are not objects of systematic and comparative research. Only when some of these institutions experience a crisis, like the monarchy in the United Kingdom, do we find research data; relatively little research has been conducted in other democratic monarchies, with the exception of Spain, which restored a monarchy in 1975. Only in new democracies where there is or was recently an option between different democratic institutions do we have some data about the preferences of the people. Given the limited number of studies and the quality of survey research in many countries, public opinion research provides us with few insights into the perception of alternative institutions in those societies. Moreover, to formulate questions about nonexistent institutions is known to tax the ingenuity of the researcher.

After years of one-party or no-party rule, in new democracies a large consensus soon develops that more than one party is essential to democratic politics. Even some of those not committed to democracy consider parties an essential part of democratic politics. This might represent a clear change from the 1920s and 1930s, when large proportions of the population felt that competition between parties was undesirable in principle and that one party, be it fascist or Communist, could better represent the interests of the people. At least that is what we can gather from the voting for antiparty parties or movements, although we have no public opinion data to know how much that vote reflected a hostility to parties or perhaps the response to other issues.

That broad consensus on the need for political parties and for party pluralism that we find in the surveys of old and new democracies, though in quite different proportions of the population, coexists with continuous criticism of political parties. The consensus goes together with a consistent low trust in parties compared to other institutions and groups. It would be natural that people would be hostile to the party they have not voted for, but the fact is that among the voters of all political parties the criticism and the distrust reach similar levels. In many countries there are good reasons to be critical of one or another party, as parties can be involved in corruption and are believed to have mismanaged public affairs in the view of many voters. However, the criticism seems to reflect something more complex, a fundamental ambivalence about the role of parties and about elected politicians, irrespective of the party voted for or the self-placement on a left/right political continuum. The proportions supporting different criticisms of parties and the behavior of elected representatives seem to be similar across the party spectrum. Public opinion research on the electoral process has provided us with many insights into the critique of different parties by those not voting for them, and sometimes by those supporting them, but has not analyzed sufficiently the pervasive criticism of all parties. While in the 1920s and 1930s the critique of political parties led to support for antiparty movements and for eliminating political parties, it is striking that today the critique and low esteem of parties coexist with a consensus on the need for them.

There are no systematic comparative studies of political parties and their functions in parliamentary or presidential democracies (Linz and Valenzuela, 1994). Though at the turn of the century prominent thinkers like Moise Ostrogorski and Max Weber (on the basis of his familiarity with the Russian's writing and the United States) were concerned with the similarities and differences and the convergent trends between political parties across the ocean, lately much less attention has been paid to the differences between European and American parties. In view of the different function performed by parties in parliamentary and presidential systems and the distinctive institutions of U.S. democracy, the critique of parties across the Atlantic cannot be the same. Sometimes, as in an American Political Science Association publication from years ago, *Towards a More Responsible Two-Party System* (1950), Americans looked with some envy to European parties. More recently, Europeans have been impressed by some features of American democracy, particularly primary elections, and without much thought about the implications they are trying to import that institution as one response to their dissatisfaction with political parties. More systematic cross-Atlantic comparative research on the public perception of political parties and their role in the democratic process would be most useful to comparativist researchers. The unhappiness of Europeans with the control of members of parliament by the party leadership and the lack of real debate owing to party discipline obviously would be inapplicable to American parties. The same would be true for the European dissatisfaction with the representation of specific local interests of constituents, particularly when we think of the dictum by former House speaker Tip O'Neill that "all politics is local," and the fact that representatives in the U.S. Congress (note the term "representative") devote much of their energies to defending specific interests of their constituents. Indeed, Americans probably feel that parties should defend broader programmatic positions and give more support to the president of their party.

Ignoring some of those differences between Europe and the United States that could be extended to parliamentary versus presidential systems, common themes can be found in the critique of parties. Indeed, in many cases incompatible opinions were held by the same respondents. Let me quickly enumerate a few of them.

We hear that parties are divisive, that they generate conflict where there is none, that they artificially divide people. At the same time we find significant numbers of people who say that in spite of all the competition between parties, overall the parties and the politicians are much the same, and that there is little choice between them. The latter is a response that makes some sense at a time of "catch-all" parties in a democracy in which all parties aspire to govern, rather than to make ideological statements. Such statements are made without the hope of governing and therefore the need to assume the responsibility to implement their ideological programs. Antisystem parties could be completely different from parties with a calling to govern, and thus conscious of the limited alternatives, particularly in a globalized economy.

People expect parties to be responsive to their wishes and to pay attention to their opinions and preferences. Public opinion research and focus groups allow politicians to be immediately responsive to the opinions and moods of the voters. Voters also feel that politicians are not acting according to their conviction nor for the long-term interest of the country when they are preoccupied with the latest polls. There is an inherent tension between the desire for responsiveness and the feeling that parties and politicians should act responsibly, even by taking positions that are unpopular when the public interest demands it. There are those who feel that parties and politicians should shape public opinion rather than just reflect it.

People, at least in Europe, feel that parties are not democratic and party members have only a limited say in the position taken by parties and the government. They feel that the party elite and more specifically the parliamentarians are disconnected from the average party member. One response has been to demand direct democracy within the parties rather than representative democracy in party congresses and the parliamentary faction of the party. The American institution of the primary seems to be one answer for this demand for internal party democracy. The paradox is that this demand coincides with a trend of diminishing numbers of people joining political parties, fewer being active in party affairs, the "death" of the party press, and other factors that signal less overall party involvement. The result is that a small number of party members are invited to elect a party leader in an internal primary, and further that relatively few of these members vote; those elected will have received only a small majority or a plurality of those votes. This means that indirectly the future prime minister is elected by a very small number of voters rather than by the parliamentary representatives elected by a large portion, plurality, or even majority of the electorate.

Another theme in the critique of parties is that there is too much disunity and too much conflict, especially between personalities and sometimes factions within a party. This critique goes together with the desire for internal party democracy, which to be meaningful would require a confrontation between leaders and potentially would result in factions. The response has been to say that the competition between leaders should not be based on factionalism but only on personality, but without candidates attacking each other.

Simultaneously we hear the critique that there is too much discipline and unity within parties as well as the complaint of why should voters trust a party to govern when the leaders are constantly bickering and fighting each other and different leaders take opposite or different positions on issues. There is considerable evidence from public opinion research in both Spain and Germany that voters reject a party in which there is considerable disunity.

Related to this issue is the feeling that party discipline, which is enforced by the whip in a contemporary parliament to control individual M.P.'s, makes representatives mere "yes" men. In every vote taken the outcome is already predetermined by the partisan composition of the legislature. This is an old critique of party democracy, in contrast to nineteenth-century parliamentarism with reasoned debate in which the interventions and speeches were aimed at convincing legislators irrespective of party affiliation. The discipline demanded by party democracy in parliamentary systems, where one of the main functions is to sustain government and to vote its policies, is not characteristic of congressional representation in presidential systems. In fact, such parties are characterized by their lack of party discipline, as we know from the United States and even more from Brazilian presidentialism.

The opposite opinion is that representatives should have their own opinions and vote according to their own convictions, without slavishly submitting to the party leadership and supporting the prime minister regardless of the position he or she has taken.

A corollary of this dilemma is the critique of parties for expelling members for lack of discipline, and on the other hand the rejection of members who bolt their party and become either independent members of parliament or move to another parliamentary group. Voters strongly feel that those who have been elected on a party list in proportional representation systems should give up their seat when they are not willing to accept party discipline. In Spain *transfuguismo* is considered unacceptable even though still protected by the principle that members of parliament represent all the voters rather than a party, and therefore should hold on to their seat until the next election in which the party and/or the voters will punish them for their party disloyalty.

TABLE 3.4   Party Discipline and Autonomy of Deputies in Spain

	Total	IU	PSOE	PP	PNV	CiU	Did not vote
			Party supported				
Directives	34.1	30.7	35.4	37.6	40.9	42.1	27.9
Own criteria	48.3	54.0	46.9	47.7	45.5	51.3	52.2
Don't know	16.7	14.3	17.0	13.8	13.6	6.6	18.8
	(2484)	(189)	(614)	(678)	(22)	(76)	(272)

NOTES: The question was: "Let us talk about the relation between political parties and deputies. There are those who say that in a democratic system the deputies should always vote in agreement with the directives set up by their parties. Others, on the contrary, think that the deputies should follow their own criteria when they have to vote, even when those do not coincide with the directives of their parties. With which of those opinions do you agree more?"
KEY: IU, Izquierda Unida; PSOE, Partido Socialista Obrero Español, (Socialist Party); PP, Partido Popular (Center-conservative party); PNV, Partido Nacionalista Vasco (Basque Nationalist); CiU, Convergéncia i Umió (Catalanist party).
SOURCE: Data from the CIS Survey "Ciudadanos y élites ante politica, Study 2240, April 1997."

Not unexpectedly, we have found citizens with opposite opinions about party discipline and independence of representatives. Indeed, data show that this division of opinions runs through all Spanish political parties in very similar proportions (Table 3.4). Certainly those who would like to see parliamentarians having more autonomy and standing for their own positions will be critical of parties. But I am also sure that most of those citizens would also feel that members who are disloyal to the party, which assured them of their seat by putting them on its list, should relinquish their seat to an alternate of the same party.

Modern societies are based on professionalism, but as Schumpeter noted, democratic politics is the politics of amateurs. There are no schools or degrees for politicians. Citizens therefore feel that the professionalization of politics, the transformation of politics into a full-time activity and sometimes a lifetime career, is one of the undesirable characteristics of many contemporary democracies. Professionalization in European systems very often means that the politician depends fully for his livelihood on compensation as a member of the legislature or other bodies, and when out of office counts on the party to find him another position or place him in the party bureaucracy. Professionalization is perceived as limiting the autonomy and thus the responsibility of politicians. Presumably it also reduces the attractiveness of politics for independent personalities. The contrast is made with the independent representatives in nineteenth-century parliaments, who were persons of independent means, very often local notables, who could afford to be defeated. There is also the Cincinnatus myth of a political leader who, after serving his country, retires to private life, originally his estate.

Many factors have contributed to this professionalization: the requirements of political activity, larger parliamentary sessions, extensive committee work, the need to keep in touch with constituents, work within the party organization, the frequent elections requiring campaigns, and, in some cases like the United States, the monumental effort in fund-raising. On the other hand, today the full-time dedication to a profession makes it impossible to be simultaneously engaged in politics and in one's private activities. It is now inconceivable that a party leader like Rudolf von Virchow, the distinguished German pathologist, would be teaching at the university and spending a few hours in parliament. American universities usually give only a three-year public service leave, and it would be difficult after a number of years in politics to return to teaching, to a medical practice, even to a law firm as a lawyer rather than a lobbyist.

Paradoxically, the same voters who criticize the professionalization of politics strongly support those measures that inevitably contribute to it. They demand that the holding of public office be incompatible with other activities. Military officers and civil servants are required to resign their positions or give up their career before becoming candidates. Business managers should not be active in their business. Rules are being proposed to prevent politicians from engaging in certain activities until years after losing office. Presumably all of these restrictions are intended to ensure that the politician will have only the public interest on his or her mind rather than other interests or career expectations. This emphasis on incompatibilities, which are often written into law, pushes politicians toward professionalization of their political career. An exception is made in many European countries for professors and teachers, who constitute a growing number of the political elite, and sometimes for civil servants, who can return to their careers. Of course at the same time that the public calls for limits on the interests and activities of their politicians, the criticism is heard that politicians live in an isolated world removed from the concerns of ordinary citizens, without daily contact with the problems faced by people in business or other occupations.

Somewhat related to the issue of professionalization is the concern raised by the continuity in office election after election. When asked, people are likely to favor term limits, while they actually reelect their representatives when they trust them. Again, there is a contradiction between the no-reelection principle and one basic characteristic of democracy, which is to make those in office accountable, to reward and punish those elected for their performance. How can we emphasize accountability if there is no possibility of making those elected accountable at the time of the next election? There is also a tension between the no-reelection principle and the demand for politicians and representatives to be experienced and knowledgeable about the issues. Anyone who has served on any committee knows that it takes some time to become familiar with the issues and the procedures for making decisions, and that a newcomer always has less input to offer than old-timers. To what extent can those elected gain experience if they are in office for only one or two terms?

Another critique that one hears in European democracies, to some extent justifiably, is that the members of parliament are unable to fight for the interests of their constituents. When there is a national policy at stake or even policies of the European community, the M.P., subject to party discipline, cannot bargain effectively for his constituents, perhaps those losing jobs because of the closing of a factory or a navy yard. The common complaint is that "my interests are not represented." In the United States this criticism is less likely. Representatives pay a lot of attention to the interests of their constituency and can fight a policy and bargain for those interests when it comes time to approve a trade agreement, for example. On the other hand, nearly everybody believes that representatives are acting for special interests. Naturally, those special interests are not perceived to be of one's own activity or community. Unfortunately, parties and politicians cannot satisfy simultaneously all the interests of their voters and at the same time be guided only by collective interests and larger policy issues and choices.

In Europe there has been a constant demand for the democratization of a large number of institutions, such as the election of representatives on supervising boards and advisory committees of those institutions. We know from research on participation and democracy in voluntary organizations that the number of people ready to be candidates and to participate in the electoral process is limited, and that these organizations are likely to be more oligarchic than democratic political institutions. The result has been that the candidates for most of those positions have been proposed by political parties and tend to be elected along party lines or left/right ideological lines irrespective of qualifications, largely because voters lack information on the individual candidates. This has led to what has been called *partitocrazia* and in Italy *lottizazione*: the distribution of offices on such boards along party lines and arranged by deals between the parties. The result has been that parties must fill many positions, sometimes with people who are clearly incompetent and even dishonest, with the blame put on the parties. Some of the critique of parties in Italy, Austria, and Venezuela, as reflected in recent elections, was based on the dissatisfaction of citizens with the presence of parties in too many spheres of society. If surveys were to ask questions separately, we would find people demanding greater democratization of all kinds of institutions, and at the same time being critical of the presence of the parties in those same institutions.

One of the greatest criticisms of politics in democracies is the role of money to pay for parties and their campaigns. This is certainly a central issue in American political life but it is far from absent in European politics. To run democratic politics and democratic parties is a costly business, particularly with the frequent elections and the need to reach people through mass media and other advertising. Nowadays people are less likely to join parties and devote their time and energy to campaigns, put up posters on billboards, and distribute leaflets, and so hired hands must be employed. Most people no longer go to a stadium or a bullring to listen to party leaders, or to rallies at the factory gate, but instead follow the campaign on television. Who is to pay for these campaigns when fewer party membership dues are flowing into party coffers?

Public financing of parties and campaigns has become one important option. Private resources of the candidate and soft money from business and labor contributions and those of other interest groups pay for the democratic process in the United States. Surveys show that most voters are not particularly willing to contribute themselves to political parties, although simultaneously they are critical of private funding and suspicious of the influence of special interests, and would like to see campaign contributions regulated and reduced. At the same time, they are far from enthusiastic about their taxes being used to pay for political parties and, to some extent, are dimly aware that public financing makes it difficult for new parties or independent candidates to run. Moreover, public financing might very well reinforce the oligarchic control of the party by the leaders. When surveys separate the questions about different alternatives, we see that none of them finds widespread support and, to some extent, that people would reject *all* possible alternatives. The democratic process should be a free good, ignoring how much it costs in a modern organized mass society. Again, whatever alternative they choose, because others may prefer other alternatives, probably there will be no majority for any alternative.

In some democracies, particularly federal democracies, there is a new source of dissatisfaction. People have voted for a party and its leader to form a government, but only a short time later they are asked to vote in state elections, for example, the German Länder and/or European Parliament elections. Those elections presumably deal with distinctive issues, but in fact very often the voters use them to express their dissatisfaction with the government they only elected shortly before. This forces the leaders of the national government to get actively involved in the other campaigns, thus detracting time and energy from governing. Presumably, a defeat in these elections will lead journalists and pundits to claim that the government has lost its mandate to govern. However, since it will continue governing, some voters may feel that their vote does not count.

I have enumerated a number of criticisms of political parties and politicians in democracies, which are shared by voters of many parties. These criticisms divide the electorate of those parties along lines that cannot be directly derived from social demographics, or even left/right ideology as reflected in self-report responses on a scale that is frequently used now in public opinion research in Europe. I have also made an effort to formulate a number of questions on the basis of some of these ambivalent attitudes and am in the process of analyzing the findings of a Spanish survey executed by the CIS using these questions.

Multinational Democracies

The breakup of the Soviet Union and Yugoslavia and the "Velvet Divorce" between the Czechs and the Slovaks have led to new questions about the viability of multinational federal states. Of course in the former Soviet Union and Yugoslavia there was no full process of democratization of the state and the drafting of a new constitution that would regulate the relation of the federal units with the state. The democratization of those units before the creation of a democratically legitimated center contributed to the crisis of the federal state and its breakup (Linz and Stepan, 1996). It is wrong to assume that in established democratic states with a multinational, multiethnic, multilingual, and multireligious population, the processes will be the same. On the other hand, many countries do not fit the model of the nation-state that we so often assume when we speak of states as if they were nations (Linz, 1993). Indeed, many of the countries that will undergo the processes of democratization in the near future are not nation-states, and any efforts toward nation building around one national core are probably doomed to failure. This does not mean that those countries will break up or should break up. Any solution has to keep in mind that people live intermingled, that sometimes one ethnic or linguistic group may be dominant in the countryside and another in the cities, making territorial secession unviable. The principle that every nation should have its own state—the principle of self-determination and the right of secession—is one of the most dangerous principles in modern politics. Equally dangerous is the belief that every state should achieve the kind of integration that modern nation-states achieved in Western Europe in the course of the nineteenth century, if not before. This idea can lead to the discrimination or oppression of minorities, if not to ethnic cleansing.

Another idea that sounds good is that of letting the people decide. As Sir Ivor Jennings at the end of World War I stated, "On the surface it seemed reasonable: let the people decide. It was in fact ridiculous because the people cannot decide until somebody decides who are the people"(1978). The holding of any plebiscite on self-determination requires that somebody defines beforehand who the voters shall be, how the fate of different territorial units should be decided, and what majority should be required. To begin with, do we speak of a majority of voters or of eligible voters? The analogy between such a plebiscite and a democratic political election is misleading, since in an election the people decide who shall govern for a limited period of time (normally four years) and will have a chance to decide again afterward, when they may change their minds. Democratic government is pro tempore, whereas states are not pro tempore. It does not seem reasonable that 50.1% of the voters should decide forever the future of a population. The establishment of higher thresholds, as sometimes required for the approval of constitutions, however, might prejudge the outcome.

In this context, politicians and journalists and even scholars talk loosely about the aspirations of nations and their struggle for freedom and independence. Sometimes they are thinking of the entire population of a territorial unit, irrespective of the ethnic, linguistic, or religious composition of that population. In other cases they assume that those sharing certain primordial characteristics like language, religion, or descent share the same political aspirations. Actually, the idea of a plebiscite imposes on a heterogeneous population a simple dichotomous choice, when in fact there could be many different preferences and alternatives.

The simple dichotomy between *us* and *them* hides the complexities of most multinational, multiethnic, multilingual, and multireligious societies. It ignores the fact that people might have multiple identities, that in the course of their life people have created ties to different communities, that families are not homogeneous, and that people have friends and ties across boundaries separating emerging national communities.

When people live in relatively defined territorial units, it is a reasonable solution for a multinational, federal, democratic state to grant special rights to minorities to use their language and govern themselves, but at the same time the state should protect within the constitutional framework the rights of minorities within a territorial majority. A number of unitary states, like Belgium, Spain, and India after independence, have turned to federalism to hold together within a democratic liberal state very diverse communities, some of which consider themselves to be nations. In some multicultural societies, like Switzerland, loyalty has always been to a state that enjoys some of the same emotional support as a nation, but that we could consider a state-nation rather than a nation-state.

Public opinion research has not provided us with many insights; research on these topics was long taboo, partly because of neglect, and in some cases because simplistic formulation of questions required respondents to answer in restrictive terms, such as "are you 'A' or 'B'"?

TABLE 3.5   National Identity in Catalonia[a]

	1979	1982	1990	1992	1996	1999 Youth study
Spanish	31	23.5	36	20	13	8
More Spanish than Catalan	7	8.2	4	8	12	21
Equally Catalan and Spanish	36	40.1	27	36	36	38
More Catalan than Spanish	12	16.9	11	21	26	17
Catalan	15	9.0	19	15	11	16
Don't know	—	2.4	3	—	2	—
	(1122)	(885)	(1064)	(2420)	(784)	

[a]The question was: Today one talks a lot about nationalities, what would you say you feel you are?
SOURCES: The 1979, 1982, and 1990 surveys were conducted by DATA, as was the 1999 survey. The 1992 data are from José Ramón Montero, Francisco J. Llera, and Pallorés, *Autonomia y Comunidades Autónomas*, p. 111. The 1996 data are from CIS, November-December survey, Study 2228, Conciencia Nacional y Regional. The 1990 data are from Orizo and Sánchez Fernández with DATA (1991).

The research I have done in collaboration with DATA (Linz, 1985a; Linz et al., 1986), replicated by my colleague Francisco Llera (1994) and the Centro de Investigaciones Sociológicas (a public survey research institute; Garcia Ferrando et al., 1994; Moreno, 1997; Moral, 1998) and other scholars, shows the importance of dual identities, the changes resulting from the "federalization" of Spain and the nation-building policies of the governments of the Autonomous Communities (Tables 3.5 and 3.6). As far as I know, only in the United Kingdom (Moreno, 1995, pp. 239–240) have several surveys asked a comparable question about British, Scottish, and Welsh identity. In this regard, public opinion research represents both a corrective and a step forward from much of the writings on nationalisms in multinational democracies.

TABLE 3.6   Identification in the Basque Country

	1979	1989	1991	1996	1999
Spanish	14.5	16.4	9	5.3	9
More Spanish than Basque	5.8	6.5	4	4.2	6
Equally Spanish and Basque	27.4	23.4	34	37.8	40
More Basque than Spanish	12.6	17.8	18	31.0	20
Basque	39.7	39.9	31	21.5	24
	(973)	(2386)	(1400)	(266)	

NOTES: The question in 1979, 1989, 1991, and 1999 was the one quoted in the text. The CIS 1996 question was: With which of these sentences do you identify yourself more? I feel only Spanish; I feel more Spanish than of my Autonomous Community; I feel as Spanish as of my Autonomous Community; I feel more (identified) with my Autonomous Community than Spanish; I feel only identified with my Autonomous Community. This change in wording obviously can affect the answers and make them less comparable. The 2% not answering have been left out of our table. I am grateful to Pilar del Castillo for making these data available.
SOURCES: The 1979 survey was conducted by DATA (Linz, 1985b), and the 1989 survey by the CIS Centro de Investigaciones Sociológicas, No. 1785 (Llera, 1986, p. 81). The February 1991 survey was sponsored by the Basque Government (Llera, 1994, p. 75). Data for 1996 are from CIS survey No. 2228, November–December 1996. The DATA Values Survey is the source for 1999.

References

Collier, David, and Robert Adcock. 1999. "Democracy and Dichotomies: A Pragmatic Approach to Choices About Concepts." *Annual Review of Political Science* 2: 537–565.

Collier, David, and Steven Levitsky. 1997. "Democracy with Adjectives: Conceptual Innovation in Comparative Research." *World Politics* 30(4): 477–493.

Diamond, Larry. 1999. *Developing Democracy. Toward Consolidation*, Chap. 2, pp. 24–64. Baltimore: Johns Hopkins University Press.

Garcia Ferrando, Manuel, Eduardo López-Aranguren, and Miguel Beltrán. 1994. *La Conciencia nacional y regional en la España de las autonomías*, pp. 15–20. Madrid: Centro de Investigaciones Sociológicas.

Hadenius, Axel, ed. 1997. *Democracy's Victory and Crisis*. Cambridge, England: Cambridge University Press.

Jennings, Ivor. 1978. "The Approach to Self-Government." Quoted in Lee C. Buchheit, *Secession. The Legitimacy of Self-Determination*, p. 9. New Haven: Yale University Press.

Lazarsfeld, Paul F. 1950. "The Obligations of the 1950 Pollster to the 1984 Historian." *Public Opinion Quarterly*, Winter, 617–638.

Lijphart, Arendt. 1984. *Democracies: Patterns of Majoritarian and Consensus Government in Twenty-one Countries*. New Haven: Yale University Press.

Lijphart, Arendt. 1999. In *Patterns of Democracy: Government Forms and Performance in Thirty-six Countries*. New Haven: Yale University Press.

Linz, Juan J. 1976. *The Breakdown of Democratic Regimes: Crisis, Breakdown and Reequilibration*. Baltimore: Johns Hopkins University Press.

Linz, Juan J. 1985a. "Legitimacy of Democracy and the Socioeconomic System." In *Comparing Pluralist Democracies: Strains of Legitimacy*, Mattei Dogan, ed., pp. 65–113. Boulder: Westview Press.

Linz, Juan J. 1985b. "De la crisis de un Estado unitario al Estado de las Autonomías." In *La España de las Autonomías*, Fernando Fernández Rodríguez, ed., pp. 529–672. Madrid: Instituto de Estudios de Administración Local.

Linz, Juan J. 1993. "State Building and Nation Building." *European Review* 1(4): 355–369.

Linz, Juan J. 1998. "Democracy's Time Constraints." *International Political Science Review* 19(1): 19–37.

Linz, Juan J., and Alfred A. Stepan. 1996. *Problems of Democratic Transition and Consolidation: Southern Europe, South America and Post-Communist Europe*. Baltimore: Johns Hopkins University Press.

Linz, Juan J., and Arturo Valenzuela, eds. 1994. *The Failure of Presidential Democracy*. Baltimore: Johns Hopkins University Press.

Linz, Juan J., M. Gómez-Reino, F. A. Orizo, and D. Vila. 1981. *Fundación FOESSA, Informe sociológico sobre el cambio politico en España 1975–1981*, Vol. 1. Madrid: Euroamérica.

Linz, Juan J., M. Gómez-Reino, F. A. Orizo, and D. Vila. 1986. *Conflicto en Euskadi*. Madrid: Espasa Calpe.

Llera, Francisco J. 1994. *Los Vascos y la Politica*. Bilbao: Universidad del Pais Vasco.

Merkel, Wolfgang. 1999. "Defekte Demokratien." In *Demokratie in Ost und West, Für Klaus von Beyme*, W. Merkel and A. Busch, eds., pp. 361–381. Frankfurt: Suhrkamp.

Montero, José Ramón, Richard Gunther, and Mariano Torcal. 1997. "Democracy in Spain: Legitimacy, Discontent, and Disaffection." *Studies in Comparative International Development*, Fall, 32(3): 124–160.

Moral, Félix. 1998. *Identidad regional y nacionalismo en el Estado de las Autonomías*. Madrid: Centro de Investigaciones Sociológicas.

Moreno, Luis. 1995. *Escocia, Nación y Razon*. Madrid: Consejo Superior de Investigaciones Cientificoa.

Moreno, Luis. 1997. *La federalización de España*. Madrid: Siglo XXI.

Orizo, Francisco Andrés and Alejandro Sánchez Fernández with DATA (1991) *Sistema de Valors dels Catalans: Catalunya dins 1 'enquesta europea de valors dels anvs 90*. Barcelona: Institut Catalá d'Estudis Mediterrainis.

Schumpeter, Joseph A. 1942, 1950. *Capitalism, Socialism and Democracy*. New York: Harper & Brothers.

4

AN HISTORICAL CONTEXT FOR ELECTION RESEARCH

SEYMOUR MARTIN LIPSET

George Mason University

What are election studies good for? Everything I suppose, but I will try to discuss some of them. Since the colloquium on which this book is based was intended to help design a major new study based on previous research, I will focus on the results of the earlier studies.

Five Pioneers

In considering mentors or intellectual predecessors, five people should be remembered. The first is Joseph Schumpeter (1883–1950), a major economist and sociologist. He formulated what has been described as the elitist theory of democracy. Schumpeter (1947) basically defined democracy realistically as a system in which the voters, the mass of the population, are able to choose between contending elites, that is, alternative candidates. He argued that participatory democracy, such as occurs in New England town meetings or small Swiss cantons, is impossible on a large scale in complex societies. Elections and parties are the key mechanisms of democracy, but without stable parties, elections are weak reeds, as the post-Soviet Russian experience illustrates. Democracy requires institutionalized competition.

The second person is Stuart Rice (1928), who holds an interesting role in the history of election research for his pioneering work on quantitative methods. He conducted the first panel study (repeat interviews with the same people) in 1924, in which he queried a sample of students from Dartmouth College, where he was then teaching, examining their vote changes from Time I to Time II. Rice also conducted a statistically sophisticated, ecological study of voting over time, also known as an area panel. He examined changes in electoral participation and analyzed the voting records of legislators, looking for patterns of cohesion.

Why was Rice so innovative and productive? When Peter Rossi (1959), then engaged in a study of the voting classics, interviewed him in the early 1950s, Rice told him that his youthful creativity was a result of his first teaching position after leaving Columbia University, at Dartmouth, located in the then sleepy small town of Hanover, New Hampshire. He and a few other new instructors wanted to get out of Hanover and return to "real" life. They decided that the only way to do so was to engage in research and to publish. Although in different fields, they agreed to press each other in their writing and publishing efforts. Rice asked himself, "What can I do?" He had written a Ph.D. dissertation involving an ecological analysis of voting in the Midwest. The topic had been given to him by Franklin Giddings, the first professor of sociology at Columbia. Giddings was a proponent of quantitative methods in social science and brought statisticians to the faculty. Rice decided to demonstrate the worth of statistical methods in the study of various political topics, and the result was his book *Quantitative Methods in Politics* (Rice, 1928). It enabled him to get out of Hanover when he secured a job at the University of Pennsylvania. Unfortunately, that was the end of his career in voting research. He published little afterward, only one monograph on methodology (Rice, 1930). His career demonstrates that you do not have to be intellectually inspired to make a major contribution.

This, of course, was not true of the third figure, my mentor in research, Paul Lazarsfeld. I could spend most of this chapter discussing his intellectual genius, his methodological and substantive contributions in scaling, and his contributions to electoral and communications research. The best course I took as a graduate student at Columbia was his Logic of Social Research. It taught students how to think multivariately, to hold factors constant, to conceptualize. Although Lazarsfeld is best known for his quantitative work, he emphasized that multivariate analysis is fundamental to approaching qualitative issues as well. In the course, he looked at classics such as

Durkheim's *Suicide* and Weber's *Protestant Ethic*, clarifying how leading social scientists formulated hypotheses and found the data with which to test them.

Lazarsfeld was interested in studying changes in attitudes and behavior on the individual level. He had been trained as a psychologist. Like Rice, but totally independent of him, he developed the idea of the panel, or repeat interviews with the same respondents over time. He looked at those who changed their votes or buying or media consumption preferences, arguing that these areas required similar approaches to decision analysis. He was also a founding genius in different subjects, such as communications research methods, market research, sociology, and voting behavior. In each area, he emphasized decision processes, that is, the factors that affect changes in preferences.

His two books on elections, both of which were coauthored, *The People's Choice* (Lazarsfeld, Berelson, and Gaudet, 1944/1948) and *Voting* (Berelson, Lazarsfeld, and McPhee, 1966), were panel studies of presidential voting in two small cities, Sandusky, Ohio (1940), and Elmira, New York (1948). This research sensitized social scientists to the importance of economic class, religion, and community environment and structure. The researchers formulated an Index of Political Predisposition (IPP) from these variables. Persons who were economically well off, Protestant, and rural tended to vote Republican. At the opposite end were the poor or working class, Catholics, and urban dwellers. These characteristics contributed to Democratic predispositions. This analytic framework also led him to an understanding of the effects of cross-pressured, contradictory, exposures, to electorally relevant stimuli, such as being (in 1940) a well-to-do Catholic or a poor Protestant who might also be a trade union member or a business person. Cross-pressured voters were more likely to be indecisive, to have unstable preferences, and to be less likely to vote. As a student of media influence, Lazarsfeld paid particular attention to the way newspapers and radio influenced voter decisions. Like structural variables, they too served to challenge or reinforce predispositions. But individuals sought to avoid conflicting influences, hence they would largely listen to speakers, or expose themselves to media, with which they agreed.

Lazarsfeld's emphasis on the effects of structural factors on voting may have stemmed from his background. Before he emigrated to America, he had been a young, politically active Marxist in Austria, where social class, religion, and rural-urban environment distinguished Socialist voters from those supporting the conservative Catholic People's Party. His academic origins in social psychology and mathematics led him to create attitude scales, which also defined where voters stood prior to an election campaign.

Mathematical or statistical elaboration of the logic underlying scales was probably the innovation of which Paul Lazarsfeld was most proud. But it should be noted that he could be a pragmatist who recognized that social reality and political choices were often simpler than the complex statistical analysis. One of his major contributions to scalar thinking was latent structure analysis, a way of specifying the underlying interrelationships of factors. Yet he knew it had practical limitations.

I once was lunching with Paul at the Columbia Faculty Club when a young collaborator on the *Voting* study, William McPhee, rushed up all excited. He reported that he had just successfully completed a latent structure analysis from the data. Lazarsfeld looked at him quizzically and asked, "What did you do that for?" McPhee was crestfallen and could only ask what he meant. Paul then said, "I've never seen a scale that for practical use was better than a simple addition of the answers. Latent structure analysis costs a lot of money. All you have to do is total up the items. Latent analysis is intellectually valuable. Its structure is something you find for intellectual pleasure, or for mathematical rigor. But it does not supply a more useful scale than pluses and minuses." His student Peter Rossi would later demonstrate statistically that for operational research purposes different indicators of class position, including the Marxist and the Weberian, yielded indistinguishable results when correlated with the attitudinal or behavioral dependent variables.

Elections are particularly important for social science analysis because they are repetitive events that have gone on for a long time, for two centuries in the United States. The records permit quantitative analyses of changes in social behavior and values, as well as the stability of cleavages over time. There are studies of the social basis of support and opposition to the Constitution in the 1780s, of continuities and discontinuities in party support from the 1790s on, of pre–Civil War referenda on race issues, of secession referenda in the South in 1860–1861, and many more (American Statistical Association, 1930; Benson et al., 1974; Jensen, 1967). The French have collected plebiscite and parliamentary election data for a century and a half. Their scholars have linked voting preferences to social and economic structures by relating electoral maps to maps tracing ecological variables. André Siegried founded a school of electoral sociology before World War I, and François Goguel has continued it in more recent times.

Americans have a long interest in polls going back to the early nineteenth century. The earliest ones were conducted by politicians and newspapers, basically to find out who would win an election. Moise Ostrogorski (1992), a Russian liberal, studied American and British politics in the 1890s. American politicians told him that they took polls before elections by having the precinct workers visit every hundredth house to ask people how they were going to vote. They conducted such interviews two or three times in an election season. They found that people made up their minds two months before elections, and that choices did not change over the last two months. This was the same conclusion reported by Lazarsfeld a half century later in *The People's Choice*, his study of the 1940 election. As noted earlier, it was the first major academic election study based on the polling of a panel. It followed by four years the use of representative national samples by George Gallup, Archibald Crossley, and Elmo Roper to report on the 1936 presidential contest. These studies led to the development of the public opinion research industry. Although most survey research has been for commercial marketing purposes, politicians, the media, and the academy have spent enormous sums of money in recent decades collecting data to understand election processes and choices. Literally tens of thousands of polls make it possible to learn a great deal by secondary analysis of survey data gathered for candidates, parties, and university-based institutes. When added together, they make more comprehensive analyses possible than separate surveys could yield.

One other early approach in American voting research must be mentioned, the single-person area panels conducted by Samuel Lubell, a journalist who is our fourth figure. Lubell, who worked in the 1940s, distrusted surveys. He preferred to study precincts, which had a record of following national trends. He would interview every person in such precincts, asking how he or she had voted last time and for whom she or he planned to vote now. He then queried the changers in depth and assumed they would be representative of shifters everywhere. The logic of this approach was the same as that of Lazarsfeld's panels, namely, to focus on those whose opinions differed from time one to time two. Lubell (1956) did well in anticipating the results of elections and in reporting on the expressions of sentiments. However, he was critical of, and not very interested in, academic research, and his approach and findings have not entered into the scholarly arena.

These sociological, structural ways of approaching the determinants of voting were supplemented in the 1950s and 1960s by a group based at the University of Michigan headed by our fifth founder, social psychologist Angus Campbell (1960). The Michigan Survey Research Center had its origins in a research program in the U.S. Department of Agriculture in the late 1930s, which moved to Ann Arbor after World War II and continues today as the major academic center for the study of electoral behavior. Many important scholars have been associated with it, Angus Campbell, Phillip Converse, Warren Miller, and Donald Stokes among them. Campbell and his collaborators expanded the compass of academic voting surveys to the nation, and reduced the number of panel (repeat) interviews to two instead of the five to seven used by Lazarsfeld in his studies of local communities. More significantly, the Michigan researchers shifted from a sociological emphasis on structure, that is, class and group membership factors, to personal, psychological variables, which "intervene" between macro events and behavior. These orientations affect the ways voters interpret political factors, particularly three: "party identification," "issue," and "candidate" orientations. The first they view as a stable sentiment, and the other two vary from election to election. Though they recognized that structural factors affect how electors react to political stimuli, they assumed that partisan or ideological sentiments are more important. More recent research, here and abroad, indicates a decline in party identification in many countries, while issues and candidates seemingly have become more important. On the structural side, class factors are clearly less significant. In general, however, diverse group affiliations, such as ethnicity, religion, and union membership, still explain much of a voter's preferences.

The Center conducts what is officially known as the National Election Study (NES), which is funded by the National Science Foundation. The NES is designed in part to document what has happened in each national election, what the salient issues are, how the major demographic groups distribute the characteristics of candidate and party supporters, and so forth. The focus on orientations involves exploring how voters respond to macro events. In other words, the

Michigan approach has been dedicated more to accounting for the outcomes of specific elections than to explaining continuing processes. It separates contests into three types — maintaining, deviating, and realigning. The researchers assume a normal or continuity vote pattern that reflects the distribution of party identifications that hold steady in maintaining elections. Short-term effects will shift party loyalties from one to another, thereby producing a deviating contest. Realigning elections take place more rarely, some suggest at intervals of thirty years or more , when significant groups of voters or regions shift their party identification, not just their vote, thus setting new standards of normality. The elections of 1894 and 1932, and possibly 1960, were realigning. The shift of white Southern voters from the Democrats to the Republicans was a realignment.

In addition to documenting and analyzing what has happened, the NES surveys include special segments or modules that reflect the interests of the different political scientists involved. These may include media effect analysis, the role of particular organizations or groups, such as trade unions, on voters, the relationship between religious commitments and voting, or the characteristics and behavior of supporters of each party.

Historical Analysis

As Stuart Rice (1928) understood, ecological (area) analysis of voting over time parallels the methodology of the panel in using aggregate election data in much the same way as survey analysts use individual responses. It not only can inform us about the correlates of party choice at a given moment, but also makes it possible to specify the characteristics of areas or groups that change from time one to time two. Quantitative studies of ecological change require that areas be comparable, something that inherently is almost impossible, except for short periods. For example, constituency boundaries can change. The Michigan Consortium for Political Research deserves considerable credit for processing voting data from the nineteenth century into census units. By analyzing these data researchers can trace through the ebb and flow of party support, the strength of party loyalties, and participation and opinion correlates, thus contributing to historical knowledge.

There are some major historical analyses whose results correspond to those of contemporary longitudinal polls. Charles Beard (1913), a great political historian writing before World War I, used ecological data to analyze support and opposition to the U.S. Constitution in referenda and conventions, and to describe the differences between the Federalists and Anti-Federalists. Beard emphasized the role of economic factors, arguing that the issues debated about the Constitution reflected interests. His conclusions have been questioned by latter-day historians, but Beard's work remains important.

Another important analysis, which like Beard's is based on ecological voting data as well as information on the socioeconomic background of elected representatives, is *The Adams Federalists* by Manning Dauer (1953). Dauer tries to answer the question, "Why did the Federalist Party collapse?" Early elections were marked by a two-party system, the Federalists led by Alexander Hamilton and the Democratic Republicans led by Thomas Jefferson. Washington had been a Federalist sympathizer, while his successor, John Adams, the second president, was firmly in the party. Adams was defeated for reelection by Jefferson in 1800. Thereafter the Federalist party gradually declined, and by the second decade it no longer was a national contender.

Dauer concludes that the Federalists declined because they did not understand the nature of democratic politics, namely, that to win, parties have to appeal to at least half the electorate, and that to do so requires compromising interests and principles. The Federalists had an urban mercantilist base and advocated Hamilton's program of building up industry and business. The country, however, was overwhelmingly rural; the great majority of the population were farmers. Most of them were not interested in an economic policy designed to build up cities and business interests. Hamiltonian industrial policy was not the way to win elections in a country of farmers. Hence, as the debate over the character of political institution issues declined in importance and economic ones became dominant, the Federalist vote for Congress steadily fell, since the party took positions that the majority of the voters did not support. Dauer demonstrates his thesis by an analysis of state and constituency voting over time.

The so-called second party system, the contest between the Whigs and the Democrats, existed from the 1830s until close to the Civil War. Voting studies indicate that the issues and correlates of party support were similar to those of the previous system, and that party organizations were strong, though the system was short-lived. Areas were either Whig or Democrat, and did not shift much. Party support moved up and down, but there was great stability in regional vote patterns. As with the first party system, the more agrarian-based Democrats maintained their strength, while the more urban, business-oriented, and elitist Whig party disintegrated, in part because the Whigs, like the Federalists, were more principled, moralistic, and less compromising. They were the party of the Protestant middle class and were severely impacted by the slavery issue.

The Democrats, then as earlier and later, were the party of the less privileged rural and urban elements, as well as of immigrants, including most Catholics. The Whigs were the party of the more well-to-do, both rural and urban. Like the Federalists, they favored business-enhancing policies, particularly "internal improvements." They supported government initiatives to build harbors, roads, and railroads to enlarge the scope of markets and to facilitate transportation and communication within the country. The more rural Democrats were against internal improvements, which they saw as subsidies to urban business.

The Whigs, however, also received strong support from some farmers, particularly those living in mountain regions, who required state-financed transportation facilities. They had difficulties getting their crops to markets and were unable to finance the needed road network. The Whigs consequently secured wide support in mountainous regions, such as Tennessee, Kentucky, and West Virginia, and in other districts that had transportation problems.

Ecological analysis demonstrates that these divisions led to counterintuitive behavior in the events leading to the Civil War. In 1860–1861, there were special elections and referenda in the Southern states that dealt with secession. Using county data, I correlated secession support with the proportion of the population who owned slaves. The analysis, which is published in *Political Man* (Lipset, 1960), indicates that areas of lower slaveholding, inhabited largely by poorer whites, voted more strongly for secession than did the more well-to-do whites in plantation regions. The latter counties, which had more slaves, gave more support to the Union.

These cleavages corresponded to the Whig–Democrat support patterns. The poor Democratic whites, though not slave owners, were largely Protestant sectarians, whose ministers preached a Calvinist doctrine of blacks being predestined to be inferiors and slaves. They were supposedly the descendants of one of Noah's sons, Ham, whose descendants were condemned to be the servants of servants because Ham had looked at his naked father and mother. The well-to-do whites, many of whom were slave owners, tended to be Episcopalian. They supported slavery for self-interested economic reasons, but did not view its preservation as a moral cause. Previously, they had been Whigs, and in the 1860 presidential election voted for a pro-union party, Constitutional Union (John Bell). The Southern Democrats (John Breckenridge), whose constituents were more likely to be poorer and to own fewer slaves than the Constitutional Unionists, became the political force that most aggressively supported secession.

After the war, the Southern Whig counties that had voted Constitutional Union were more likely to become Republican. This meant that the poor mountain Whigs in the South were also more disposed to vote Republican, although the Republican Party was the party of the urban middle class and of big business. In 1936 when Franklin Roosevelt's New Deal policies produced an emphasis on economic class divisions between the parties, the poorer farmers of Kentucky, Tennessee, and other areas continued to vote Republican. They were still voting for internal improvements, as in the 1840s, which had been the issue that made them Whig and consequently Republican. Given that the social structure of the Southern rural and small town communities had not changed much, that they remained Scottish-Irish sectarians and small farmers, this population continued with the same party, even though that party's role and meaning in the larger system had changed.

There are some interesting parallels to this in France. French scholars have been interested in why agrarian regions with highly similar economic and other structural conditions differ in their electoral allegiances, some voting left and others right for well over a century. French electoral sociologists have pointed to continuities in voting in these areas from 1848 to the post–World War II era. During the 1930s and 1950s this sometimes meant support for the Communists or for extreme right-wing parties. The explanation of why rural areas voted for or against the Communists or de Gaulle may be related to the way they had voted following the 1848 revolution. The differences were produced by the diversity in their fiefdoms before the French Revolution of 1789, that is, to which Catholic monastic orders they had been bound. Those who had been under the Dominicans—the Dominicans were more liberal and tolerant, and dealt well with their serfs—remained Catholic and voted conservative in the twentieth Century. Their descendants remained loyal to the Church and followed right-wing politics. The areas controlled by the much more authoritarian Jesuits became irreligious, leftist, and Communist. The Jesuits had treated their serfs badly, and therefore their descendants have been anticlerical. In sociologically identical areas, rural party loyalties were determined by the ways the Jesuits and the Dominicans had dealt with their ancestors a couple of hundred years earlier. Of course, these kinds of historical continuities are evident only in small communities that have not changed much. They do not apply to Paris or Marseille, nor to Chicago or New York.

Systematic quantitative historical electoral analysis is still in its infancy. Lee Benson (1961), Richard Jensen (1983), and Paul Kleppner (1970) have played important roles in developing this field. From studying voting behavior in the later part of the nineteenth century, they have shown that religion and ethnicity, together with economic role, were the dominant variables separating Democrats and Republicans. In the nineteenth century, the latter had a base among Protestant evangelicals and sectarians (it still does) and had absorbed the anti-Catholic Know-Nothings, while the Democrats had drawn heavily from Catholics and others of recent immigrant stock. In many local and state elections, though not national ones, the nineteenth-century Republicans were openly anti-Catholic. Conversely, the Democrats, particularly in the large Northern cities, were closely involved with the Catholic Church, which was the denomination of most immigrant workers. The election results demonstrated this division.

Although the church–state issue, which affected continental politics, did not exist in its clerical–anticlerical form in the United States, election history, as noted, demonstrates the importance of religious diversity as a source of political difference. Except for the Lazarsfeld studies, academic students of voting, as well as pollsters, seemed surprisingly unaware of its importance until 1960 when Kennedy ran with heavy Catholic support. The election of 1928, when Al Smith's Catholicism was a major issue, should have sensitized them. But the early pollsters did not even ask about religious affiliation.

The Michigan Consortium has sought to facilitate historical analysis. It has recorded votes by census units from before the Civil War to the present. Through use of these data, historians may reliably document how voters behaved in the past, how stable party alignments have been, how ethnic group allegiances have varied over time, and many other relationships and patterns. Extant research has demonstrated the significant influence of culture cleavages on voting in the nineteenth century. Such research documents that the Republicans were more ascetic, pro-Prohibition, and antigambling, and the Democrats more libertine and less moralistic. Indeed, back in the old days Democratic conventions were marked by much greater consumption of alcohol than were the Republican conventions.

Participation in Recent Years

Participation in elections has differed greatly over time. The variations in turnout have affected outcomes, since the extent of nonvoting is quite different among various social groups. Election statistics indicate that from 80 to 90 percent of the male electorate voted in the late nineteenth and early twentieth century. There can be some suspicion of the validity of these reports, since over 100 percent were reported as casting ballots in a number of counties. Voting rates dropped precipitously in the 1920s after women received the franchise through the passage of the women's suffrage amendment in 1919. Newly enfranchised voters do not turn out in large numbers; sizable abstention rates are characteristic of their behavior. Factors associated with higher voting rates are education, income, majority ethno-religious status, and age (the middle-aged voting more, the young voting the least), and, as noted earlier, lesser exposure to cross-pressures. Political competitiveness, as reflected in the number of parties or candidates, or in the United States in the narrowness of the gap between the two parties in given constituencies, will increase turnout. The United States currently has the lowest rate of voting among the world's stable democracies—50 percent for president, 35 percent for Congress, and around 20 percent in primary nomination elections. Only Switzerland rates as low. These two nations are also similar with respect to affluence and extent of personal satisfaction, and are low in partisan ideological divisions. Motivation to vote may be adversely affected by lower levels of politically relevant concerns.

In seeking to explain why the United States has such low voting rates, researchers have emphasized that it is more difficult to vote here than in other countries. In America, it is necessary to register to vote, sometimes months before elections, during periods when there is little discussion of or interest in electoral politics. Elsewhere, citizens are entered on the voter list by a public authority, in which case there is only one decision to make, whether to vote or not. The evidence clearly indicates that reducing registration requirements in different states increases the percentage who vote, though it is still far less than in other democracies.

1998: Explaining the Vote

Much of the discussion that preceded the congressional election in 1998 focused on the possible differential impact of rates of voting among various groups. The general assumption has long been that those designated by pollsters as "likely voters" are disproportionately white, middle to upper class, heavily Republican, and anti-Clinton. In fact, pro-Democratic groups like African-Americans and trade unionists voted more heavily than usual in 1998 as a result of sophisticated and well-financed campaigns to get out the vote among them. The 1998 vote for Congress, especially for the House of Representatives, was divided almost evenly between the two major parties.

Although the Republicans won a tiny 1 percent plurality, they lost seats, thus violating the repeated finding that the "out" party, the nonpresidential one, invariably gains in off-year elections. The small Democratic increases may reflect the validity of another generalization cited earlier that has held up during the twentieth century in most countries: incumbents gain when times are good and lose when they are bad. But issue saliency is also important.

The evidence does not permit a conclusion about the impact on the election of the effort to impeach and convict Clinton. A sizable majority of the population repeatedly told pollsters that they did not like Clinton as a person, that he was immoral, but that he had done a good job as president. They opposed both the investigation of the Lewinsky affair and his threatened conviction following impeachment. On the other hand, close to two-thirds of voters favored a congressional censure and/or conviction. Only a third were in favor of letting him off scot-free.

Conclusion: The Need to
Contextualize Election Campaigns

Do polls have an impact? They certainly do. Bill Clinton would not be president of the United States today were it not for the existence of polls. The surveys saved him by showing that the majority of the American people wanted him to continue as president. In the absence of these surveys, most of the Representatives and Senators would have assumed that the anti-Clinton articles and editorials and Washington elite opinion reflected the will of the general population. The polls gave him a rationale and public support for staying on.

Whether polls affect election outcomes by declaring winners in advance, in effect by creating a "bandwagon" effect, has been a much debated subject. The academic consensus is that they do not have an impact, that national predictions do not affect individual voters. On the other hand, Elisabeth Noelle-Neumann, a leading German pollster, suggests that voters are responsive to the climate of opinion in their immediate circles. In *The Spiral of Silence*, Noelle-Neumann (1993) suggests that political minorities are socially intimidated, keep quiet, and thereby help to create consensus within groups. It should also be noted, however, that even if national poll results do not affect individual voting much, they can help determine outcomes by affecting campaign activists and financial contributors to increase or decrease their level of involvement.

This discussion points out major lacunae in election research, the analysis of the effect of issues, and the ways that larger social, economic, and political contexts affect campaigns. The 1998 exit poll data indicate that the social alliances that have existed since the Great Depression are still intact. A *New York Times* article (Connelly, 1998, p. A20) summarized these survey findings as follows:

> Candidates from the party of the incumbent President tend to be favored by voters who believe their economic situation has improved. In 1980, 1994 and 1996, the Democratic candidates were backed by a majority of voters who said their financial situation had improved. And voters appear to turn against the incumbent party when they believe their situation has worsened. Most of the voters who described their family as being either less well off or the same voted for Republicans candidates, as they did in 1994 and 1996.
>
> There are still some signs of the social alliances that have existed since the great Depression. For example, less affluent voters, those with annual income under $30,000, gave the majority of their votes to the Democrats. Black, Hispanic and Jewish voters remained strongly Democratic. Voters who lived in a household with a union member continued to support the Democratic candidate, as did urban voters.
>
> By contrast, voters whose income exceeded $30,000 and white Protestants voted for Republican candidates. Republican candidates were favored by suburbanites, as well as by those who live in small towns and rural areas.

Lazarsfeld's predisposition factors are still here. For example, less affluent voters, those with annual incomes under $30,000, gave the majority of their 1998 votes to the Democrats. Black, Hispanic, and Jewish voters remained strongly Democratic. Voters living in a household with a union member continued to support the Democratic candidate, as did urban voters. Catholics, it should be noted, have changed, in tandem with the growth of a sizable middle class among them. But holding income constant, they remain significantly more Democratic than Protestants.

It is also noteworthy that the orientations of the two major parties since 1932 may be described as communitarian and welfarist (the Democrats) and libertarian and antistatist (the Republicans). The groups that are disproportionately communitarian are the Catholics, the Jews, the Blacks, and the Hispanics, whereas Protestants of long-term native, English, or German origin are more prone to hold libertarian beliefs. These value emphases hold up within the same economic class categories. Ironically, the libertarian-disposed groups, reflecting their Protestant sectarian background, are more inclined to be moralistic with respect to issues such as sexual behavior and orientation.

The same predisposing factors divide liberals and conservatives, the left and the right, Democrats and Republicans. Within such continuities the vote moves up and down inside the demographic or value groups, varying by socioeconomic conditions, issues, campaign strategies, the mobilization of groups, and finances, while the media influence the proportion voting and the appeal of the parties. We need to know a great deal more about the determinants of election cycles as distinct from the business cycle and personal predispositions. Would that the curiosities and theoretical interests of the founding figures, of Schumpeter, Rice, Lazarsfeld, Campbell, and Lubell, were revived by the students of politics in the twenty-first century.

References

American Statistical Association, Committee on Social Statistics. 1930. *Statistics in Social Studies,* Stuart A. Rice, ed. Philadelphia: University of Pennsylvania Press.

Beard, Charles. 1913. *An Economic Interpretation of the Constitution of the United States.* New York: Macmillan Co.

Benson, Lee. 1961. *Concept of Jacksonian Democracy: New York as a Test Case.* Princeton: Princeton University Press.

Benson, Lee, et al. 1974. *American Political Behavior: Historical Essays and Readings.* New York: Harper & Row.

Berelson, Bernard R., Paul F. Lazarsfeld, and William N. McPhee. 1966. *Voting: A Study of Opinion Formation in a Presidential Campaign* (originally published in 1954). Chicago: University of Chicago Press.

Campbell, Angus, et al. 1960. *The American Voter.* New York: Wiley.

Connelly, Marjorie. 1998. "A Look at Voting Patterns of 115 Demographic Groups in House Races." *The New York Times,* November 9, p. A20.

Dauer, Manning J. 1953. *The Adams Federalists.* Baltimore: Johns Hopkins University Press.

Jensen, Richard J. 1967. *The Winning of the Midwest: A Social History of Midwestern Elections, 1888–1896.* New Haven: Yale University Press.

Jensen, Richard J. 1983. *Grass Roots Politics: Parties, Issues and Votes, 1854–1883.* Westport, Conn.: Greenwood Press.

Kleppner, Paul. 1970. *The Cross of Culture: A Social Analysis of Mid-Western Politics.* New York: Free Press.

Lazarsfeld, Paul F., Bernard R. Berelson, and Hazel Gaudet. 1948. *The People's Choice: How the Voter Makes Up His Mind in a Presidential Campaign,* 2nd ed. (1st ed., 1944). New York: Columbia University Press.

Lipset, Seymour M. 1960. *Political Man: The Social Basis of Politics.* New York: Doubleday & Co.

Lubell, Samuel. 1956. *The Future of American Politics.* New York: Doubleday/Anchor Books.

Noelle-Neumann, Elisabeth. 1993. *The Spiral of Silence: Public Opinion, Our Social Skin.* Chicago: University of Chicago Press.

Ostrogorski, Moise. 1992. *Democracy and the Organization of Political Parties.* New York: Macmillan Co.

Rice, Stuart. 1928. *Quantitative Methods in Politics.* New York: Knopf.

Rice, Stuart Oscar, ed. 1937. *Methods in Social Science: A Case Book.* Chicago: University of Chicago Press.

Rossi, Peter. 1959. "Four Landmarks in Voting Research." In *American Voting Behavior,* Eugene Burdick and Arthur J. Brodbeck, eds., pp. 5–54. Glencoe, Ill.: Free Press.

Schumpeter, Joseph. 1947. *Capitalism, Socialism, and Democracy.* New York: Harper and Brothers.

5

CONTEXT AND COMPARISON IN ELECTION RESEARCH: THE ISRAEL NATIONAL ELECTION STUDY

ASHER ARIAN AND MICHAL SHAMIR

A good election study is not designed to produce accurate pre-election predictions, to build political strategy, or to recommend campaign tactics for a particular election, important as these side benefits might be. Rather, a good election study is based on solid social science and aims to reveal regularities associated with this crucial mechanism of democratic politics. Like other basic research, results of such studies may eventually be applied to election campaign management and media accounts of elections. But this is not their objective, and they should not be judged by whether or not they meet this fleeting purpose.

Election studies allow us to explore this institution of social choice, and the ways in which it mobilizes citizen participation. These two subjects point to different foci and levels of analysis. On one level, we are interested in the electoral process: in organization, networks, and communication patterns, the election campaign and electoral competition, the performance of political parties and the media, and the resulting party system and public policy. On a different level, we are interested in individuals: their turnout, modes of electoral participation, and voting patterns.

The major research tool in election studies has been the opinion survey, which is most suited to explore the individual level. Indeed, the societal level is often ignored in election studies. However, survey data may also be used creatively to provide system-level analysis if the right questions are asked. A good election study incorporates other data and methodologies, including observation, interviews with participants, and the study of relevant documents. Considering the dominance of the mass media in general and of television in particular, media content analysis is also important. Community studies in the Columbia University tradition are still valuable; an excellent recent example is Huckfeldt and Sprague (1995).

Election studies need to be anchored in the broader social and political context because elections are only part of politics. But since national election studies are undertaken in the highly charged atmosphere of the campaign, they provide a promising platform from which to observe deep political, cultural, and social processes. The form of government, the structure of social cleavage, the national agenda, and the nature of the information environment are examples of such contextual factors. As an example, consider the introduction of a new electoral system whereby a proportional representation system for the elected members of the Knesset (the Israeli parliament) was augmented by a provision calling for the direct election of the prime minister using a winner-take-all system. This electoral reform in 1996 dramatically affected voting behavior, the election campaign, the political parties, the party system, and the relations among the different branches of government. Thus, the prime minister was directly elected, but he was dependent on majority support in the Knesset. The two-vote system (one for prime minister and one for the Knesset) encouraged voters to split their votes, increasing the representation of small, factional parties. As the Knesset became more factionalized, the power of the two large parties shrank. Moreover, the prime minister had to spend more time, energy, and resources to keep the coalition together (Arian and Shamir 1999).

To be truly useful, theoretical issues should drive election studies, patterns and generalizations should be explored, and comparative ramifications should be elucidated. Theory and comparison allow for the meaningful assessment of any single election. The idiosyncratic election studies of a specific country become generally useful when they are designed to allow comparative analysis in time and space, either of previous elections in the same system or of elections in different states or countries.

We know a good deal about "the not so simple act of voting" (Dalton and Wattenberg 1993). Theories of voting behavior are explicit and detailed regarding the different considerations voters utilize and the factors that influence them. The sociological model of Columbia (Berelson et al. 1954; Lazarsfeld et al. 1948; Rose 1974), the social psychological University of Michigan model (Campbell et al. 1960; Sears 1993), and the rational choice variations (Downs 1957; Fiorina 1981) have been found useful in various settings. We should focus on the task of specifying the contexts and the conditions under which each model is most useful and when various factors will dominate or be minimized. The same goals should guide studies in election communication. Country names need to be replaced by variables (Przeworski and Teune 1970), as should election years in longitudinal one-country studies. We must work harder to combine individual- and system-level data and analysis.

Finally, national election studies should sustain dynamic analysis and the study of continuity and change. Potent theoretical tools are available using concepts such as realignment and dealignment, the "frozen party systems," "postmodern culture shift," or the "particularization of vote choice" hypotheses (Burnham 1970; Dalton et al. 1984; Franklin et al. 1992; Inglehart 1990; Lipset and Rokkan 1967; Key 1955, 1959). To support insightful use of these concepts, time series and repeated measures of both system-level gauges and individual-level indicators are needed.

These goals have been rendered feasible as a result of theoretical advances and the revolution in empirical data resources that have occurred over the last few years. Relevant comparative and longitudinal data sets are becoming available at little or no cost. Data archives such as the Interuniversity Consortium for Political and Social Research (ICPSR) at the University of Michigan and the Zentralarchiv für Empirische Sozialforschung (ZA) at the University of Cologne offer a variety of comparative and longitudinal data collections. The ICORE collection of election studies on national parliaments in Europe at ZA, or the American National Election Study from 1948 on (available on CD-ROM), provide access to data undreamed of by an earlier generation of researchers.

Another example is the Comparative Study of Electoral Systems (CSES) project, in which we participate. It is a large-scale compara-

tive project that explores elections as an institution together with citizens' role in them, incorporates context, and systematically combines individual- and system-level data. The project is a collaborative program of teams of election researchers from over fifty
consolidated and emerging democracies. The goal of this collaboration is to collect data that will shed light on how the institutions that
govern the conduct of elections affect the nature and quality of democratic choice. CSES concentrates on the impact of electoral institutions on citizens' political beliefs and behaviors; the nature of political and social cleavages and alignments; and the evaluation of
democratic institutions and processes.

This theoretical focus calls for the maximization of cross-national
variation and sample size and the combination of individual- and
system-level data. The research agenda, the study design, the data
modules, and the organizational structure of CSES were constructed
through a broad-based process of discussion among directors of
election studies around the world over several years and meetings.
Each national team is in charge of data collection in its respective
country, and is also responsible for securing the funding and assur-
ing the quality of the data collected. A common questionnaire module has been constructed, which is included in the national election
study. This module is pretested through a series of pilot studies conducted in several countries and consists of questions measuring the
major concepts, as well as demographic variables. In addition, collaborators provide macrolevel data on electoral laws and other institutional arrangements, political parties, electoral alliances, and the
election context. These micro- and macrolevel data are deposited at
the central archive (ICPSR) for further processing and dissemina-
tion. The data are placed in the public domain as soon as they have
been processed. Currently microlevel and macrolevel data sets are
available for ten countries ("Comparative Study of Electoral Systems, 1996–2000," Center for Political Studies, University of Michigan, Ann Arbor, Mich. http://www.umich.edu/~nes/cses. October
24, 2000).

By coordinating the collection of electoral data across countries,
the Comparative Study of Electoral Systems project strives to advance our understanding of electoral behavior and democratic politics in a way not possible through the secondary analysis of existing
data. Being a collaborative program of cross-national research
among national election studies teams, CSES succeeds in joining spe-

cific country and election contexts with common research questions. The research agenda and the construction of micro- and macrolevel data sets open the way to analysis that combines system-level and individual-level factors. Because the data are made available as soon as they are merged and archived, it is now up to us in the research community to make good use of them to advance our knowledge about institutions and elections.

The Israel National Election Study

It is much easier to characterize a good election study than to conduct one. National election studies in Israel began in 1969, and the format established then has been continued. The two basic elements in our election study are a preelection survey and an edited volume. The survey comprises face-to-face interviews with a national sample. At least one survey was carried out in each election year; in certain years, more than one survey was conducted, and in a few cases a postelection survey was added. In 1988 and 1999, a panel design was used. Through 1977, the samples were drawn from the adult urban Jewish population. In subsequent years, they were representative samples of the adult Jewish population as a whole, not including kibbutzim and Jewish settlements in the territories under Israel's control; since 1996 they also included Israeli Arabs. The sample size is usually around 1200; in 1988 it was close to 900, and in 1969 over 1800. The data find their way to the public domain shortly after each election and are available through the Israel Social Science Archive at the Hebrew University (http://ssda.huji.ac.il).

The second element of the Israel election study is *The Elections in Israel* series. Following each election, contributions are solicited among scholars of Israeli society and politics. Eight books have been published covering the 1969 to 1996 elections (Arian 1972, 1975, 1980, 1983; Arian and Shamir 1986, 1990, 1995, 1999). The next volume is currently being compiled and written for the 1999 national elections. Each book covers the election from various perspectives, focusing on voting behavior, cleavages, political parties and candidates, the election campaign and the media, coalition building, and public policy. Submitted articles are refereed; contributors come from various institutions in Israel and abroad and from different disciplines. Most are political scientists, but sociologists, anthropologists, economists, and communication scholars have contributed. Many of the chapters rely on the survey data we have collected; other authors use their own survey data of specific groups or ecological voting data. Still others rely on documents, interviews, various degrees of participant observation, and content analysis of party platforms, print, and electronic campaign advertising. Each book in the series thus brings together leading social scientists who represent diverse intellectual traditions using different methods and data, thus providing a broadly based and interdisciplinary account of the election.

This procedure allows us to overcome a nagging feature of the study of Israeli national elections—the scarcity of resources. There is no regular support for election studies in Israel, and funds for more elaborate research designs and data collection plans are not available. We would like to research campaign dynamics and political communication along the lines of the Canadian National Election Study introduced in 1988 (see Johnston in Chapter 6 of this volume). Since we are not able to do this, our approach—based on the cooperation of other scholars in our book series—partially offsets this liability and allows a broadly based account of the election in spite of the limited budget.

National Election Studies, Collective Identity, and Comparative Politics

The repeated use of the same questions in our election surveys over time has yielded important results (see Shamir and Arian 1999). Consider the study of culture, multiculturalism, and identity. Although these topics are now being given great attention in the social sciences generally, especially in political science and comparative politics, surprisingly this has not been the case for electoral research. Compared to other subfields of comparative politics, electoral research has been largely unconcerned with the role of culture, as with other grand theoretical issues of political science (Barnes 1997, 117–118), even though sociodemographic variables have always loomed large in election studies. Most countries, including Western democracies, are culturally diverse. Ethnic, racial, linguistic, religious, regional, and other differences form the basis for collective identity and for cultural, social, and political strife. Everything we know tells us that electoral politics are not immune to these forces, and that we would be most likely to find the traces of these factors in the voting booth. Periodical national election studies can provide snapshots that allow us to study such important societal phenomena through systematic and longitudinal analysis, while contributing to comparative voting literature at the same time.

Comparative electoral research suggests that voting has become more individualized and less structured by social groupings; the bases of electoral mobilization and choice have changed from social cleavages to cognitive mobilization and issue cleavages. Traditional social cleavages—class in particular, but also religion, ethnic affiliation, and the like—have become less important in explaining electoral behavior in advanced industrial democracies, while issue voting is becoming more important in the calculus of voters. Moreover, our ability to account for voting decisions in these party systems is declining (Dalton and Wattenberg 1993; Franklin et al. 1992). Taking multiculturalism and identity into account permits us to reconsider the generalization and prediction of declining social cleavages.

Issues differ in their potential to generate group allegiance. Some issues may be only weakly related to specific social groupings, as the postindustrial literature argues; other issues can connect and reinforce existing cleavage structures by providing new reasons for the same people and groups to support the same parties. Identity questions are of the latter type and they trigger group allegiance. Thus the extent to which the vote is related to group characteristics of voters depends at least in part on the nature of the issues on the agenda.

By identity we mean consciousness boundaries that divide groups into different communal and social entities, and often divide them also territorially or geographically. Identity marks meaningful distinctions between group members and outsiders, commonality within the group in terms of some consequential social category, group goals, and value orientations. Identity requires self-awareness of membership in the group and psychological closeness to it. Understood and applied in this fashion, the concept of identity binds together sociological, psychological, and economic approaches to voting behavior and directs attention to social groups, issues, value priorities, and self-interest. When identity dilemmas capture the agenda, generalizations about electoral behavior in advanced industrial societies may be misguided since these dilemmas often amalgamate issue- and social-group-based voting. We would still expect an increase in the importance of issues in voters' considerations, but not necessarily a decline in the amount of the vote variance explained by social structure, either on its own or in conjunction with attitudinal variables.

Dilemmas of identity are at the heart of the major cleavage dimensions in Israeli politics, and they have become more salient in electoral competition over time. We focus here on the Jewish majority, and within it we conceptualize two identity dimensions that are themselves interrelated. The external identity dimension refers to the questions of geographical borders and relations with Israel's neighbors and the rest of the world. The issue of the occupied territories represents this dimension in concrete terms. The internal dimension of identity relates to the nature of the Jewish state in terms of citizenship, nationhood, and religion. Israeli Arabs are one side of this debate. For most Israeli Jews the notion of Israel as a Jewish state provides a common denominator, but the meaning assigned to it differs dramatically across groups and forms the basis for what has developed into a conflict between subcultures. It is often defined in terms of religious versus secular, primordial versus civil, Jewishness versus Israeliness, or Eretz Israel versus the state of Israel, in Kimmerling's apt phrase (1985). The two identity dimensions are closely related, as Eretz Israel (the Land of Israel) is strongly embedded in both geography and religion.

In Israel from the late 1960s through the 1990s, the simultaneous impact of social-group-based voting and of issue voting is clear. In many Western countries, issues involving postbourgeois versus materialist values, gender, public versus private consumption, and state employment have gained ascendancy. In Israel, these issues have energized only limited publics and have not become as central, critical, and engulfing as the major issue dimension in Israeli politics: the territories and the Israeli-Arab conflict. The questions involved in Israel touch on essential dilemmas of national self-definition. The peace process, the Oslo agreements, and the questions of territorial compromise are the policy expression of the dilemmas of collective identity regarding geographical boundaries and Israel's relations with other nations, in particular its Arab neighbors and, even more specifically, the Palestinians. Internally, the debate over the collective identity of Israel as a Jewish and democratic state has intensified. These two identity dimensions are interrelated and strongly tied to social groups. Voting in Israel has become more structured, and the issues embodying these dilemmas have become a more important determinant of the vote over time. Religious, Sephardim, less educated, and lower-status hawks voted for Netanyahu, for the right-wing Likud and for religious parties, whereas the left—Barak and Peres, Labor and Meretz—received a disproportionate share of secular, upper-class Ashkenazi dovish votes.

Table 5.1 establishes this pattern for the period of 1981–1999, using the prime-ministerial vote in 1996 and 1999; prior to the introduction of the direct election of the prime minister, the right-left bloc vote for the Knesset (parliament) was used. This dependent variable can be used meaningfully only for the elections since 1981, which mark the clear emergence of the bipolar structure of the party system. A similar pattern holds in the analysis of the vote for the two major parties, Likud and Labor, throughout the period for which we have survey data, from 1969 through 1999. The distinction between these two parties has become less meaningful as the contest generated by the direct election of the prime minister has won most attention, and we do not reproduce it here.

For each year, we present two regression analyses, performed only on respondents who disclosed their voting intention. First we analyze voting behavior with reference to the major sociodemographic variables (age, gender, density of dwelling, education, income, religious observance, and ethnic background) to allow for the most comprehensive test of the role of social-group-based voting. In the second stage we combine these sociodemographics with indicators for the major issue dimensions in Israeli politics (the socioeconomic issue, the territories issue, and the state–religion issue). These analyses provide an additional test of the potency of the sociodemographic variables over time when controlling for policy concerns, and also allow us to examine the changing role of issues over time. For the wording of the questions and details about the samples, see Shamir and Arian (1999), Appendices A and B.

Comparing the total percentage correct predictions in the two-step regression models, we find that the sociodemographic model achieved between 67 and 74 percent correct predictions, with no clear trend over the years. The contribution of issues (beyond the socioeconomic variables) increased from 1984 on, compared to earlier elections. In the analysis of the Likud–Labor vote (not presented here), issues added between 0 and 5 percent up to and including 1981. In 1981, issues added 3 percent to the right–left bloc equation, and from 1984 they added between 8 and 16 percent correct predictions.

136

TABLE 5.1 Logistic Regressions: Right–Left Bloc, 1981–1992, and Prime-Ministerial Candidate, 1996–1999

Variable	1981 (N=1249) B	(s.e.)	1984 (N=1259) B	(s.e.)	1988 (N=873) B	(s.e.)	1992 (N=1192) B	(s.e.)	1996 (N=1168) B	(s.e.)	1999 (N=1075) B	(s.e.)
I. Sociodemographic												
Age	-0.07*	(0.03)	-0.14***	(0.04)	-0.12**	(0.04)	-0.14***	(0.03)	-0.10**	(0.04)	-0.06*	(0.03)
Gender	-0.43**	(0.17)	0.11	(0.18)	—a		0.05	(0.17)	-0.60***	(0.17)	-0.27	(0.16)
Density of dwelling	0.36**	(0.13)	0.29	(0.17)	0.43**	(0.16)	0.19	(0.13)	0.46**	(0.15)	0.36*	(0.18)
Education	-0.01	(0.09)	-0.10	(0.10)	-0.45**	(0.15)	-0.27*	(0.10)	-0.23*	(0.10)	-0.28*	(0.12)
Income	0.05	(0.09)	0.00	(0.09)	-0.01	(0.09)	0.05	(0.07)	0.14	(0.08)	-0.12	(0.07)
Religious observance	-0.68***	(0.10)	-0.66***	(0.12)	-0.81***	(0.13)	-1.01***	(0.11)	-1.18***	(0.13)	-0.95***	(0.11)
Ethnic background	-0.46**	(0.18)	-1.68***	(0.20)	-0.39*	(0.20)	-0.82**	(0.18)	-0.57**	(0.18)	-0.52**	(0.17)
	N=723b	67%c	N=676	74%	N=596	71%	N=821	72%	N=771	73%	N=795	68%
II. Sociodemographic and issues												
Age	-0.05	(0.04)	-0.08	(0.50)	-0.09	(0.06)	-0.10*	(0.04)	-0.03	(0.04)	-0.05	(0.04)
Gender	-0.45*	(0.18)	0.25	(0.24)	—a		0.04	(0.21)	-0.52**	(0.21)	-0.27	(0.21)
Density of dwelling	0.32*	(0.14)	0.24	(0.22)	0.41*	(0.21)	0.23	(0.17)	0.50**	(0.18)	0.14	(0.20)
Education	0.12	(0.10)	0.03	(0.13)	-0.46*	(0.20)	-0.39**	(0.12)	-0.02	(0.12)	-0.30*	(0.15)
Income	0.02	(0.10)	-0.07	(0.12)	-0.02	(0.12)	-0.06	(0.09)	0.08	(0.09)	-0.22*	(0.10)
Religious observance	0.52***	(0.11)	-0.60***	(0.14)	-0.67***	(0.17)	-0.75***	(0.15)	-0.87***	(0.15)	-0.31*	(0.15)
Ethnic background	-0.59**	(0.20)	-1.65***	(0.26)	-0.05	(0.27)	-0.80***	(0.23)	-0.56*	(0.22)	-0.56*	(0.22)
Territories	0.62***	(0.10)	1.08***	(0.11)	1.30***	(0.12)	1.11***	(0.09)	1.32***	(0.11)	1.55***	(0.13)
Socioeconomic	-0.36***	(0.10)	-0.96***	(0.18)	-0.67***	(0.13)	-0.39**	(0.12)	-0.23*	(0.12)	-0.47***	(0.13)
State–religion	-0.23**	(0.08)	—a		-0.13	(0.13)	-0.29**	(0.11)	-0.38***	(0.10)	-0.51***	(0.13)
	N=682	70%	N=682	83%	N=536	86%	N=750	82%	N=758	81%	N=761	84%
		(+3%)d		(+9%)		(+15%)		(+10%)		(+8%)		(+16%)

NOTE: Dependent variable: vote for right–left bloc 1981–1992; prime-ministerial candidate 1996–1999.

aNot available.

bSample size. For details on the samples, the wording, and the coding of the variables, see Shamir and Arian (1999), Appendices A and B.

cTotal percentage of correct predictions.

dChange in percentage of correct predictions.

* $p \leq .05$, ** $p \leq .01$, *** $p \leq .001$.

In Israel, issue voting has increased over time, but the predictive potential of sociodemographics (and of sociodemographic and attitudinal variables in combination) has not declined. We maintain that the source of this pattern lies in the identity dilemmas raised by the issues on the agenda and their interrelationship with group characteristics. This is most clearly indicated in Table 5.1 by the two issue variables of the territories and state–religion relations, and by the religious observance variable that distinguishes between secular and orthodox voters.

The issue of the territories is the most influential issue factor in all equations in Table 5.1. It grew in importance from the 1984 election onward, when it emerged as the overriding dimension ordering the party system. It is still dominant, however, it is important to note that the state–religion issue has been increasing in importance over time, and by 1996 had become second to the socioeconomic issue.

Religiosity was measured by a question asking the degree to which an individual observes the strictures of rabbinical Jewish law (Halacha). This measure of religious observance is based on behavior but indicates at the same time one of the most meaningful definitions of an individual's social affiliation and identity in modern Israel. Among the sociodemographic variables, religiosity has become the most meaningful social distinction. Its impact on the vote increased up to 1996. In 1999 it weakened somewhat, but the role of the state–religion issue increased. The religiosity variable was strongly related to the policy issues of state–religion relations ($r = 0.47$ in 1996; $r = 0.50$ in 1999) and the future of the territories ($r = 0.29$ and 0.36, respectively), which represent the two identity dimensions. Taken together, these results indicate that the internal and external identity dimensions became more important factors in electoral politics, in a mutual reinforcement process between group membership and issues.

The Politics of Identity in Israel

The 1990s signaled the ascent of the politics of identity in Israel. Prime Minister Rabin's assassination on November 4, 1995, and the May 1996 elections encapsulate these processes most concisely. Both events are best understood in terms of difficult and absorbing collective identity dilemmas, and both raised the question of identity in a very pointed manner. These processes have deeper and distant roots associated with various social, cultural, economic, and political changes within Israeli society. But they have become more salient with the progress in the peace process between Israel and the Palestinians, and with the electoral reform featuring the direct election of the prime minister.

Yitzhak Rabin's assassination, and the 1996 elections that followed, were framed in terms of a struggle between two value orientations, politically labeled "right" and "left" and culturally identified as "primordial" and "civil" (Kimmerling 1985). The political assassination was set in the context of collective identity and symbols, in which the public debate focused on drawing political, cultural, and social boundaries. The slain Rabin came to symbolize the "Israeli," the civil, the "peacenik," the left side of the dichotomy. He had a personal history of leadership in war and courage in the politics of making peace, as demonstrated by his shaking hands, both physically and figuratively, with Palestinian Liberation Organization leader Yasser Arafat. These provided the background for his tragic assassination by a right-wing religious extremist at the end of a Tel Aviv mass rally ironically entitled "Yes to Peace, No to Violence."

The 1996 elections took place six months later, the first elections to be held under the new electoral system. The direct election of the prime minister set the two candidates against each other: Rabin's successor, Shimon Peres, on the left, and Benjamin Netanyahu on the right. The election was framed as a stark choice between the candidates, a choice between the two value orientations (see contributions in Arian and Shamir 1999). The winner-take-all feature of the race for prime minister, the election campaign, the close election results, and the mobilization patterns of the contenders manifested the conflict over collective identity, and dramatized the (ostensible) dissensus. Perhaps the best expression of this division was to be found in the campaign slogan used near the end of the campaign by the ultraorthodox hawkish Habad Hassidim: "Bibi [Netanyahu] is good for the Jews." This gave the impression that the country was divided between right-wing religious hawks and left-wing secular doves. Like Yitzhak Rabin's assassination, the race for prime minister underscored the major value conflicts over the definition of Israel as a Jewish state, the peace process, and the close association between the two. After the elections, the standoff between these two groups became a dominant frame used by the media and politicians of both sides. The 1999 elections continued that focus, except by then Netanyahu had basically accepted the principle of mutual recognition with the Palestinians and the idea of returning territories for peace, and he himself became an "issue" in the elections.

Notwithstanding the media framing, the election studies of 1996 and 1999 also revealed the consensual underpinnings of the value structure of much of the Jewish electorate, which was more unified than divided. The majority of Jewish voters had opinions on the various aspects of the politics of identity, but only a minority espoused extreme positions. They preferred peace and a Jewish democratic state to the fantasy of greater Israel—the land of Israel and its post–1967 war boundaries. By 1999, after three years during which Netanyahu had reluctantly pursued the Oslo accords, the process itself had become part of the consensus. Opposition to the Oslo process shrank, and the "National Unity" list, the right-wing alternative to the Likud and Netanyahu, which campaigned for "greater Israel" and outright opposition to the Oslo process, obtained only 4 seats in the 120-member Knesset.

As shown in Table 5.1, the connection of the vote with religiosity and with the issues embodying the two identity dimensions increased over time. Of the two identity dimensions, the external one involving "the old issue" of territorial compromise still outweighs by far the internal dimension in distinguishing between right-wing and left-wing voters (and also between Likud and Labor voters, not shown here). However, the nature of the controversy appears to have changed. As of this writing, the value conflict has been decided for peace and against greater Israel, and a large majority today supports compromise with the Palestinians and with the Arab world. The debate that rages is still fierce, but it is now cast less in metaphysical terms of divine promises and national destiny and more in the pragmatic terms of borders, the nature of security arrangements, and the eventuality of a Palestinian state. Differences in opinion are still wide, but as ideology and values give way to pragmatic arrangements with respect to territory, the identity connection is bound to weaken, and the first-time decline in the impact of religiosity on the vote in 1999 may be a sign of it.

At the same time, the internal collective identity dimension has gained in power in structuring the vote and the party system. In the 1999 elections, Shinui was a party with one delegate in the outgoing Knesset, and seemed to be doomed to extinction. It recruited an outspoken journalist to head its 1999 list, built its campaign solely on an anti-haredi (extreme orthodox) message, and leaped in size to six seats. The left-wing Meretz party, which combines a dovish and secular agenda, grew from nine to ten Knesset members. On the other side, the religious parties increased their share of seats in the current Knesset to twenty-seven from their previous record high of twenty-three seats in 1996, based mostly on the spectacular rise of the ultraorthodox Sephardi party Shas, which grew from ten to seventeen seats.

The strife between religious and secular and between Jewish and democratic Israel is still on the agenda. The contrast was on view in the Labor-Meretz government of 1992 and 1996, and the Netanyahu right wing and religious coalition that replaced it. When Labor took office in 1992, many seemed to want a stronger expression of secular values in Israel, evidenced by the 1992 pre-election survey that found an unprecedented low in the percentage supporting public life according to Jewish religious law (29 percent compared to 43–51 percent in previous years). In 1996, after four years of the left-wing coalition of Labor and Meretz with its secular image and outlook, this trend was reversed and there was a demand for more "Jewishness"; support for public life according to Jewish religious law soared to its highest rate ever (53 percent). By 1999 it had shrank again to 33 percent. More than an indication of instability, these figures signify the reticence of the public to identify with extremes and a yearning for a middle ground that combines the Jewish and democratic features of Israel. Our survey data suggest this, as do various civil society initiatives in the last few years. Post-Netanyahu politics seems to indicate that political elites are moving in this direction.

The close relationship between the internal and external dimensions of identity is the result of long-term processes, but it manifested itself dramatically in the 1996 election and in Rabin's assassination. Religion was always related to nationalism, but the two have become more closely intertwined since 1967, as religious authorities provided legitimization for keeping the territories taken in the war of that year, thus establishing the link between the people, their history, God, and the land. The settlement movement, Gush Emunim, and the National Religious Party played key roles in the long-term process of linking religion and nationalism in public opinion and in coalition politics. Fueled by the growing strength of the ultraorthodox non-Zionist (haredi) camp, and especially the Shas party, the schism along the internal identity dimension sharpened. The term "hardal" (literally meaning mustard), an acronym for haredi and "dati leumi" (national religious), captures this process of growing overlap between the two dimensions of collective identity within the religious sector. National religious Jews grew closer to the haredim in their religious observance, and the non-Zionist ultraorthodox community became more nationalistic regarding the Arab–Israeli conflict.

In our last two election studies we included several items intended to measure more extensively the collective identity dimensions (the wording of the questions is presented in Shamir and Arian 1999, Appendix B). Exploratory factor analyses conducted in both surveys showed that external and internal identity were indeed separate dimensions, but were strongly correlated. The external identity scale was defined by orientation to the Israeli–Arab conflict: the territories, the peace talks, a Palestinian state, the Oslo agreements, and the value priority of greater Israel ($\cdot$ = 0.81 in 1996, 0.79 in 1999). The internal identity scale included the value priority of democracy, the primary identity as Jewish or Israeli, the state–religion issue, and the primacy of democracy or Jewish religious law ($\cdot$ = 0.68 in 1996, 0.65 in 1999). The two scales correlated strongly as expected (r = 0.60 in 1996 and 0.56 in 1999).

Both scales were constructed as continua and not as dichotomies, but for shorthand purposes we labeled their poles: for the external identity scale, the poles were Doves and Hawks; for the internal identity scale, the poles were Israeli and Jewish. We focus now on the intersection of the two scales, presented in Table 5.2. We cut each of them into three, with the extremes representing a quarter to a third of the sample and the middle category the rest. This categorization is arbitrary, but the intersection of the groups is of interest. In this way, nine scale types are generated and provide a richer mapping of the orientations and politics of collective identity than the separate dimensions; the nuances here are all important. The sizes of the categories indicate their strong interrelationship. The "consistent" identifications of those identifying as Hawks and as Jewish and those identifying as Doves and Israeli are large. Scale type 1 made up of respondents with Dovish and Israeli identity contains 18 percent in 1996 and 19 percent in 1999. Scale type 9 of Jewish Hawks includes 15 percent of the two samples. The "inconsistent" combinations on the other hand are very small (category 3 of those with Dove and Jewish identities comprises 1 percent in both 1996 and

TABLE 5.2   The Intersection of External and Internal Identity Scale Types, 1996 and 1999

	External scale type	Internal scale type	1996 (%)	1999 (%)
1	Dove	Israeli	18	19
2	Dove	Middle	10	9
3	Dove	Jewish	1	1
4	Middle	Israeli	8	11
5	Middle	Middle	22	16
6	Middle	Jewish	10	11
7	Hawk	Israeli	2	5
8	Hawk	Middle	13	12
9	Hawk	Jewish	15	15
Total			99	99
(N)			(1039)	(902)

1999; those with Hawk and Israeli identities, category 7, make up 2 percent of the sample in 1996 and 5 percent in 1999).

The other important characteristic of the scale is the large number of respondents falling in the middle rather than at the extremes, another indication of our previous claim that the public is less polarized than it may seem. Twenty-two percent in 1996 and 16 percent in 1999 belong to the middle–middle category; about 60 percent in both years belong to the middle category on at least one of the identity dimensions.

We have already pointed out that the two identity scales are very strongly related to the vote, but we can gain additional insights by looking at vote intentions by scale type. Table 5.3 contains the results for the 1996 and 1999 prime-ministerial vote. Among those identified as Hawks measured by the external identity scale (scale types 7, 8, and 9), the vast majority intended to vote for Netanyahu (rather than for Peres in 1996 or for Barak in 1999) irrespective of their internal scale position. The numbers are astounding. The vote for Netanyahu varied between 85 and 96 percent. The mirror image is obtained among the voters identified as Doves. Between 92 and 97 percent voted for Peres in 1996, and 94 to 99 percent voted for Barak in 1999 (the 71 percent for category 3 represents 5 out of 7 respondents). The external identity dimension drove these two

TABLE 5.3 Prime Minister Vote Intentions by Identity Scale Type, 1996 and 1999

	Dove Israeli 1 (%)	Dove Middle 2 (%)	Dove Jewish 3 (%)	Middle Israeli 4 (%)	Middle Middle 5 (%)	Middle Jewish 6 (%)	Hawk Israeli 7 (%)	Hawk Middle 8 (%)	Hawk Jewish 9 (%)
Prime Minister Vote Intention, 1996									
Netanyahu	3	7	8	28	48	69	88	89	96
Peres	97	93	92	72	52	31	12	11	4
Total	100	100	100	100	100	100	100	100	100
(N)	(186)	(95)	(13)	(67)	(191)	(89)	(17)	(116)	(135)
Prime Minister Vote Intention, 1999									
Netanyahu	1	6	29	29	58	69	91	85	96
Barak	99	94	71	71	42	31	9	15	4
Total	100	100	100	100	100	100	100	100	100
(N)	(158)	(79)	(7)	(86)	(114)	(80)	(34)	(85)	(121)

groups of resolute respondents, and the internal identity dimension made virtually no difference.

The middle external category is much more interesting in this context. For the category as a whole, voters are positioned between the extremes. In 1996, scale type 5 voters, the middle-middle category, split their vote just about in half; in 1999 this category was smaller in size and split 42:58 in favor of Netanyahu. But in the middle external identity position, internal identity was very important in both 1996 and 1999. It accounted for a 40 percent difference in voting behavior among internal identity groups, a sharp contrast to the lack of power of internal identity in the Hawk and Dove external identification groups.

Internal identity mattered mainly among those who are not defined on the external dimension. It is important to reiterate that they comprise a large portion of the Jewish electorate. The opposite is not true; that is, within each internal identity category, including the middle one, external identity matters, and to a similar degree.

An appropriate conceptualization of Israeli politics—not only of electoral politics—must take account of the full spectrum of the dimensions of collective identity that we have discussed, and not just the extreme Dove and Hawk positions, as is often done. Since voting behavior of resolute Doves and Hawks was virtually predetermined, the fight for votes depended largely on appeals to those in a middle position on external identity, those whose vote decisions were strongly influenced by their internal identification, but also by other factors. The 1996 elections largely were driven by the overlap of the external and internal dimensions. By 1999 the two identity dimensions were still predominant and their overlap impressive, but they were joined in the election campaign by other concerns—and especially the assessment of the performance of Prime Minister Netanyahu.

Conclusion

We have used election studies to explore the politics of identity in Israel. This emphasis extends beyond elections to other political institutions, to culture, and to policy. Prediction of the result of a specific election might be a subsidiary result of such a study, but it is not the primary focus. More important is the use of the election study for exploring trends of change and continuity. And, as we have shown, both are plentiful in the Israeli case. The politics of identity has become a major feature of Israeli society, and they are revealed in elections. Our national election studies aid us in delving into their nature, and we have explored the meanings of internal and external collective identity concerns, their considerable overlap, their social roots, and their translation into political choices.

But we have also used the Israeli election studies to go beyond the specific case. The issues that captured the agenda in Israel may be unique, but the nature of these issues leads us to broader issues of multiculturalism and collective identity. These foci can enrich the comparative voting literature. Issues based on ethnic, racial, linguistic, religious, or regional diversity and collective identity characterize most countries, including Western democracies. Neglecting these factors weakens the generalizations of students of electoral behavior. Taking them into account directed us to a reconsideration of the prediction of declining social cleavages, and to the expectation of finding social cleavages of greater potency and an increase in issue voting at the same time. In its last two national elections, Israel demonstrated precisely these simultaneous forces. The legacy of the classic election studies and the sociological, attitudinal, and economic approaches built on them is alive and well as it adapts itself to the changing world that is marked by increased globalization and individualism, but not less by strong particularistic tendencies and multiculturalism.

References

Arian, Asher, ed. 1972. *The Elections in Israel—1969*. Jerusalem: Jerusalem Academic Press.

Arian, Asher, ed. 1975. *The Elections in Israel—1973*. Jerusalem: Jerusalem Academic Press.

Arian, Asher, ed. 1980. *The Elections in Israel—1977*. Jerusalem: Jerusalem Academic Press.

Arian, Asher, ed. 1983. *The Elections in Israel—1981*. Tel Aviv: Ramot Publ.

Arian, Asher, and Michal Shamir, eds. 1986. *The Elections in Israel—1984*. Tel Aviv: Ramot Publ.

Arian, Asher, and Michal Shamir, eds. 1990. *The Elections in Israel—1988*. Boulder, Colo.: Westview Press.

Arian, Asher, and Michal Shamir, eds. 1995. *The Elections in Israel—1992*. Albany: State University of New York Press.

Arian, Asher, and Michal Shamir, eds. 1999. *The Elections in Israel—1996*. Albany: State University of New York Press.

Barnes, Samuel H. 1997. "Electoral Behavior and Comparative Politics." In *Comparative Politics: Rationality, Culture, and Structure*, Mark I. Lichbach and Alan S. Zuckerman, eds., pp. 115–141. Cambridge, England: Cambridge University Press.

Berelson, Bernard R., Paul F. Lazarsfeld, and William N. McPhee. 1954. *Voting: A Study of Opinion Formation in a Presidential Campaign*. Chicago: University of Chicago Press.

Burnham, Walter Dean. 1970. *Critical Elections and the Mainsprings of American Politics*. New York: W. W. Norton.

Campbell, Angus, Philip E. Converse, Warren E. Miller, and Donald E. Stokes. 1960. *The American Voter*. New York: Wiley.

Dalton, Russell J., and Martin P. Wattenberg. 1993. "The Not So Simple Act of Voting." In *Political Science: The State of the Discipline II*, Ada W. Finifter, ed., pp. 193–218. Washington, D.C.: American Political Science Association.

Dalton, Russell J., Scott Flanagan, and Paul Beck, eds. 1984. *Electoral Change in Advanced Industrial Democracies*. Princeton: Princeton University Press.

Downs, Anthony. 1957. *An Economic Theory of Democracy*. New York: Harper & Row.

Fiorina, Morris P. 1981. *Retrospective Voting in American National Elections*. New Haven: Yale University Press.

Franklin, Mark, Tom Mackie, Henry Valen, et al. 1992. *Electoral Change: Responses to Evolving Social and Attitudinal Structures in Western Countries*. Cambridge, England: Cambridge University Press.

Huckfeldt, Robert, and John Sprague. 1995. *Citizens, Politics, and Social Communication: Information and Influence in an Election Campaign*. Cambridge, England: Cambridge University Press.

Inglehart, Ronald. 1990. *Culture Shift in Advanced Industrial Society*. Princeton: Princeton University Press.

Key, V. O. 1955. "A Theory of Critical Elections." *Journal of Politics* 17: 3–18.

Key, V. O. 1959. "Secular Realignment and the Party System." *Journal of Politics* 21: 198–210.

Kimmerling, Baruch. 1985. "Between the Primordial and the Civil Definitions of the Collective Identity: 'Eretz Israel' or the State of Israel?" In *Comparative Social Dynamics*, Erik Cohen et al., eds., pp. 262–283. Boulder, Colo.: Westview Press.

Lazarsfeld, Paul, Bernard Berelson, and Hazel Gaudet. 1948. *The People's Choice: How the Voter Makes Up His Mind in a Presidential Campaign*. New York: Columbia University Press.

Lipset, Seymour M., and Stein Rokkan, eds. 1967. *Party Systems and Voter Alignments*. New York: Free Press.

Przeworski, Adam, and Henry Teune. 1970. *The Logic of Comparative Social Inquiry*. New York: Wiley.

Rose, Richard, ed. 1974. *Electoral Behavior: A Comparative Handbook*. New York: Free Press.

Sears, David O. 1993. "Symbolic Politics: A Socio-psychological Theory." In *Explorations in Political Psychology*, Shanto Iyengar and William J. McGuire, eds., pp. 113–149. Durham, N.C.: Duke University Press.

Shamir, Michal, and Asher Arian. 1999. "Collective Identity and Electoral Competition in Israel." *American Political Science Review* 93(June): 265–278.

6

CAPTURING CAMPAIGNS IN NATIONAL ELECTION STUDIES

RICHARD JOHNSTON

University of British Columbia

What an election study is good for depends on the election. Different contexts throw up different challenges, which lead election study teams in different countries to idiosyncratic design choices. The local culture of granting agencies is also reflected in study design. And whether or not earlier design choices are wise, they constrain—but sometimes liberate—later ones. The Canadian Election Study is a case in point, because circumstances certainly allowed it, but could be said to have forced it, to become the prime site for the study of campaigns. This chapter considers the rationale that led to the 1988 design change, basic elements of the recent designs, and some characteristic results. It concludes by addressing general questions about campaigns as objects of study.

The Possibility of Campaign Effects

As recently as the late 1980s, the very idea that campaigns might influence election results was anathema to political scientists. For a campaign to be anything other than the mobilization of preexisting bodies of sentiment and affiliation, mass media had to be a critical source of stimuli for voters. But the dominant view was still that media effects were minimal (Klapper 1960). To be sure, beachheads had been established for capturing media effects and, thus, capturing campaign dynamics. The U.S. National Election Study (NES) opened itself to measuring within-year change, first by expanding the traditional pre/post panel design to include waves before and after the presidential primaries in 1980 (hearkening back to the Columbia University studies of the 1940s) and then, most consequentially, by creating a "rolling cross section" (henceforth, RCS) as an adjunct to the 1984 study (Bartels 1988; Brady and Johnston 1987). Iyengar and Kinder (1987), although not focused on campaigns, produced evidence that mass media did have an impact in the domain of attitudes. Even though none of these studies suggested that a *general* election could turn on mass media stimuli, they nonetheless opened avenues of both conceptualization and measurement.

About this time, Canadian elections seemed ripe for studying media effects and campaign dynamics. All along, Canadian campaigns had been short and fierce, as Canada reproduces most essentials of the Westminster parliamentary system. Usually, the start date for a campaign is a secret closely guarded by the governing party. The campaign spans less than two months. The stakes are very high, as the winner almost always forms a single-party government, usually with an outright majority of seats in the House of Commons. This reflects the fact that Canada uses a single-member plurality electoral formula, the traditional "First Past the Post" system.

Figure 6.1 illustrates the postwar legacy to 1984, with a reconstruction of the Liberal Party's share of campaign-period vote intentions from postwar Gallup polls. Each panel starts with the last poll before the official beginning of a campaign,[1] concludes with the election result itself, and tracks all polls in the interval. For each election, the share is plotted relative to an estimate of the "normal" Liberal vote for the period.[2] Panels A, B, and C depict variants on a story of weak to null campaign effects. Movement is certainly visible in each panel and each subperiod seems to have its characteristic dynamic, but all three panels depict movement *toward* the period norm, and variance in shares relative to the normal outcome shrinks as election day approaches. The implication seems to be that the effect of the campaign is mainly to anticipate a deadline. By that deadline, voters have fully accessed the considerations that, all along, constituted the party system. The pattern is altogether reminiscent of the claim, in Gelman and King (1993), that campaign-period polls

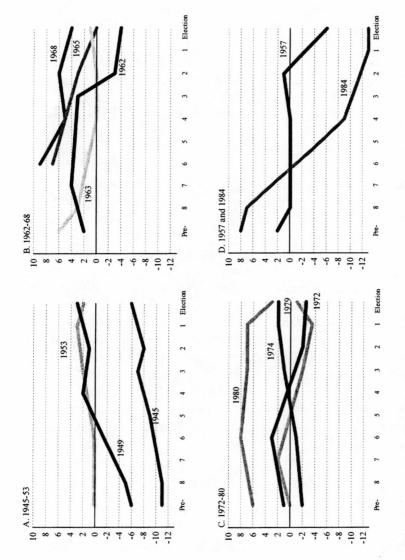

FIGURE 6.1 Liberal standing by week of campaign, 1945–1984. Entries are deviations from period normal vote (1945–1957 = 47 percent; 1962–1984 = 41 percent); 1958 is omitted. SOURCE: Gallup Canada.

do a poorer job of predicting outcomes than do models employing information publicly available well before the campaign starts.[3]

But two exceptions stand out. In 1957 and 1984, the Liberal Party started out well ahead of the period average for the preceding years but ended up well below and even further away from that average. If the result was ineluctably fated and only masked by early polls, fate was not in control of forces typical of the preceding system. And the new forces, whatever they were, did not reveal themselves until late. In 1957 the Liberal collapse came only at the campaign's very end, after the last poll was conducted. The 1984 drop began earlier, but only after a key debate among party leaders. Hindsight reveals the governing coalition to have been fragile, as each election terminated a period of alignment. But no one predicted such carnage beforehand. It seems reasonable to infer that each campaign itself was critical to unmasking the weakness, that the damage could have been slighter or avoided altogether, even if only as a stay of execution.

If the 1957 and 1984 results positively beg longitudinal analysis, the same seems true even for the other, less compelling cases. The variation of trajectories and the mere fact that trajectories presented themselves force us to ask awkward questions. What sort of movement counts as a campaign effect? Does any systematic shift qualify? Conversely, does the absence of movement imply that the campaign was pointless, and that votes might just as well have been cast at the beginning as at the end? For that matter, is movement in vote intentions the only or even the most important thing to track? What, in any case, is so special about that period we call a campaign? For that matter, when is a campaign a campaign? In short, Fig. 6.1 suggests that an election study should be designed to take the campaign *period*, if not necessarily the campaign strategy and counterstrategy, seriously.

Capturing Campaign Effects

This brings us to the 1988 election and its corresponding Canadian Election Study. The Canadian Election Study series is among the oldest in the world, dating back with only one gap to 1965. But the Canadian granting agency has resisted creating a presumption in favor of the studies, such that proposals are left to the decentralized initiative of the research community. There is no guarantee that any proposal will emerge, or that there will be only one. Up until 1988, successive teams were only modestly concerned to replicate their predecessors' instrumentation. On the eve of the 1988 election, then, there was little time series, in the sense of the U.S. NES, to preserve. As a result, few resisted a proposal that year for the Canadian studies to take a dramatic turn and become a prime site for the investigation of campaign dynamics.

The 1984 election's campaign dynamics, as captured in commercial polls, loomed particularly large in the decision to shift the Canadian Election Study to a campaign-sensitive mode. Earlier Canadian studies were simply unable to capture any short-term movement. Like the U.S. NES, they employed in-home interviewing and clustered samples. Unlike it, they were strictly postelection ventures. Not even the modest biweekly release of a fresh sample in some U.S. pre-election waves was mirrored, or even possible, in the Canadian design. The lack of a pre-election wave perfectly illustrates the point in this chapter's opening paragraph. As a Westminster system, the Canadian system leaves enormous discretion in the hands of the prime minister to determine the date of an election call. In-home fieldwork constitutes too ponderous a machine to mobilize within days or even weeks of a campaign's start. To mount any sort of campaign-period wave required moving the study to the telephone. By 1988, telephone technology for surveys was pretty much the private-sector norm, and Computer-Assisted Telephone Interviewing (CATI) opened up a world of sample control and experimentation that was hitherto unimaginable.

If moving to the telephone made preelection interviewing possible, the form that fieldwork might take remained open. One alternative was to adapt the structure of the 1980 U.S. NES and the 1987 British Election Campaign Study, which involved multiple interlocking panels over the campaign and precampaign period.[4] The precampaign wave would establish the baseline, the distribution of dispositions in advance of the crush of campaign stimuli. Staged waves within the campaign would permit some narrowing of the temporal span for identification of campaign effects. The panel property permits identification of transitions at the individual level. This, of course, is the basic logic of the classic Columbia studies, the 1940 Sandusky and 1948 Elmira panels (Lazarsfeld et al. 1944; Berelson et al. 1954). Projected onto a national scale, however, such a design is extremely expensive. Because they used reinterviews, the campaign waves would be subject to panel mortality, and thus would not be true cross sections. The timing of waves would not necessarily correspond to the campaign's own rhythms; the more widely spaced the waves, the greater the difficulty of identifying causes of observed shifts. And would the shifts we observe correspond to those occurring in the electorate at large, or would the instrument effect of pre-election interviewing condition response to campaign stimuli?

For all of these reasons we looked to the alternative adumbrated by the 1984 U.S. NES, the primary-period rolling cross section. Once we decided on a campaign-period wave, it was only a small further conceptual leap to take the total sample and distribute it over the whole campaign. This requires, first, generating at random enough telephone numbers to yield a preordained total of completed interviews.[5] Second, the total body of numbers must be assigned to "replicates," or miniature subsamples, all of whose numbers are released on a single day. In the Canadian case, one replicate was released per day of fieldwork. But the number of such replicates released per day can vary, in fact, such that daily sample density can be boosted for periods when statistical power is especially desirable, such as when events might follow in tightly spaced sequence, as around a debate. The critical thing at this point is that each replicate mirror the total sample and that assignment to replicates be essentially random, just as with the initial drawing of the sample.[6] The third critical thing is to apply the same clearance strategy to each replicate. A telephone number once released to sample must remain open, if not yet contacted, for exactly the same number of days as each other such number and should go through the same daily and weekly cycle of callbacks.

Figure 6.2A shows the 1993 pattern, which is quite representative: between 80 and 85 percent of completed interviews occur four or fewer days after the day their telephone numbers are released to the field.[7] Figure 6.2B illustrates the resultant day-to-day pattern of completions. The first three days yield samples that are small, and biased toward respondents who are easy to reach. By day four, the total take approximates the average for the rest of the campaign. Thereafter, day by day, the profile of daily-release replicates constituting each day's completions varies only by sampling error.[8]

The resultant sample is a true cross section, no more and no less than any other cross section. In this it is no different from, say, the first wave of the U.S. NES, and many analyses can proceed as do

A. Lag between release and completion

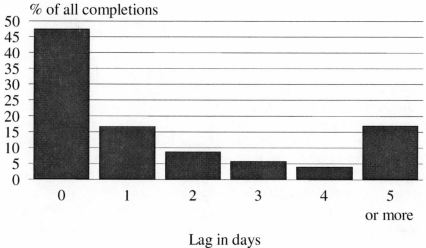

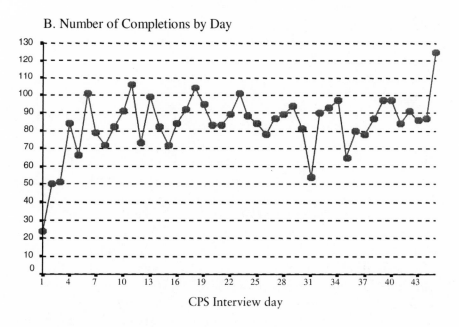

FIGURE 6.2   Distribution of interviews.

garden variety U.S. ones, with the whole sample treated as a one-shot data set. Just as it is common with the U.S. NES to treat post-election variables as cross-sectional data points (crossing one's fingers and hoping for the best), so is it with the Canadian data, which also reproduce the basic U.S. pre/post setup. Now, to the extent that true dynamics occur over the course of a U.S. campaign, they should be reflected in the pre-election wave of the U.S. NES, given its lengthy fieldwork period.[9]

The problem is that self-consciousness about time is difficult to sustain where the data structure distracts analysts from its temporal heterogeneity and where capture of that heterogeneity requires controls based on a model of respondent accessibility. A properly conducted rolling cross section essentially requires no such controls, as *the date of interview is, in effect, a random event.* Thus, analysis can focus on events in real time almost without controls. Graphical analysis becomes straightforward, as variables can be displayed against time more or less in their natural state. Establishing the impact of some event or sequence sometimes requires just a simple temporal partition. If one has a working theory of causal direction, variables inside the survey data set can tell a longitudinal story (Brady and Johnston 1996; Johnston and Brady 2001). Data generated outside the data set, for example, volumes and valence of news coverage and advertising, can be loaded into the data set on the basis of date of interview. In principle, none of this requires controls. Controls often make sense, of course, in the interests of elaboration. Testing models of the impact of persuasive communication (McGuire 1968, 1969; Zaller 1992), for example, requires controls both for exposure to such communication and for the probability of yielding to its persuasive content. So long as media use and party or policy commitment variables are included in the data file, such controls are straightforward.

Beyond this, the primary argument for adding variables to an impact analysis is to increase statistical power. Power is inescapably a major issue where a sample is partitioned, all the more so if the partitioning is down to individual days. Actually, the probability that individual days will be compared is almost nil. Still, quite short intervals may tempt the analyst and so sampling error for relevant periods can be quite large. When measurement error is also significant, identification of effects from the campaign, if it is possible at all, may require a multivariate setup with covariates. The covariates are not controls that reflect respondent accessibility. Rather, they are variables that affect the dependent variable but that may be of no particular theoretical interest to us. What they do is reduce regression error in predictions of the dependent variable, which in turn reduces standard errors for coefficients on the independent, campaign-dated variables of interest.

For all this, Canadian Election Studies are panels after all. But the panel wave comes after the election. The postelection wave allows us to make a cumulative record of the event, for example, to record the respondents' actual votes, as opposed to their intentions. Repeating certain items allows us to track impact from the campaign, indeed to test the effects of differing lapses of time between interviews. Repetition also helps us assess reliabilities for items. Finally, asking certain questions after election day affords special insight into movement before that same day. In the following section I present an example in relation to the impact of a debate among party leaders.

Three Representative Trajectories

The three campaigns since Canadian studies shifted to the RCS design each illustrate a different paradigmatic pattern. This is indicated by Fig. 6.3, which reproduces the basic logic of Fig. 6.1 in a more refined form, thanks to daily sampling. First, note that each series omits the first few days of fieldwork, as interviews completed on those days are unrepresentative of the total and, second, that the 1997 campaign was much shorter than its predecessors.[10] The 1988 event saw the government party begin with a comfortable lead, lose the lead, and win it back. In one sense, it featured high drama. In another, it only reproduced the main elements of the then current party system. In the next election, 1993, the government party entered with a weak position and saw that weakness turn into a rout. The 1993 outing, as in 1957 and 1984, ended a period of alignment, but with even more dramatic effect. The 1997 election takes us back to the normal pattern of the postwar years, especially 1962 to 1980 (see Fig. 6.1C). The Liberal government share at the start was misleadingly high, but the campaign burned the excess off.

Of 1997, not much more need be said. A case could be made that a leaders' debate hurt the Liberals, but only temporarily. This is indicated by the dip of the normalized Liberal line below zero, followed by a partial recovery. But the line could as easily be read to embody

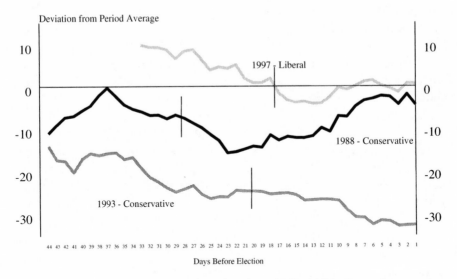

FIGURE 6.3 Government standing by day, 1988–1997. Seven-day moving average; vertical lines indicate dates of debates.
SOURCE: Canadian Election Studies.

a steady downward drift, which the debate neither accelerated nor decelerated. Nevitte et al. (2000) interpret the pattern as a temporary debate effect, based on the record of all five parties in the race. The Conservative line (not shown) unquestionably surged after the debate, in company with a fairly widespread consensus that the Conservative leader, Jean Charest, performed best.[11] The surge stalled and went into reverse, a reverse that has not been analyzed in any depth. The impulse of the debates may only have decayed. Certainly, media coverage of the party grew after the debates and then fell back, especially in Quebec. But coverage also shifted direction after the debate, initially being more positive, then moving back toward neutrality.[12] The latter may have reflected increasing criticism from other parties. Or some voters who were initially drawn to the Conservatives may have pondered the fact that the party's surge was still going to leave it out of contention for all but a handful of seats.

The 1988 campaign, although it delivered the same government-party share at the end as at the beginning, was a memorable event. The reading in Johnston et al. (1992) is that the Conservative recovery was not automatic, certainly not all of it.[13] The critical drop in

Conservative share followed a debate that was much remarked on at the time and that produced a near-consensus about who performed best: John Turner, the Liberal leader. The debate also primed what thereafter was the campaign's only issue, the Canada–U.S. Free Trade Agreement (FTA), precursor to NAFTA. Unusual for an issue in an election campaign, opinion on the FTA moved.[14] So in the days after the debate nothing worked for the Conservatives: their chief opponent had his reputation enhanced, the trade agreement they were defending was losing popularity, and as it did it became absolutely central to the vote. Both opinion on the FTA and Conservative support began to recover not too many days later. But support for the Liberal party (not shown) also continued to rise. With just over one week to go, then, the Conservatives seemed poised to lose their parliamentary majority, which, given the stakes, would have entailed outright loss of power. Then Conservative support surged. Where the first five points in recovery had taken eleven days, gaining the final eight points required only four days.[15] The path of recovery—slow initially, rapid at the end—seems to be the opposite of the sequence implied by simple decay of the debate-induced impulse. Evidently, the Conservatives had to work to win the election back.

Figure 6.4 makes some points about winning the election back. The figure also attempts to illustrate the complexity of debate effects. The point here is to illustrate how RCS data can be mobilized to test propositions in the communications literature. One obvious question about a debate is whether actually watching it on television makes any difference, or whether interpretation of the event is entirely mediated by journalistic interpretations or by viewers' subsequent attention to news broadcasts. Panel A, accordingly, compares daily vote intentions between debate viewers and nonviewers.[16] Seeing the debate indicates more than exposure to its content. It also reflects chronic media habits and may also, directly or indirectly, reflect party bias. In the RCS proper, we cannot begin asking about debate viewership until after the debate has occurred. As a result, alternative interpretations of debate processes are hard to assess. But many of these problems can be solved by repeating the debate questions in the *postelection* wave. With the postelection question we can retroactively divide respondents interviewed before the debate according to whether or not they eventually watched it. The predebate viewer/nonviewer difference on the criterion variable can then simply be taken out, which normalizes values to the start of the post-debate period. Here the criterion is the percentage intending to vote Conservative. The first entry in Fig. 6.4A is for the day before the debate and all values are relative to the mean for viewers and non-viewers, respectively, for the week before the debate.

The debate's immediate effect was greater for those who actually saw it than for those who did not. The total drop in Conservative share among viewers was nine points. Among nonviewers the drop was five points. Awkwardly, the very short term effect was barely—if at all—larger among viewers, as in the first two days after the debate each group dropped four to five points. Debate watchers continued to drop, hitting bottom about a week after the event. No less awkwardly, this group also reversed itself spectacularly, such that by the end Conservative support among debate viewers was higher than on the eve of the debate. Debate viewers are thus more responsive to *something*. How much of this something is the directly viewed content of the debate?

Panel B in Fig. 6.4 looks to an obvious alternative source, the content of television news. Entries here are predicted values for the impact from six days of lagged news values; as in Panel A, respondents are divided between those who saw the debate and those who did not. The news value is the daily balance of treatment of John Turner, the winner of the debate.[17] Positive coverage of Turner surged after the debate, which helped bring the Conservative share down. But only debate viewers responded, and for them the predicted drop in Panel B rivals the observed drop in Panel A. Presumably, this is not so much because they saw the debate in particular, but because they are generally attentive and responded to the changed interpretation of the event. As Turner coverage drifted back to neutrality and then went negative as other parties, the Conservatives in particular, fought back, debate watchers were predicted to drift back with it. The news had *no* net effect on debate nonviewers. As a gauge of news impact, this is reassuring. We would expect that relatively inattentive respondents would also be relatively unaffected by news values. Now, McGuire (1968, 1969) alerts us to the possibility that they might be more responsive if they receive the information, but this particular avenue seems not to be the active conduit. But *some* conduit is active, for Panel A indicates that nonviewers did swing, however modestly, in the same direction as viewers. Is this the impact of personal influence (Katz and Lazarsfeld 1955)?

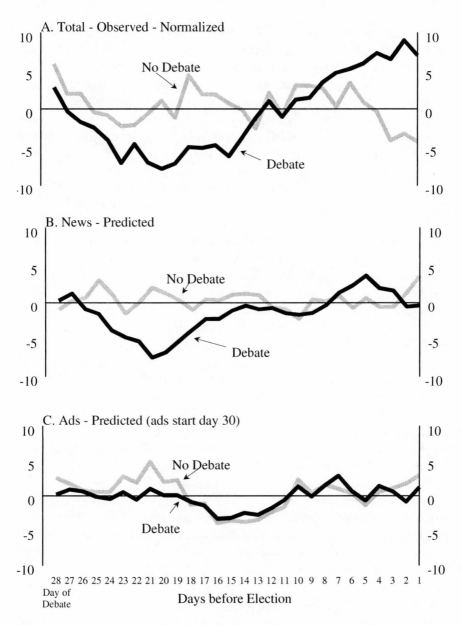

FIGURE 6.4   1988 Debate–news–ads interaction (net percentage-point shift in Conservative Party support). Moving averages: seven-day for A and five-day for B and C.

It cannot be the impact of advertising. Advertising did have an impact, according to Panel C, but not until well after the debate.[18] By law, party advertising could not start until two days before the debate. Also, impact from advertising tends to be displaced further back in the lag structure, as we might expect from a stimulus that voters do not seek out (Johnston et al. 1992). Together, these considerations dictate that advertising is unlikely to bite, if at all, until well after the debate. In 1988, this meant that the Liberal Party advertising may have prolonged the impact of the news. For nearly two weeks after the start of the legal advertising period, only the Liberal Party mentioned its own leader, always in a favorable light and always in connection with the main issue. Only with little more than two weeks left were the Conservatives able to focus their counterattack. Before this point, they scarcely mentioned John Turner. After this point, they scarcely mentioned anything else. They did defend the Free Trade Agreement, but almost always in a manner that also impugned Turner's credibility as an interpreter of the document. This is reflected in the upturn in the predicted line in Panel C. Advertising impact may be greater for nonviewers than for viewers, but the difference seems small. And advertising cannot account for the final, dramatic Conservative surge among debate watchers.[19]

The most startling campaign was in 1993, and this remains a formidable challenge for analysis. The campaign clearly undid the governing Conservative Party. The Conservatives were obviously unlikely to win right from the start, as according to Fig. 6.3 they began the campaign with a share well below the norm of the preceding decade. Yet the Conservatives would still have held on as the Official Opposition. The Liberals opened with roughly the same share and did not seem at all assured of the seat majority they eventually secured. But then, about two weeks into the campaign, the Conservatives dropped some 10 points in a matter of days. They eventually dropped another 10 points, most of these also in a few days.[20] These shifts, and the complements elsewhere in the system, constitute a realignment. The next, 1997 election, as we have seen, did not disturb these waters much. For students of alignment and realignment, of the long-run, constitutive forces of party systems, the 1993 Canadian data set is arguably the most valuable anywhere, precisely because of its ability to capture movement in the very short run and also to isolate the precipitating circumstances for the long-run shift.

Although the particular event is still a goad to analysis, this much can be said from work to date. Even at its starting point, the Conservative position was probably tenuous. In interelection popularity it reached historic lows by 1991. Some of its recovery from those lows seems to be part of a quasi-autonomic cycle of decay and recovery, not unlike those observed in Britain. But some of the recovery was induced by the Conservative leadership campaign, which induced a convention effect rather like those observed in the United States by Holbrook (1996).[21] The convention did give the Conservatives the initially most popular leader, Kim Campbell, as confirmed by early leader ratings in the CES.[22] Dissipation of this advantage seems to be the key to the first Conservative dive. What induced the dissipation was a controversy over policy, which can be stylized in terms of how far to the political right Campbell was prepared to go in deficit politics and attacks on the welfare state. She was reluctant to move right, but the very raising of the question and her inconclusive reaction spooked supporters on her party's left. Overnight, this produced a net five-point loss to the Liberals. More consequential over the full campaign was the hemorrhage on the other side, for among Conservatives welfare-state opponents outnumbered supporters. Her lack of forthrightness arguably left her party vulnerable to defection to Reform, a party altogether opposed to an expansive welfare state.[23]

Three things are striking at this point, however. First, although the content of the controversy involved the deficit and the welfare state, the indicators that moved in advance of the vote all referred to the person of Kim Campbell.[24] Voters did not shift position on any issues, unsurprisingly, and perceptions of the Conservatives' position on the key issue moved only slightly and not for keeps. The party was not very credible before the controversy and became only slightly less so after. At this point, then, the repulsive force was channeled through Kim Campbell. Second, although the controversy was about social policy and was refracted through the lens of Campbell, defection from the Conservative Party was immediately structured by an issue that played no role whatsoever in the immediate controversy. This was voters' orientation to French Canada and Quebec. Pro-Quebec defectors went overwhelmingly to the Liberal Party, and anti-French ones to the Reform Party. In no sense had the issue been primed (Iyengar and Kinder 1987).

The widening of the issue gap shows how flow induced by short-term factors is likely to follow channels prepared by social structure and history. The Conservative Party, although accommodationist on French–English relations under Campbell and her immediate predecessors, had been for decades the primary pole of anti-French sentiment. The fact that, when in power, the Conservative Party did not yield to its anti-French supporters was a key element in the initial rise of the Reform Party. Reform's position on French–English, Canada–Quebec relations was already clear to voters, again as revealed by placement items. Reform was thus a political presence and likely to win a number of seats in Alberta and British Columbia. But observers commonly asked at this point why Reform seemed to have stalled. I suspect that one thing blocking Reform's path was voters' ignorance of what else Reform stood for. This leads to the third striking thing: the campaign became the platform for dispelling that ignorance and, as awareness of Reform's position spread, so did the party's attractive power. But so did the party's power to repel, and in the campaign's later stages Reform's support was further refined as it shed ill-suited newcomers.

If the early shifts embodied a compound of personal judgment and issue positions, the final stage introduced a third consideration, namely, strategic information. Remarkably few polls were published during the campaign, not just in contrast to other countries but also to the 1988 campaign.[25] The early Conservative drop was thus not a matter of public record until nearly two weeks after it occurred, and the last two-and-a-half weeks of the campaign revealed a dramatically altered strategic field. Moreover, in Alberta and British Columbia, where Reform started strongest, the days just before the publication of the key polls saw a surge in expectations for the party's chances of winning locally.[26] At this point, Reform was competitive but in no sense dominant. In both provinces, about as many voters claimed a Conservative as a Reform intention and the balance of these two had not shifted. Reform's gains, as reflected in national polling numbers and the 1993 CES, were entirely in places of erstwhile weakness, driven by "sincere" (as opposed to sophisticated) motives. What changed in the Far West was not so much Reform's actual strength as voters' awareness of it. Thereupon, the strength was reinforced. But so was the position of the Liberal Party, as Conservatives who feared Reform's impact on national unity deserted to the sole remaining party with nationwide support.

The 1993 campaign leaves at least three lessons. Its first striking feature was that many of its key movements, even though they undid an old alignment, were, in a sense, self-propelled. At least one issue seam along which the Conservative electoral coalition unraveled, French–English relations, was largely prefigured. No advertisement and no news story primed this, but once general unraveling began, the seam just opened up. The final, strategically driven moves also required little conscious direction. Polls presented a reasonably accurate picture of the changed landscape and voters updated accordingly. Voters in a position to sense Reform's local strength were able to anticipate those polls. Even the first push that undid Kim Campbell did not seem all that powerful when it was first made. The pivotal drop in Conservative share was largely accomplished before the first party advertisement was legally allowed to appear.

Second, the basic structure of choice shifted as each stage of the campaign yielded to the next. Early in the campaign, leadership considerations were critical. Campbell's popularity helped to neutralize unhappiness with her party. Put another way, leadership coefficients in regression estimations of vote intention were powerful cross-sectionally at this point. So were they longitudinally, as the drop in her popularity alone took her party down. But once the Conservatives' share dropped its first 10 points, leadership lost power as a factor affecting choice. Issues gained power, but not because any party reoriented its rhetoric. Rather, Reform's distance from the other parties on the welfare state, formerly unremarked, now became visible. The agenda shifted because the choice set, as perceived, shifted. Finally, strategic considerations kicked in, as the long-standing assumptions about relative viabilities were overturned. To say that strategic considerations gained power is not necessarily to say that strategic, or second-choice, voting became more ubiquitous. Many voters, indeed, now felt licensed to vote as they really wished.

Third, as a direct corollary of the second point, interpretation of the meaning of the result and of the root causes of the realignment would have been next to impossible from a postelection study, or even from a campaign wave that started only toward the end. By the end, the Conservatives had dropped so far that there remained, in a sense, too little variance in their support left to explain. Leadership was no longer very relevant, for instance, yet was clearly a key part of the full story. Strategic reasoning commonly requires actual shifts to manifest itself. Here too a cross section would say little.

Discussion

In the Canadian context, the rolling-cross-section design was a nearly costless choice. Traditional in-home interviews were always a cumbersome approach in a thinly populated country, so much so that they made even a simple pre/post design impossible. To realize the benefits of preelection interviewing, the Canadian study simply had to move to the telephone. Once that move was made, controlled release of pre-election samples was the next obvious step. Whatever analytic benefits the RCS brings in its own right, this design detracts least from certain other goals of an election study. It is a true cross section, for instance, so that secondary analysts uninterested in time as a factor still have a massive sample with extensive coverage of most standard election study variables. And it is particularly well suited—it *is* the paradigmatic form—for continuous monitoring of an electorate.

Why not incorporate a precampaign panel into the design? Given enough resources, there is no reason to resist this for a subset of campaign-wave respondents. The methodological concern with instrument effects can be addressed by keeping another subset out of the precampaign wave, by analogy to the early Columbia studies. Where resources are tight, however, the case for making the campaign wave the first one is strong. A classic argument for a panel is to lay down a baseline. In the RCS, however, early interviews are, in a sense, the baseline, and the continuous monitoring of time allows aggregate estimates of change relative to that base. I would make the partisan assertion that aggregate change is—or ought to be regarded as—the change of primary interest. Given that the data are being collected by a survey, aggregation need not be for the whole sample, as the latter can be partitioned however the analyst wishes, so long as the partitioning factor is roughly stable over time. Analysis of the 1988 debate, news, and advertising effects in this very chapter is a case in point. If the concern is to distinguish purely cross-sectional from purely longitudinal variation, this is certainly possible, as Brady and Johnston (1996) and Johnston and Brady (2001) show. An analyst who absolutely requires a baseline should give serious consideration to the *postelection* wave as a workable substitute for a precampaign reading.

Meanwhile, the RCS presents itself as a sensitive gauge of factors operating in campaign time. The design does not commit us to any particular conception of those factors. They could even be the conservative, equilibrating forces that dominate our conception of U.S. presidential campaigns (Gelman and King 1993; Bartels 1992). Although there seems to be no gainsaying that finely tuned strategies matter little for such campaigns, the fact remains that much of what we think we know about factors internal to those campaigns remains supposition. It makes sense to understand the forces for equilibration before history comes along and makes fools of us.

The 1993 Canadian example reminds us that not all campaign factors originate in the minds of political consultants. The width of certain group or issue cleavages can shift if the standing of parties at various policy distances from each other also shifts. Strategic considerations in voters' minds may also be relevant and may also shift. This is especially likely in multiparty elections under an electoral formula that punishes "coordination failure" (Cox 1997), which is precisely the Canadian situation.[27] The 1993 election also indicates that where an active force is required to perturb the system, the force need not be very powerful itself. Certainly, the media exchanges that detonated the Conservative coalition in 1993 did not seem that startling at the time. Their effect derived as much from the fragility of their target as from the intensity of the news stimulus.

This naturally makes one ask if campaign effects are a peculiarly Canadian disease. I doubt that this is so, but if it were the case would go as follows. Canada is geographically and socially diverse, like a Belgium projected onto a whole continent, as it were. As such, its representational and electoral system should be sensitive to social complexity, being inclusive and proportional. Instead, its system is almost pure Westminster: single-member plurality elections yielding, most of the time, single-party majority governments. But the overarching structure is barely able to contain the ferment down below. Containment failure was signaled early on by the appearance of "third" parties, as for years Canada was the only Westminster system with a multiparty Parliament.[28] And sometimes it is signaled by massive, often sudden phase shifts, a pattern of punctuated equilibria. These shifts may occur—perhaps are most likely to occur—right in the middle of campaigns, for it is that high-stimulus environment that signals to voters the range and viability of alternatives.

And what if Canada is peculiar? Then I submit that Canadian elections, and Canadian election studies, ought to be seen in relation to elections and election studies in general rather as the U.S. Congress is seen in relation to legislatures and parliaments in general.

The principles illustrated in congressional studies are not peculiar to the United States. Congress is the place to test these principles because it is the only legislature sufficiently out of partisan control to exhibit the requisite variance. If Canadian elections are truly peculiar, they are so for kindred reasons. Canada would be the place where parties' strategic choices induced by the universalistic logic of the single-member plurality system most often fail. This failure opens an analytic window on electoral choice, a window that stays open for only a few weeks at a time. If this describes Canada, then a campaign-sensitive instrument is practically a necessity for understanding the long run as much as the short run of its elections.

Notes

The Canadian Election Study data analyzed in this chapter come from the 1988, 1993, and 1997 surveys. Principal investigator for 1988 and 1993 was the author. For 1997 the principal investigator was André Blais. Co-investigators in 1988 were Blais, Henry E. Brady, and Jean Crête; for 1993, Blais, Brady, Elisabeth Gidengil, and Neil Nevitte; and for 1997, Gidengil, Nevitte, and Richard Nadeau. Each study was funded by the Social Sciences and Humanities Research Council of Canada. Fieldwork was carried out by the Institute for Social Research, York University, under the direction of David Northrup. The author thanks Elihu Katz and Yael Warshel for materially improving this text but exempts all the above persons and institutions from blame for any remaining errors of fact or interpretation.

1. This is possible only where such a poll can be reasonably identified. The Canadian Gallup poll was still a rather fugitive enterprise before 1970, such that in a few cases many months intervened between a poll and the calling of an election. In 1968, for instance, the last Gallup poll was conducted before the party convention that selected Pierre Trudeau as Liberal leader. The bubble of Liberal support induced by this is better indicated by the first poll after the campaign began than by a poll from many months before.

2. The normal estimate is simply the Liberal Party's average share across all elections defining a period. Shares to 1957 are calculated against the average for the so-called "Second Party System" (Johnston et al. 1992). Elections from 1962 to 1984 inclusive are calculated relative to the "Third Party System." The one missing election, 1958, was the sole majority-government victory by the Progressive Conservative Party, a classic "deviating election" in the Campbell et al. (1960) sense.

3. This claim is echoed in Bartels (1992). The missing link in the Canadian case is a model to identify and translate precampaign information.

4. A brief account of the 1980 U.S. study can be found in Bartels (1988, p. 318). The 1987 British campaign study was an offshoot of the general-

purpose 1987 British Election Study. A detailed description can be found in Miller et al. (1990, pp. 21–26).

5. The response-rate model must take into account certain peculiarities of rolling-cross-section fieldwork, which will be considered below.

6. Practically speaking, assignment to replicates involves some stratification by area code.

7. Missing from Fig. 6.2A are numbers that do not yield an interview.

8. The very last day illustrates how circumstances can bedevil even the most scrupulously stable clearance strategy. On that day, appointments for later interviews are no longer possible even as interest in the campaign reaches its peak. The result is a naturally occurring surge in completions.

9. To the extent that the character of survey response about an election changes as the event recedes into the past, there may be longitudinal factors at work in any protracted *postelection* fieldwork period as well, a potentially awkward fact.

10. The meaning of "period average" is less obvious in this figure than in Fig. 6.1. For the Conservatives in 1988 and 1993, the average is calculated over the 1988 and 1984 results. If it seems odd to treat a two-election period as, in effect, a "party system," I do not see an alternative. The period average for the 1997 Liberals is calculated similarly, over the 1993 and 1997 results. Full characterization of the 1984–1993 and 1993–present periods in relation to the earlier history of Canadian party systems is not yet possible.

11. Over three times as many respondents (36 percent) gave his name as the winner as any other, a slightly smaller percentage than could name no winner. This percentage neither grew nor shrank over the three weeks that followed the debate.

12. The media discussion reflects Nevitte et al. (2000).

13. Movement in the Conservative share before day 35 or so is a mystery to us and probably was not a real campaign phenomenon. Where all other shifts that can be compared to the record of published polls are corroborated, this one is not. We suspect that the problem lies in the time required to learn the final ropes of managing rolling-cross-section fieldwork.

14. No other issue in any of the three Canadian campaign studies saw its opinion distribution move. The relative importance of certain issues shifted, as happened with the FTA. The point is worth making that the rolling-cross-section format is well adapted to address the issues raised by Merrill Shanks in Chapter 7 of this volume.

15. Indeed, the daily tracking without smoothing suggests that the late surge probably spanned only two days.

16. Over 60 percent of 1988 CES respondents claimed to see the debate. The percentage is probably biased upward, although by how much we do not know. Some of the report may have been of news reports just after the event. It is reassuring that this percentage was basically stable for the bal-

ance of the campaign. If the percentage is too high, the effect should be to reduce the measured impact of viewership.

17. For more detail on media variables and on the estimation model, see Johnston et al. (1992). Values are not normalized to the previous week's level, as little is gained by it. First, they come from a calculation identity without a nonzero intercept; the mean value thus is pulled off zero only to the extent that coverage is biased, which overall it was not in 1988. Second, media values are the same for both viewers and nonviewers; what differs between viewers and nonviewers are the coefficients for each lag term, where all six lagged values appear in each respondent's data line, such that lags are self-weighting by viewership. Predicted values for the eve of the debate thus carry information from almost a week before.

Entries for the media estimations are smoothed by five-day moving averages only. For these estimations, smoothing does not reduce the visible impact of survey sampling error, as there is none in the estimated values (as opposed to error in the estimation equation). If there is sampling error, it is in the adequacy of prime time in the country's largest media market as a gauge of news coverage. The day-to-day flux, in any case, is in news values as actually measured. There is little point in capturing every minuscule turn in predicted values. Smoothing thus stopped when the loss of consecutive-day sign shifts seemed greatest, which for media factors was at five days.

18. Daily advertising values are similar to news values. The time devoted to positive and negative mentions of John Turner was summed across all party ads for the major networks' Toronto prime time broadcasts. Negative time was subtracted from positive for a net reading. See also note 17.

19. Neither, of course, can the news.

20. The seven-day moving average makes each shift seem less sudden than inspection of the raw tracking suggests it really was.

21. This account of interelection popularity is based on Johnston (1999). The following narrative and interpretation synthesize Johnston et al. (1994) and a manuscript still in progress.

22. The CES employs 100-point leader rating scales akin to the "feeling thermometers" used in the U.S. NES to rate candidates and groups.

23. Popular commentary emphasizes an unwise remark by Campbell to the effect that the campaign was no place to discuss policy. The remark aptly summarizes her political problem, but her party's 10-point drop had already occurred by the time she uttered it.

24. The indicators in question include scales for respondents' own positions on major issues, five-point issue placement items for parties akin to the seven-point scales in the U.S. NES, and trait ratings for leaders, also akin to those in the U.S. NES.

25. Between 1988 and 1993, economic adversity had made media outlets less willing to pay for polls and polling firms less willing to give their find-

ings away for promotional purposes. At the same time, the countrywide uniformity of the 1988 context was supplanted by an intensely regional pattern in 1993. In 1988, polls could get by comfortably with samples of around 1000. In 1993, many polls involved 3000–4000 respondents.

26. The indicator of expectations was a 0–100 "chances" scale, adapted from the 1984 U.S. primary study.

27. Cox defines a strong electoral system as one that punishes similar groups that fail to agree on a single candidate when only one can win. The usual consequence is the election of a candidate from another, smaller, but better-coordinated affinity. Where there is a need to coordinate in this sense, voters may do the coordinating by using poll information to determine which of the competing but acceptable candidates is best placed to win.

28. This line of argument was first made with incredible prescience by Lipset (1960).

References

Bartels, Larry M. 1988. *Presidential Primaries and the Dynamics of Public Choice.* Princeton: Princeton University Press.

Bartels, Larry M. 1992. "The Impact of Electioneering in the United States." In *Electioneering: A Comparative Study of Continuity and Change*, David Butler and Austin Ranney, eds., pp. 244–277. Oxford: Clarendon Press.

Berelson, Bernard R., Paul F. Lazarsfeld, and William N. McPhee. 1954. *Voting: A Study of Opinion Formation in a Presidential Campaign.* Chicago: University of Chicago Press.

Brady, Henry E., and Richard Johnston. 1987. "What's the Primary Message: Horse Race or Issue Journalism?" In *Media and Momentum: The New Hampshire Primary and Nomination Politics*, Gary R. Orren and Nelson W. Polsby, eds. Chatham, N.J.: Chatham House.

Brady, Henry E,. and Richard Johnston. 1996. Statistical Methods for Analyzing Rolling Cross-Sections with Examples from the 1988 and 1993 Canadian Election Studies. Paper presented at the Annual Meeting of the Midwest Political Science Association, April 18–20, 1996, Chicago.

Cox, Gary W. 1997. *Making Votes Count: Strategic Coordination in the World's Electoral Systems.* Cambridge, England: Cambridge University Press.

Gelman, Andrew, and Gary King. 1993. "Why Are American Presidential Election Polls So Variable When Votes Are So Predictable?" *British Journal of Political Science* 23: 409–451.

Holbrook, Thomas M. 1996. *Do Campaigns Matter?* Thousand Oaks, Calif.: Sage.

Iyengar, Shanto, and Donald R. Kinder. 1987. *News That Matters: Television and American Opinion.* Chicago: University of Chicago Press.

Johnston, Richard. 1999. "Business Cycles, Political Cycles and the Popularity of Canadian Governments, 1974–1998." *Canadian Journal of Political Science* 22: 499–520.

Johnston, Richard, and Henry E. Brady. 2001. "The Rolling Cross-Section Design." *Electoral Studies*, in press.

Johnston, Richard, André Blais, Henry E. Brady, and Jean Crête. 1992. *Letting the People Decide: Dynamics of a Canadian Election.* Stanford: Stanford University Press.

Johnston, Richard, André Blais, Henry E. Brady, Elisabeth Gidengil, and Neil Nevitte. 1994. The Collapse of a Party System? The 1993 Canadian General Election. Paper presented at the Annual Meeting of the American Political Science Association, September 1–4, 1994, New York.

Katz, Elihu, and Paul F. Lazarsfeld. 1955. *Personal Influence.* Glencoe, Ill: Free Press.

Klapper, Joseph T. 1960. *The Effects of Mass Communication.* Glencoe, Ill: Free Press.

Lazarsfeld, Paul, Bernard Berelson, and Hazel Gaudet. 1944. *The People's Choice.* New York: Duell, Sloane, and Pierce.

Lipset, Seymour M. 1960. "Party Systems and the Representation of Social Groups." *European Journal of Sociology* 1: 50–85.

McGuire, William J. 1968. "Personality and Susceptibility to Social Influence." In *The Handbook of Personality Theory and Research*, Edgar F. Borgatta and William W. Lambert, eds., pp. 1130–1187. Chicago: Rand McNally.

McGuire, William J. 1969. "The Nature of Attitudes and Attitude Change." In *The Handbook of Social Psychology*, Gardner Lindzey and Elliot Aronson, eds., 2nd ed., Vol. 3, pp. 136–314. Reading, Mass.: Addison-Wesley.

Miller, William L., Harold D. Clarke, Martin Harrop, Lawrence LeDuc, and Paul F. Whiteley. 1990. *How Voters Change: The 1987 British Election Campaign in Perspective.* Oxford, England: Clarendon Press.

Nevitte, Neil, André Blais, Elisabeth Gidengil, and Richard Nadeau. 2000. *Unsteady State: The 1997 Canadian Federal Election.* Toronto: Oxford University Press.

Zaller, John R. 1992. *The Nature and Origins of Mass Opinion.* Cambridge, England: Cambridge University Press.

7

WHAT ABOUT ISSUES?

MERRILL SHANKS

University of California at Berkeley

Before each presidential election, social scientists who are responsible for major surveys concerning voting behavior must make a series of detailed decisions concerning the data that will be collected before, during, and after that campaign. The general design and specific questions that are adopted for such surveys play a decisive role in determining—and limiting—the kinds of questions that can be answered through postelection analyses of the resulting data. Some researchers use survey data from the most recent election to extend our understanding of general trends or processes, such as partisan "realignment" or the stability of partisan and policy-related predispositions, based on continuing measures that have been used over several elections. Many researchers, however, will also be interested in new or unique aspects of the survey data that were collected during the most recent campaign, in order to clarify the issues or topics that appeared to shape voters' decisions in that specific election.

Researchers of that sort typically ask: "What was the most recent contest between major party candidates really *about*, other than a struggle between rival leaders for congressional seats and presidential authority?" Most, if not all, researchers of this sort and their eventual readers want to know which aspects of the opposing campaigns, or which substantive issues, seemed to have played the most important roles in shaping voters' eventual decisions, in addition to their reactions to the personal (or nongovernmental) qualities of the opposing candidates and their prior identifications with one of the major political parties.

This chapter discusses the evolution of research based on national surveys concerning the role of substantive or *policy*-related issues in U.S. presidential elections, beginning with the treatment of those topics in *The American Voter* (Campbell et al., 1960). The first section of this chapter identifies alternative perspectives concerning the electoral relevance of policy-related controversies that have emerged since the appearance of that influential book, both before and after the creation of the National Election Studies (NES). The second section reviews the major conclusions concerning this topic from the author's own research, based on the extended analysis of NES data for the 1992 election in *The New American Voter* (Miller and Shanks, 1996) and a subsequent analysis of the 1996 election (Shanks et al., 1999). The third, and final, section introduces an alternative approach to answering these kinds of questions about policy-related voting, based on a comprehensive series of survey questions about potential "governmental objectives," and discusses the potential implications of that approach for future election surveys.

This chapter begins by reviewing alternative perspectives and approaches concerning these kinds of survey-based analyses, but it is primarily devoted to specific procedures and results that are closely tied to the author's point of view. Other researchers can, and do, approach the same questions with a different set of analytic objectives and methodological assumptions. This discussion, however, is based on the author's conviction that electoral scholars need to spend *more,* not less, time discussing the implications of different perspectives concerning the specific questions we should try to answer—and the assumptions required for specific interpretations of statistical results—in addition to the more practical questions associated with the design of future election surveys.

The Role of Policy Issues:
The American Voter and its Critics

After four decades, contemporary research on voting behavior is still influenced by the concepts, methods, and general conclusions that were introduced in *The American Voter.* No other book on voting behavior or American elections has been more frequently cited, and analyses of voters' decisions in contemporary elections are still discussed in terms of that pathbreaking work's conclusions based on the elections of 1952 and 1956. In some respects, that book represented an extension of research that was initially reported in *The Voter Decides* (Campbell et al., 1954), based on the first national survey that was entirely devoted to a presidential election. This sequel to *The Voter Decides*, however, addressed many more aspects of voting behavior in presidential elections, so that it quickly became the focal point for continuing electoral research in the United States and several other countries.

The American Voter provided the first comprehensive explanation of electoral decisions made by ordinary citizens, including the option to vote or abstain as well as the choice of one presidential candidate instead of another. The analyses of turnout and candidate choice presented in *The American Voter* reviewed the full range of potential explanations of voters' decisions that had been suggested by other scholars, including a variety of external factors that are determined outside voters' own lives or experiences as well as their attitudes toward political issues, parties, and candidates. External or nonpolitical factors that were discussed because of their potential impact on electoral behavior included voters' social or economic status (or class) and their relationships with various social groups, as well as electoral laws and other institutional arrangements in which elections take place. The most influential chapters in *The American Voter*, however, concentrated on the conceptualization and measurement of different types of political attitudes, and the apparent influence of those attitudes on vote choice. This emphasis on attitudes or opinions concerning explicitly political topics included an extended discussion of voters' continuing identifications with one of the major political parties and the (relatively infrequent) circumstances in which those identifications may change, as well as the ways in which voters acquire positive or negative impressions about major candidates for president.

In addition to these general contributions to our understanding of voters' electoral decisions, *The American Voter* presented three kinds of statistical results concerning the role of voters' attitudes toward *policy*-related controversies. These three types of evidence were based on:

- the degree to which voters mentioned reasons for "liking" or "disliking" one of the major party candidates that were expressed in terms of some aspect of domestic or foreign policy;

- the degree to which potential voters possessed the kinds of information and opinions that should be present if their vote is directly influenced by their own policy-related preferences; and
- the proportions of voters whose comments about politics demonstrated different "levels of conceptualization" concerning ideological or issue-related attitudes toward politics.

Each of these contributions concerning the role of policy-related issues is discussed briefly below, followed by alternative perspectives and procedures that have been advocated by scholars who were critical of that aspect of *The American Voter.*

Policy-Related Reasons for Liking or Disliking a Candidate

In an introductory chapter devoted to basic concepts and causation, the authors of *The American Voter* outlined a "field theoretical" approach to electoral explanation. In that formulation, the electoral choices made by individual voters were seen as determined by a variety of attitudinal "forces" that are located at different points in a general "funnel of causality." In this framework, psychological or attitudinal elements that may have some direct influence on the vote were designated as "political" as well as proximate to the ultimate dependent variable, whereas elements that have only an indirect influence on the vote were described as "nonpolitical" or "external to the voter" and were located at a point that is "more remote in the funnel."

On the basis of this perspective, most of the analyses of vote choice in *The American Voter* were based on the answers to open-ended questions that asked respondents if there was "anything in particular" about a particular candidate that "might make you want to vote for" (or against) that person. If the respondent indicated any positive (or negative) views about a given candidate, the interviewer probed for all of the specific "reasons" involved, and recorded each response in verbatim form. The coded versions of these responses to open-ended question about the candidates and parties were seen as an approximate representation (if not direct measurement) of the "field of forces" that could be used to explain each voter's choice for president. Using those responses, *The American Voter* was able to summarize voters' candidate-related attitudes in several different ways, for the content of individual responses to these general questions about the candidates and parties can be grouped or combined to describe voters' attitudes toward more general topics or domains as well as the specific concerns associated with each response category.

Most of the results based on these "reasons for choice" in *The American Voter* utilized constructed measures that summarized all of the responses to these open-ended questions in terms of six general "dimensions" concerning: the personal attributes of the Republican candidate (Eisenhower), the personal attributes of the Democratic candidate (Stevenson), groups that are active in politics and group-related interests, the comparative records of the two parties as managers of government, issues that were defined in terms of domestic policy, and issues concerning foreign policy. These six measures were designed to capture both the *partisan direction* and *intensity* of each voter's attitudes toward these six general elements of a given electoral contest. These measures were then used to document the extent to which the national distribution of attitudes toward each element operated to the (net) advantage of one candidate or the other. For example, voters' attitudes toward domestic issues and attitudes toward groups that were active in politics appeared to have provided some aggregate support for Adlai Stevenson in both 1952 and 1956, whereas attitudes toward foreign policy and toward the parties as managers of government appeared to have made some contribution to Dwight Eisenhower's victories in both of those elections. In general, however, voters' partisan attitudes based on domestic and foreign policy were seen as less important in shaping the aggregate results of those elections than partisan attitudes that were defined in terms of the candidates, social groups, or the parties as managers of government.

Alternative or Critical Perspectives

After *The American Voter* was published, other researchers suggested that its open-ended questions about the candidates and parties did not provide a satisfactory account of the electoral influence of policy-related controversies. In general, such scholars were concerned about the validity of these kinds of explanations, on the grounds that survey respondents are not very good at reconstructing the sources of their positive or negative impressions of the candidates. Some researchers were prepared to use the open-ended questions to summarize voters' overall evaluations of the major candidates and parties, but did not believe that the responses to those questions could be used to assess the role of particular issues—especially because many of those responses are expressed in terms of broad topics or domains (e.g., "because of his position on education") instead of specific policy issues. Other researchers were concerned that any measure based on the simple number of responses that appeared to favor (or oppose) a given candidate concerning a particular issue or topic could seriously underestimate the electoral relevance of that topic. Much of the history of the electoral field since *The American Voter* can be described in terms of this kind of disagreement concerning the accuracy of explanations (of vote choice) based on open-ended questions concerning voters' positive or negative impressions of the candidates. Throughout this period, electoral analysts have simply not been able to agree about the validity of the substantive "reasons" provided by voters to explain their own evaluations of the candidates.

In part because of influential studies in social psychology (Nisbett and Wilson, 1977) and widespread concerns about the kinds of answers that are (and are not) produced by those open-ended questions, many researchers recommended that electoral surveys include *structured questions* (with fixed response alternatives) for *each* potential issue or substantive topic that may serve as a source for some candidate evaluations. The most frequent form of this kind of criticism was implicit, in that many researchers appeared to believe that the open-ended questions emphasized in *The American Voter* should be ignored (if not eliminated) in favor of structured questions about particular topics or issues, in order to assess their influence on voters' choices for president. This general trend in measurement-related preferences (away from open-ended questions) eventually involved every type of political attitude that might be used to explain voters' choices for president.

At first, criticism of this sort concentrated on the potential influence of voters' preferences concerning *policy*-related controversies. In particular, several researchers advocated new structured questions to measure voters' own policy preferences concerning major conflicts within the society for which the parties and candidates took quite different positions, including racial integration, the war in Vietnam, urban unrest or crime, and various aspects of social welfare (Page and Brody, 1972; Miller and Miller, 1976). By the late

1970s, the same kinds of recommendations were extended to several other types of electoral explanations, including proposals for new structured questions that could be used to capture voters' evaluations of the candidates' personal qualities (Kinder et al., 1980; Funk, 1997), voters' retrospective evaluations of the incumbent administration's performance (Fiorina, 1981), and voters' prospective assessments of the candidates' effectiveness in handling particular aspects of national life, such as crime, employment, or health care.

This growing support for abandoning open-ended questions in favor of structured questions about voters' attitudes toward specific topics (including policy-related controversies) has not been based on methodological studies that "resolved" the underlying issues. Prominent scholars continue to rely on the traditional open-ended questions (Asher, 1992; Kelley, 1983; Wattenberg, 1991), and relatively little work has been done to compare substantive conclusions about a given election that are based on analyses of parallel (or matched) variables that are constructed from responses to general open-ended questions versus structured questions about the same topics. (For exceptions to that general omission, see Miller and Shanks, 1996, and Shanks, 1999.) Furthermore, some analysts have emphasized the need for caution concerning the validity of any causal interpretation of relationships between respondents' own policy-related preferences and vote choice (Brody and Page, 1972). Other participants in these discussions have been concerned about the sheer number of survey questions that will be needed if election surveys are to continue the traditional open-ended approach as well as asking structured questions about each potentially relevant topic, for all of these questions may not "fit" within a single interview. Despite these reservations, however, the campaign to expand such measures based on structured (and precoded) questions has only intensified over time.

In response to *The American Voter*'s conclusions about the (limited) influence of voters' policy-related preferences, some scholars suggested that a quite different picture would emerge if researchers used alternative approaches for both survey measurement and analysis. In particular, several researchers suggested that policy-based sources of voters' decisions should be represented in terms of a "spatial model." In that formulation, policy-related preferences are measured with the same policy alternatives (and metric) as their perceptions of the candidates' positions, and voters are assumed to choose the candidate whose combination of positions is closer or more proximate to their

own—based on some kind of transformation to convert multiple issues into a single metric for the overall "distance" between voters and
candidates. This kind of explanation was influenced by models of "rational choice" developed in economics, but it could also be interpreted
as a multivariate extension of the requirements for policy-related voting that had been outlined in *The American Voter* (discussed below).
Implementation of this approach required new survey questions concerning respondents' perceptions of the candidates' positions, as well
as some way to assign a greater "weight" to policy issues that are
more important to the respondent. Alternative procedures for using
respondents' perceptions of the candidates are beyond the scope of
this chapter, as are various attempts to measure the salience or importance of specific issues to individual respondents.

Some scholars also produced larger estimates concerning the influence of policy-related preferences by adopting different assumptions
about causation. Because of *The American Voter*'s emphasis on the
stability and pervasive influence of partisan identification, some critics suspected that some of that book's conclusions about the (limited) role of policy-related preferences could be attributed to its
treatment of party identification. In particular, alternative models
were developed during the 1960s and 1970s in which voters' policy
preferences (or other kinds of "issue-related" opinions) were treated
as causes of their partisan identifications, based on the assumption
that those identifications are as "endogenous" as other kinds of political attitudes. Based on those revised assumptions, policy-related
preferences could be shown to have a major *indirect* impact on vote
choice—through their influence on party identification–in addition
to their direct influence on such choices (Jackson, 1975; Page and
Jones, 1979; Franklin and Jackson, 1983).

In retrospect, these alternative formulations based on the "endogeneity" of partisan identifications may have selected the wrong aspect of *The American Voter* to criticize. Subsequent research concerning the relative stability of different political attitudes has made
it fairly clear that voters' partisan identifications do have the kinds
of pervasive effects on other attitudes as well as vote choice that
were outlined in *The American Voter*, and that those identifications
are not highly responsive to short-term forces. (They are also not entirely "fixed," as suggested by occasional caricaturelike references to
party identification as an "unmoved mover" that shapes all other
political attitudes, but those identifications are not very responsive

to short-term forces within a single campaign.) At this point, scholars have not obtained any convincing evidence concerning the extent to which voters acquire (and sustain) their continuing identifications with one of the major parties because its typical positions concerning major policy issues are closer to their own. For the same kinds of methodological reasons, we also have no compelling evidence concerning the strength of the opposite process, in which voters acquire their own policy-related preferences through a form of persuasion, based on the leadership of the party with which they identify. The relative magnitudes of these mutually reinforcing processes over time represent a continuing puzzle for most students of contemporary politics. Our uncertainty about the relative magnitudes of these two processes, however, should not interfere with efforts to assess the apparent effects of other kinds of attitudes on vote choice *after we control for party identification*—including the electoral relevance of specific policy-related controversies.

Empirical Requirements for Policy-Based Voting

Another aspect of *The American Voter* that continues to influence contemporary research concerns the kinds of opinions that individual voters must have before any analyst should conclude that their vote choice could have been influenced by their attitudes toward a particular policy-related controversy. In particular, the authors of *The American Voter* suggested that any linkage between voters' own policy-related preferences and their choice for president should not be seen in terms of policy-based voting *unless* the voter has some understanding of the issue, has a position on the issue with at least a minimal level of intensity, and perceives that one candidate or party has a position that is closer to the respondent's than the other.

Results provided in *The American Voter* suggested that many (if not most) voters did not meet all of these requirements concerning most specific policy-related issues. These conclusions, however, were met with some skepticism among other social scientists. Many potential critics, of course, were simply unfamiliar with the low levels of information or sophistication concerning politics that are exhibited by many (if not most) respondents in any representative sample of the national electorate. Other scholars, however, suggested alternative ways that policy-related issues might still have some influence on vote choice, even though a majority of citizens fail to meet the criteria for policy-related voting as outlined in *The American Voter* (Carmines and Stimson, 1980; Lodge et al., 1989; Miller and Shanks, 1996). These alternative formulations are beyond the scope of this general review, but they have seemed increasingly plausible given the intensity of the conflicts over civil rights and the Vietnam War during the 1960s and 1970s and the subsequent emphasis on opposing (liberal versus conservative) policies by both Democratic and Republican leaders.

In practice, analysts have often suggested some (at least tentative) conclusions about the influence of specific policy-related controversies without any information about some of these requirements. Information from respondents about their perceptions of the candidates' positions on a given issue is often unavailable, and many analysts have to operate without any information about the importance or salience of a given issue to the respondent. Thus, there may be no way to directly test the extent to which respondents' apparent positions on a given issue are based on any real interest or involvement. Furthermore, there is reason to believe that some of those apparent perceptions (of candidate positions) are not based on any real information. The respondent's own position may resemble his or her perception of a candidate's position because of two alternative processes that are quite different from the (presumed) process in which the respondent pays enough attention to the campaign to learn the candidates' actual positions. In one of these alternative processes, the respondent is "persuaded" to adopt the position that has been advocated by a candidate who is favored for some other reason, so that the respondent's own position changes to increase that individual's "proximity" to the candidate on that issue. In the other process that is not based on accurate perceptions, voters simply assume that the candidate they support must agree with their own opinions on an issue, so that apparent perceptions of the candidates are adjusted through "projection" to fit the respondents' own policy preferences (Brody and Page, 1972).

Differences Among Voters in
Political Sophistication or Information

Contemporary research concerning the electoral relevance of policy-related attitudes is also influenced by *The American Voter*'s findings concerning substantial differences among voters in the extent to which they understand the concepts or issues involved. To document those differences, *The American Voter* presented a distribution of all potential voters into four basic "levels of conceptualization" concerning political issues or ideology, based on their responses to open-ended questions about the candidates and parties. Each respondent was assigned to one of the following four categories, based on a detailed inspection of that individual's verbatim responses, as recorded on the original interview schedules:

- Level A, called "ideology and near-ideology," was used for respondents whose comments included the kinds of concepts or terms that are usually associated with ideological interpretations of politics, and for a second group of respondents who mentioned several specific issues of public policy without any apparent integration based on abstract or "ideological" concepts. Even after combining these two types of respondents, only 12% of the entire 1956 sample could be classified as either "ideologues or near-ideologues," and that figure rose to only 15% among those individuals who actually voted in that election.

- Level B, called "group benefits," was used for respondents whose comments referred to visible benefits involving specific groups within the populations, such as farmers, poor people, or small businesses, or others who benefited from a single policy issue. Because of the interpretations given to national politics by the leaders of such groups, this classification was sometimes described in terms of "ideology by proxy." On the basis of several types of group-related references, 42% of the total sample was assigned to level B, or 45% of those who voted.

- Level C was used for respondents whose comments involved references to the "goodness" and "badness" of the times, in which one candidate or party is seen as either the hero or the villain, without any conflicts over alternative policies or group-related benefits. Respondents of this type constituted 24% of the entire sample and 23% of actual voters.

- Level D was used for respondents who exhibited "no issue content," either because their comments were limited to unspecified positive or negative reactions to one of the parties or candidates or because they offered no comments that dealt with political or governmental topics. Individuals in this residual category represented 24% of the entire sample and 17% of those who voted.

The above description of the American electorate in terms of these basic levels, and the fairly small proportion of potential voters in the "ideological or near-ideological" level, represent one of the most influential aspects of in *The American Voter*. Other scholars have questioned both the accuracy and interpretation of this particular measure concerning voters' "levels of conceptualization" (Smith, 1989), and contemporary analysts emphasize measures of political *information* instead of sophistication (Luskin, 1987; Zaller, 1992). Most contemporary researchers, however, recognize that substantial numbers of voters can appear to have a "preference" concerning some policy issues without having enough information about that topic to form such an opinion (Converse, 1964), and that the influence of voters' own policy-related preferences on their vote may be "conditioned" by the amount of political information or sophistication that they possess. Conditional relationships of this sort, in which the (true) impact of a given policy-related attitude on vote choice may be much smaller for voters with less political information or sophistication, are outside the scope of this chapter. Such possibilities, however, represent a continuing source of concern in contemporary electoral research.

Issue- or Policy-Related Explanations in *The New American Voter*

After 1977, continuing support for the new National Election Studies made it possible for researchers to explore alternative approaches to electoral explanation, and to introduce new structured questions concerning several types of policy-related controversies. In particular, new measures were developed to summarize voters' general beliefs or values concerning several broad policy-related domains, including equality and morality (Feldman, 1983), race or racial discrimination (Kinder and Sanders, 1996), and responsibilities of government versus the private sector (Marcus, 1992), as well as new questions concerning a variety of specific issues. On the basis of those new measures and perspectives, this author and Warren Miller carried out a series of analyses of the 1992 election that became the core of *The New American Voter* (Miller and Shanks, 1996). Those analyses reviewed the apparent electoral effects of a wide variety of potential explanations, but one of its primary purposes was to document—and emphasize—the ways in which voters' attitudes toward policy-related conflicts may influence their choices for president.

In many respects, the analysis of the 1992 election in *The New American Voter* concentrates on the same conceptual and method-ological issues that are summarized here. Most of its statistical re-sults concerning the role of issue- or policy-related attitudes, how-ever, were based on a specific multiple-stage model that also included other potential explanations of vote choice. In particular, the analyses of the 1992 and 1988 elections presented in *The New American Voter* are based on an overall model in which all of the voter characteristics that may have some impact on their choice for president are classified into six broad stages, each of which is defined in terms of the types of explanatory variables involved:

Stable Social and Economic Conditions
Partisan Identification *and* Policy-Related Predispositions
Current Policy Preferences *and* Perceptions of Current Conditions
Retrospective Evaluations of the President Concerning Government "Results"
Impressions of the Candidates' Personal Qualities
Prospective Evaluations of the Candidate and the Parties

In this model, any characteristic of voters within a given stage may be influenced by any variable that has been assigned to a previous stage, and the impact of any characteristic on vote choice may be mediated by any of the (intervening) variables that have been as-signed to later stages in this process.

The Electoral Relevance of Policy-Related Predispositions

Using this overall explanatory model, the initial policy-related re-sults presented in *The New American Voter* were defined in terms of voters' general orientations or *predispositions* toward broad policy-related topics, instead of specific policy issues. As discussed above, the National Election Studies had sponsored several measurement development projects concerning voters' general beliefs of several policy-related domains, including their general attitudes toward equality, morality, and the allocation of general responsibility (for many outcomes) between the federal government and the private sector. Based on those measures and the above multiple-stage model, the analyses of vote choice in 1992 presented in *The New American Voter* suggested that choices between Bill Clinton and George Bush were *substantially* influenced by voters' general beliefs about equality, about morality, *and* about the role of the federal government, as well as their (even more general) self-designations as liberals, moderates, or conservatives.

In addition, similar kinds of results were presented concerning the electoral impact of voters' general attitudes toward several groups that are closely associated with continuing conflicts over federal policy, including homosexuals, Christian Fundamentalists, unions, and large corporations, and the apparent influence of general attitudes toward U.S. international involvement and lingering disagreements associated with the Vietnam War. Another summary measure concerning voters' general beliefs about race and racial discrimination was also strongly related to vote choice, but its apparent effect was reduced to nearly zero when the analysis involved statistical controls for the other predispositions listed above.

In general, the "apparent total effect" presented in *The New American Voter* for each of these predispositionlike measures was based on a multivariate analysis that controlled for voters' other policy-related predispositions, as well as their partisan identifications and a standard set of social or economic characteristics. As discussed below, the apparent impact of a given policy-related attitude can be fundamentally affected by the analyst's decision concerning the specific set of other policy-related measures that are "held constant" or "controlled." The negative conclusions about the influence of voters' attitudes toward race (mentioned in the preceding paragraph) is simply the most striking illustration of this general principle.

The Role of Current Policy Issues

The next stage of the overall explanatory model used in *The New American Voter* is defined in terms of all the specific issues that were emphasized during the campaign. This set of potential explanatory variables was defined in fairly broad terms, but it was limited to those aspects of public opinion that were defined in terms of some current or potential activities of the federal government. In addition, all of those potential issues were classified into two general types, depending on whether they were based on a general consensus or a visible policy-related conflict concerning the objectives (or priorities) of the federal government.

The most visible or familiar example of the first of these two types of issues is based on voters' impressions of the current "state of the economy." Most (if not all) electoral analysts believe that there is a general consensus among voters about the federal government's responsibility for the general condition of the national economy, and that the current administration is often punished when economic conditions are poor and may be rewarded when the economy is in "very good shape." Relatively few aspects of public opinion rest on this kind of consensus, however, so that most "issues" concerning the current or potential activities of the federal government rest on some kind of conflict or disagreement about governmental policy.

Based on this distinction and the multiple-stage model discussed earlier, *The New American Voter*'s analysis of the 1992 election examined a substantial number of survey questions devoted to current policy issues, including all of the questions about federal spending in specific programmatic areas as well as the traditional NES "7-point scales." From this substantial collection of potentially relevant issues, only five measures concerning voters' preferences on specific policy issues were found to exhibit visible (or significant) relationships with vote choice after we controlled for the other significant issues in this list, perceptions of the economy, and all of the policy-related predispositions discussed above, as well as party identification and social or economic characteristics. In particular, voters' own preferences concerning the following aspects of federal policy appeared to play some role in shaping their choices for president in 1992:

- assistance to the poor;
- military strength and use of military forces;
- appropriateness of military service by homosexuals.;
- a possible increase in federal income taxes; and
- financial support to parents of students in private schools.

In addition to reviewing alternative estimates concerning the apparent electoral influence for particular measures concerning policy-related predispositions and current issues, *The New American Voter* also discussed the combined influence of all policy-related preferences in both of those explanatory themes. Initial conclusions about the combined explanatory power for all policy-related attitudes were based on the relationship between vote choice and a simple average of each respondent's scores on all of the policy-related measures (concerning general predispositions or specific issues) that appeared to play some role in shaping voters' decisions. The standardized regression coefficient for that summary measure is as large as the corresponding coefficient for partisan identification, when both variables are included in the same explanatory equation, along with stable social and economic characteristics. This same general conclusion is also supported by a second, and more complex, kind of analysis that is introduced near the end of the book. The details of those analytic procedures are beyond the scope of this chapter, but they do permit the analyst to assess the combined relevance of all the variables that have been selected for intensive analysis within each of the above explanatory themes—thereby assessing the relative "importance" of all the evaluations of the incumbent president, or all of the personal qualities of the candidates, as well as all of the respondents' own policy-related predispositions and current policy preferences.

Similar kinds of results have been produced for the 1988 and 1996 elections, and this author suspects that the demonstrated kind of rough parity in electoral relevance between partisan identifications and the combination of all policy-related attitudes has been a persistent feature of most U.S. presidential elections since 1972, if not before. Unfortunately, however, it is difficult to compare these kinds of summary results (from 1988, 1992, and 1996) with similar kinds of results from elections before 1988, because those earlier surveys did not include the same kinds of questions concerning policy-related predispositions and the same range of measures concerning current policy issues.

It should also be noted that the present essay does not discuss the "importance" of specific explanatory variables or more general explanatory themes (such as policy-related predispositions or current policy issues) in accounting for the *aggregate results* of a given election. The last analytic chapter in *The New American Voter* presents a series of analyses that compare the 1988 and 1992 elections in terms of the importance of specific types of explanatory variables. Those analyses provide separate comparisons concerning the role of each factor in explaining individual differences in vote choice and their (often quite different) importance in producing the aggregate results of the election. For example, voters' partisan policy-related preferences concerning one (specific) issue may have played a substantial role in making some voters vote for one candidate and other voters vote for his opponent, but those attitudes may not have made any overall contribution to the aggregate results of the election—because voters' attitudes toward that issue were fairly evenly balanced between the two opposing "positions." The logic and results of those comparisons, however, are beyond the scope of this essay.

Differences from The American Voter

The foregoing results concerning the overall (or combined) importance of policy-related preferences have no counterpart in the statistical results provided in *The American Voter*. It should be noted, however, that the general character of the result concerning the combined influence of policy-related attitudes *is* quite different from the impression that most readers have obtained from that classic book. In retrospect, it seems plausible, if not certain, that voters' attitudes toward major policy issues did have less influence on their preferences for Eisenhower or Stevenson during the 1950s than similar kinds of policy-related issues in subsequent decades. Since the 1960s, the two major parties have advocated opposing positions on an increasing number of highly visible conflicts over national or federal policy, so that voters' own preferences concerning those controversies may have played a more prominent role than in the 1950s.

Unfortunately, the evidence necessary to make direct comparisons of this sort between decades is simply not available because of fundamental changes in the format and content of the questions used in the national surveys conducted during those elections. For that reason, we cannot compare elections in the 1950s to more recent elections in terms of the apparent combined influence of all policy-related predispositions and current policy preferences. As a consequence, we do not know whether this "new" aspect of *The New American Voter* (based on its increased emphasis on policy-related voting) represents a real shift in the sources of voters' deci-

sions or simply a change in the kinds of survey questions that have
been used to support such analyses.

Continuing Questions About the Role of Specific Issues

The procedures and results discussed in *The New American Voter*
were intended to stimulate general discussion within our field concerning several types of potential explanatory variables, as well as to
contribute to our understanding of the 1992 and 1988 elections. In
presenting these analyses, however, the authors were quite aware of
continuing questions or uncertainties about the accuracy or validity
of their results. In particular, other researchers (or the authors) have
emphasized continuing issues or uncertainties regarding three general aspects of the approach and procedures used in *The New American Voter*.

The first of these questions concerns the possibility that voters'
own attitudes concerning issue- or policy-related topics may be influenced by their prior choice of candidate—that is, persuasion. As
discussed earlier, these kinds of general concerns about causal direction and change over time have led to an increased use of multiple-
year panels in each of the NES surveys since the 1988 election, and
to the use of "continuous monitoring" in recent surveys of the
Canadian elections (Johnston et al., 1992) and the Annenberg
School for Communication survey of the 2000 election. The rest of
this chapter, however, will set aside these general issues concerning
survey design and causal inference and concentrate on other concerns about the substantive content of issue- or policy-related
analyses.

A second major source of continuing uncertainty is based on the
possibility that the pool of explanatory variables concerning specific issues of policy-related topics does not include adequate measures for some of the relevant policy-related topics — so that influence of some (missing) topics is inappropriately attributed to other
issues or predispositions. This general possibility is discussed at
some length in the final section of this chapter. Before turning to
that possibility, however, an extension to *The New American Voter*
based on NES data from the 1996 election has emphasized a third,
and final, source of general uncertainty about the influence of policy-related attitudes, based on a pervasive competition for explana-

tory credit between specific policy issues and general policy-related predispositions.

Potential Confusion Between General Predispositions and Specific Issues

Since the publication of *The New American Voter*, the same analytic procedures have also been used to assess the impact of alternative explanations for voters' choices in the 1996 presidential election (Shanks et al., 1999). In that essay, several explanatory variables are shown to have apparent effects on vote choice that are fairly similar to those from the 1992 and 1996 elections. For some familiar explanations, however, voters' choices in 1996 appeared to have been influenced in quite different ways. In particular, voters' general attitudes toward *equality* and *morality* did *not* appear to play any independent role in shaping voters' choices, when the analysis controls for other policy-related predispositions as well as party identification. Voters' general orientations toward these two familiar domains exhibited bivariate relationships with vote choice that were just as strong as in 1992, but their independent influence appears to have disappeared because of their stronger relationships with other predispositions—particularly those based on voters' "ideological" self-designations (as liberals, moderates, or conservatives) and their partisan identifications.

Furthermore, voters' choices in 1996 appeared to be influenced by fewer specific issues concerning federal policy than in 1992, after we control for more general policy-related predispositions and party identification, as well as any other specific policy issues (concerning different topics) with significant effects. In 1992 and 1988, several policy issues maintained significant apparent effects on vote choice after the analysis controlled for all general predispositions as well as the other specific issues. In 1992, however, the only two specific policy issues that maintained a significant relationship with the vote after all of those competing variables are controlled involved *equal rights for homosexuals* and the government's role concerning *health insurance*.

These negative results concerning some issues, however, are clearly dependent on the analyst's decision to control for more general policy-related predispositions as well as other policy issues and party identification. In particular, voters' policy preferences concerning *tax reduction* (the centerpiece of the 1996 Republican campaign) and *assistance to the disadvantaged* (a traditional emphasis in most previous Democratic campaigns) *do* appear to have played some role in shaping voters' choices for president *if* the analysis does *not* control for ideological self-designation and attitudes toward "limited government." This extension to *The New American Voter* also discusses a variety of alternative estimates concerning the electoral relevance of several other policy issues (including specific controversies concerning abortion, defense spending, education, the environment, and race), and reviews the kinds of analyses in which they do (and do not) appear to have some independent influence on vote choice.

At this point, the only conclusion about the impact of specific policy-related attitudes in the 1996 election that seems "safe" from controversy is that electoral scholars *do not agree* on the most appropriate estimates for such effects *or* the kinds of analysis that should be used to produce such estimates. It is still relatively early in the life cycle of publications concerning the 1996 presidential election, but it is already clear that the electoral field includes several different perspectives concerning how researchers should assess the influence of specific kinds of policy-related attitudes, and that these differences in approach can produce substantial differences in substantive conclusions (Abramowitz, 1995; Kinder and Sanders, 1996; Alvarez and Nagler, 1998). In general, each of the following perspectives appears to be supported by one or more prominent scholars within the field:

- There is no need to worry about the potential competition between explanatory variables that are based on structured questions about general predispositions versus specific policy issues, because these kinds of analyses should be based on the "reasons" for choice provided by respondents' answers to open-ended questions (i.e., we should rely on the traditional "likes and dislikes" concerning the candidates and the parties instead of measures based on structured questions).
- This kind of explanatory competition between general predispositions and specific policy issues is not really a problem, because the desired analysis focuses on evaluations of the candidates' past or fu-

ture "performance" with respect to fairly consensual governmental objectives (such as the state of the economy)—and is not concerned about the role or impact of any policy-related conflicts.

- This kind of question is not seen as a problem, because the analyst accepts the assumptions about causality used in *The New American Voter*, in which policy-related predispositions are assumed to be causally prior to specific issues, and the analyst also believes that there are no serious omissions of important predispositions or issues.

- There is a potential problem, despite the analyst's general acceptance of the assumptions used in *The New American Voter*, because some important issues are not included in the analysis, so that the electoral influence of some specific issues is inaccurately allocated to one or more predispositions.

- There is a serious problem with the kinds of policy-related effect estimates discussed above from *The New American Voter*, because some specific issues have an impact on general policy-related predispositions, as well as (or in addition to) the reverse process in which voters' opinions about specific policy issues are shaped by their general policy-related predispositions and partisan identifications.

- This kind of question is not really a problem, because the analyst should concentrate on the combined influence of voters' policy-related attitudes within broad policy-related domains (e.g., "economic inequality") instead of trying to assess the influence of specific policy issues (such as spending on food stamps).

- This kind of problem is not important because the analyst does not believe it is appropriate to control for *any* general policy-related predispositions, including ideological self-designation as well as beliefs about particular domains or group-related attitudes—although the analyst would choose to control for party identification.

- This kind of problem does not arise, for the same reasons as the previous position (based on the rejection of any controls for more general policy-related predispositions), but the analyst also believes that party identification should not be controlled when estimating the total effects for any specific policy issue.

All of the above perspectives are clearly present within the community of researchers who provide some kind of explanation for voters' decisions in presidential elections. With this kind of variety in basic purposes and assumptions, we should not be surprised over continuing disagreements about the "most important" factors that were involved in shaping voters' decisions in any given election.

An Alternative Approach to Issue-Related Measurement

In most national elections, voters have opinions about a large number of different topics, problems, or other kinds of "issues" that *may* play some role in shaping their impressions of national leaders or candidates. How should election surveys classify this large collection of potentially relevant topics in order to develop measures of voters' opinions concerning all of the topics involved? Put somewhat differently, what strategy should electoral researchers use in developing survey-based measures that provide the most efficient and comprehensive coverage of all the potential issues that may have had some impact on vote choice—so that they can examine the relationships between each of those measures and vote choice after the election is over? Or, what kinds of perceptions, concerns, or policy-related preferences on the part of individual citizens should be measured because the major candidates may succeed in activating those attitudes in their efforts to influence voters' choices for president? Similarly, which of these different kinds of attitudes should be used to explain variations in the level of popular approval (or disapproval) of the incumbent president and congressional leadership?

This section is based on a general conviction that satisfying answers to the preceding questions will not be obtained without a comprehensive reformulation of the way in which election surveys approach the measurement of voters' opinions about current or potential "issues." The primary objective for this and related presentations is to encourage discussion among electoral analysts concerning alternative approaches to such a reformulation. As background for those discussions, this section presents the rationale and selected results from a recent project in which many survey organizations joined forces to test one (specific) approach to the substantive questions outlined here. In particular, these results are based on a pilot version of the Survey of Governmental Objectives (SGO), which was conducted after the 1996 election, based on five different batteries of questions about current or potential objectives for the U.S. federal government.[1] As explained below, each of these question formats is designed to capture a different way in which many different topics may become an electoral "issue."

Introduction to the Survey of Governmental Objectives

Based on the substantive rationale concerning alternative types of issues in the introduction to this chapter, all SGO96 interviews began with the same five batteries of questions. Each of these batteries contained a fixed sequence of items based on the same type of "issue" concerning several different (current or potential) objectives. The initial battery of questions asked for respondents' perceptions of current conditions with respect to implicit objectives for which a broad consensus (presumably) exists concerning the federal government's general responsibilities. Questions in the four subsequent batteries are defined, respectively, in terms of the "seriousness" of different potential problems, the "appropriateness" of specific potential objectives, preferences concerning the level of "effort" that the government should be putting into alternative objectives, and preferences concerning the level of federal spending in other policy areas (where relative priority is usually discussed in terms of spending instead of effort). All of these questions (in all five batteries) were asked before any other political questions, including vote choice and all evaluations of presidential and congressional leaders.

After the initial battery of questions about current conditions, the sequence of items within each subsequent battery shifts frequently between objectives that are more frequently advocated by conservatives and those more frequently emphasized by liberals. The intended effect within each battery was to quickly expose all respondents to some statements about national or governmental objectives (or problems) with which they would easily agree and to other objectives that they would clearly reject, and to ensure that all respondents continued to be asked about some objectives that they supported and about some that they opposed. These planned switches between objectives that appealed to conservative versus liberal voters also reduced the likelihood that respondents would provide answers based on an inappropriate "response set." In each of the following sections, statistical results for specific questions are reviewed in the order they were asked, rather than grouping the stated objectives into more general topics, or into those frequently emphasized by liberals versus conservatives.

Perceptions of Current Conditions for Consensual Objectives

As emphasized above, each SGO96 interview began with a series of questions that asked "how close" the respondent thought current conditions in the United States were to goals or objectives that are presumably shared by the overwhelming majority of Americans. In particular, each respondent was asked how close the country was currently to:

- having a strong economy;
- where most people can walk in their neighborhoods without much danger of theft or violence;
- where almost any citizen who wants to work can find a job;
- having an effective defense against any military attack on this country or its allies;
- where citizens who work hard over time have a decent chance of achieving financial success; and
- where most of today's teenagers will have a good standard of living when they are adults.

Respondents used the same set of response categories to describe the nation's current situation for each of these aspects of national life, ranging from "very close to," "somewhat close to," "not too close to," to "a long way from" the stated condition.

The percentages who chose these fixed categories are not strictly comparable across the six conditions, because of differences between topics in the thresholds used to define positive or desirable conditions. Nevertheless, many observers will be interested in comparing different aspects of national life in terms of the percentages who described the United States as "very" or "somewhat" close to the above (stated) circumstances. Thus, 56% of SGO96 respondents saw the United States as very or somewhat close to having a "strong economy," 57% saw the United States as very or somewhat close to where "citizens who work hard over time have a decent chance of achieving financial success," 64% saw the country as very or somewhat close to where "almost any citizen who wants to work can find a job," and 72% saw the country as very or somewhat close to having an "effective defense" against any military attack. In contrast, only 32% saw the current United States as very or somewhat close to where "most people can walk in their own neighborhoods without much fear of theft or violence," and only 39% said that the country was very or somewhat close to where most of today's teenagers will have a "good economic standard of living when they are adults."

Relatively few aspects of national life can be described in terms of implicit goals or objectives that are almost universally shared or accepted. In the course of testing and revising the SGO96 interview schedule, questions about several current "conditions" (such as universal access to health care) were rewritten in terms of the perceived seriousness of a suggested national problem (discussed below) because several test respondents did *not* agree with the implicit appropriateness of that objective for the federal government.

Assessments of "Seriousness" for Alternative Potential Problems

The second major battery in the SGO96 questionnaire asked respondents to evaluate a series of suggestions concerning potential "problems" for the country as a whole. In particular, respondents were asked to classify each of the following suggestions as "not really a problem," a "small problem," a "serious problem," or an "extremely serious problem":

- the size of the federal budget deficit;
- the number of black people who face discrimination in hiring or promotion;
- the condition of our environment and natural resources;
- the amount of poverty in the United States;
- the number of people who have to pay the federal government too much in taxes;
- the number people who can't afford health insurance;
- the number of people who commit crimes and then aren't punished severely enough by the justice system;
- the amount of illegal drug use;
- the number of middle-income people who are likely to face economic difficulty over the next 10 years or so; and
- the amount of crime that you think will be faced by the average person 20 years or so from now.

Most of these suggested problems were seen as either "serious" or "extremely serious" by a clear majority of respondents. Thus, 88% of SGO96 respondents said that "the number of people who commit crimes and then aren't punished severely enough" was a serious or extremely serious problem, the same percentage as for "illegal drug use," followed by 87% for "the number of people who can't afford health insurance," 75% for "the size of the federal budget deficit," 73% for "the amount of poverty," and 71% for "the amount of crime that will be faced by the average person in 20 years." Several of these suggested problems, however, were *not* viewed so unanimously, and substantial numbers of respondents classified some suggestions as only a "small problem" or "not really a problem." Thus, 56% of the SGO96 sample regarded "the number of black people who face discrimination in hiring or promotion" as a small or nonexistent problem, followed by 35% for "the number of people who have to pay . . . too much in taxes," and 33% for "the condition of our environment and national resources." The two major parties in the United States have emphasized quite different sets of problems for the country as a whole, and SGO96 respondents were no different in that respect.

Preferences Concerning the Appropriateness of Alternative Governmental Objectives

The third basic SGO96 battery asked each respondent about the appropriateness (or inappropriateness) of a substantial list of potential (or suggested) objectives for the federal government. For each of these suggested objectives, we expected that many respondents would clearly prefer that the federal government *should* try to achieve that objective, while another group would say that the government *should not*. This battery of questions was designed to document those aspects of national life where we expected to see a substantial amount of conflict concerning the federal government's basic purposes or objectives. For many potential objectives, however, we were unsure how much conflict (or agreement) we would find. In particular, each respondent was asked if the federal government should—or should not:

- Make sure that every American who wants to work can find a job;
- Maintain military forces that are stronger than those of any other country;
- Use American military forces to try to stop internal fighting or civil wars in other countries;

- Try to reduce the size of the income differences between rich and poor Americans;
- Make it illegal to sell or distribute pornography to anyone;
- Give racial minorities some preferential treatment in hiring for government jobs;
- Make sure that all public school students have the opportunity to pray as a part of some official school activity;
- Make persons with higher incomes pay a larger percentage of their income in taxes than persons with lower incomes;
- Tax an individual's income from capital gains at a much lower rate than all other types of income, including salaries and wages;
- Allow homosexuals to serve in the U.S. armed forces;
- Give tax credits or vouchers to people who send their children to private schools;
- Put any restrictions on abortion;
- Make sure that all Americans have health insurance;
- Cut income taxes in some way;
- Eliminate the Department of Education in Washington; and
- Add an amendment to the U.S. Constitution that requires the federal budget to be balanced every year.

Several of these suggested objectives were accepted by substantial majorities. Thus, 83% said that the federal government *should* "maintain military forces that are stronger than those of any other country," followed by 74% for making sure that "all Americans have health insurance," 67% for cutting income taxes "in some way," and 64% for making sure that "every American who wants to work can find a job." Smaller majorities indicated that the federal government should "allow homosexuals to serve in the U.S. armed forces" (59%), change the U.S. Constitution to add an amendment that "requires the federal budget to be balanced every year" (58%), make sure that "all public school students have the opportunity to pray as a part of some official school activity" (57%), make "persons with higher incomes pay a larger percentage of their income in taxes than persons with lower incomes" (56%), and make it "illegal to sell or distribute pornography to anyone" (55%).

Other suggested objectives, however, were opposed by majorities of SGO respondents, led by 70% who thought that the federal government *should not* "give racial minorities some preferential treatment in hiring for government jobs," 68% who thought that the federal government should not "eliminate the Department of Education in Washington," 54% who thought that the government should not "use American military forces to try to stop internal fighting or civil wars in other countries," 54% who thought the federal government should not "put any restrictions on abortion," and 52% who opposed giving "tax credits or vouchers to people who send their children to private schools." Of the sixteen questions about suggested objectives in this battery, nine are more often advocated by conservative leaders and seven are more frequently advocated by liberal leaders. Because of the visibility of these ongoing conflicts, we expected that SGO respondents' views concerning the appropriateness of these potential objectives would be strongly related to their electoral choices and evaluations in 1996.

Preferences Concerning the Priority of Alternative Governmental Objectives

In many aspects of national life, the federal government is already engaged in activities or programs that are designed to reach fairly consensual objectives, but political leaders and voters may still disagree concerning the relative priority of those objectives—whether the federal government is putting too much emphasis on that objective, about the right amount, or not enough. In other words, important policy-related conflicts may exist concerning the relative urgency or priority of specific governmental programs, even though most citizens agree about the appropriateness of those objectives.

To describe such disagreements about relative priority or emphasis, the SGO96 questionnaire included two batteries of questions with the same kind of priority-related response categories. The first of these batteries asked respondents for their preferences concerning the amount of "effort" that the federal government should be placing on each (stated) objective, compared to its current activities. The objectives covered by this battery concerned the environment, punishment of criminals, job discrimination against blacks, regulation of businesses, job discrimination against homosexuals, legal immigration, illegal drugs, job discrimination against women, and gun control. For each of these objectives, respondents were asked to choose between "more," "the same," or "less" effort than the federal government is currently devoting to that objective, with additional response options for "no effort at all" and "don't know."

For five of these nine objectives, a majority of SGO96 respondents expressed a preference for "more effort" by the federal government. In particular, 83% said they wanted the government to put more effort into "making sure that people convicted of violent crimes are punished severely," and the same percentage (83%) wanted more effort on "punishing people caught with any illegal drugs." Somewhat smaller majorities favored more effort on "protecting the environment and natural resources" (62%), "restricting the kinds of guns that people can buy" (also 62%), and "restricting the number of legal immigrants" (57%). In contrast, only a minority of respondents preferred that more effort be invested in each of the other four areas, led by 49% for "trying to stop job discrimination against women," 36% for stopping "job discrimination against blacks," 33% for stopping "job discrimination against homosexuals," and only 28% for "eliminating many of the regulations that businesses have to follow"—which also had the highest percentage who preferred less (or no) effort by the federal government (25%). We anticipated that disagreement about the priority of these nonbudgetary objectives would also be clearly related to voters' electoral preferences in 1996.

The final battery of questions about alternative governmental objectives in the SGO96 questionnaire concerned the relative priority of different governmental activities where such preferences are often expressed in terms of governmental expenditures or "spending." The fifth SGO battery asked respondents if they thought the federal government should spend more, the same, or less money than it does now (or no money) on food stamps, the military, health care for poor people, nuclear missile defense, health care for retired persons or the elderly, social security benefits, assistance to poor mothers with young children, financial assistance to college students, and financial assistance to public schools.

Only two of these objectives or programs received majority support for increased spending, led by "health care for elderly people" (56%) and "financial assistance to public elementary and secondary schools" (53%), but none of these programs received less than 20% support for more spending (as was true for "providing food stamps to poor people"). The largest percentages in favor of less (or no) spending were for "providing food stamps to poor people" (30%), followed by "developing a system that would defend the U.S. against a nuclear missile attack" (21%), "providing assistance to poor mothers with children" (17%), and "maintaining a strong military defense" (15%). Because of the visibility of ongoing budgetary conflicts between the Clinton administration and Republican congressional leaders as well as between Clinton and Dole, we expected that several of these disagreements concerning federal spending would be sharply related to electoral preferences and evaluations.

Highlights Concerning the
Electoral Relevance of Specific Issues

Based on the different types of "issues" and alternative electoral explanations discussed above, how useful are the five batteries of questions in the 1996 Survey of Governmental Objectives in differentiating between voters who chose Bill Clinton for president from those who chose Bob Dole? To be sure, each question concerning a current condition, the seriousness of a specific problem, the appropriateness of a particular governmental objective, or the priority for a specific objective (in terms of effort or spending) was included in this pilot survey because some researchers suggested that it might be useful in explaining electoral choices or evaluations in 1996. Before this study, however, we encountered a substantial amount of disagreement in expectations concerning the *size* of the relationships that were likely to emerge between each of these questions and vote choice. To answer these kinds of descriptive questions, the following paragraphs summarize the basic relationships with vote choice (between Clinton and Dole) for each individual question within the five basic batteries.

Of the six SGO conditions within battery one whose distributions were reviewed in the previous section, three exhibit relationships with vote choice in 1996 that appear to support the simple pattern of incumbent reward or punishment discussed in the introduction of this chapter. The relationships between respondents' vote choice for president and their perceptions of the economy, safety from crime, and the effectiveness of U.S. military defense were at least consistent with the idea that positive perceptions of current conditions concerning consensual governmental objectives may lead to increased support for the incumbent administration, and negative conditions lead to a decline in that support. Thus, the percentage who supported Clinton (instead of Dole) went down by 35% as we shift from voters who saw the United States as "very close" to having "a strong economy" to those who saw the country as "a long way" from that desirable condition. Similar, although somewhat weaker, differences of that sort can be seen for perceptions of Americans' safety in their own neighborhoods (with a difference of 27%) and the effectiveness of U.S. defense against military attack (with a difference of 26%).

This simple interpretation, however, may not be appropriate for some of the objectives that we had presumed to be consensual, for the other three conditions in this battery exhibit the opposite tendency, with support for Clinton going up (not down) as perceptions of current conditions in those areas go from positive to negative. In particular, support for Clinton goes up (or support for Dole goes down) by 28% as we shift from voters who thought the United States was "very close" to a situation in which "almost any citizen who wants to work can find a job" to those who thought the country was "a long way from" such a condition, with intermediate divisions of the vote for those who selected one of the less extreme responses to that question. On the basis of that result, it seems plausible that the relationships between perceptions concerning crime and national defense are also at least partially produced by the policy-related tendency of voters who are more supportive of additional military expenditures and "tougher" policies against criminals to prefer more conservative candidates—instead of a simple mechanism in which the Clinton administration is rewarded for positive conditions and punished for negative ones. Because of this ambiguity, we have set aside the potential electoral consequences of voters' perceptions of current conditions for most of what follows.

SGO respondents' evaluations of the "seriousness" of alternative suggestions concerning potential national problems (based on the second SGO battery) were almost universally linked to vote choice in ways that suggest the policy-related appeal of contrasting agendas emphasized by the two parties and their candidates, rather than simple reward or punishment for the incumbent. Very large differences (in vote choice) can be seen between respondents who thought a given suggestion was "not a problem" or only a "small problem" and those who called it an "extremely serious" problem. These differences include a 45% increase in the percentage who supported Clinton as we shift from respondents who thought that "the number of black people who face discrimination in hiring or promotion" is not a problem (or only a small one) to those who saw it as an extremely serious problem. Similarly, support for Clinton rises by 44%

as we move from individuals who thought "the number of people who can't afford health insurance" is not a problem (or only a small one) to those who saw that problem as extremely serious. Similar patterns can be seen for "the condition of the environment and natural resources" and "the amount of poverty."

In contrast, support for Clinton goes down (or support for Dole goes up) as we move from voters who saw several of the traditional conservative concerns as "not a problem" (or only a small one) to those who saw such problems as extremely serious. Substantial differences of that sort can be seen for assessments of the federal deficit, the number of people who pay too much in taxes, and three different assessments of problems that are defined in terms of crime. Those differences in voting behavior, however, can also be seen as consequences of disagreement (or conflict) about the importance of those problems instead of simple incumbent punishment. As emphasized earlier, a key hypothesis concerning the electoral relevance of these assessments concerns the degree to which voters may be attracted to the party or candidate that emphasizes an "agenda" of national problems that comes closest to their own.

The third, and longest, battery of questions in the 1996 SGO questionnaire was designed to identify potential objectives for which American citizens exhibit substantial levels of disagreement about the role or responsibility of the federal government. For each of the potential governmental objectives included in this battery, some SGO-affiliated researchers expected to see a relationship between respondents' opinions about its appropriateness and their electoral preferences in 1996. They were not disappointed.

Four of these questions exhibited differences in vote choice of over 40%, based on the differences between groups of respondents who thought that the federal government should—or should not—"make sure that every American who wants to work can find a job" (43%), "allow homosexuals to serve in the U.S. armed forces" (42%), "make sure that all Americans have health insurance" (52%), and "eliminate the Department of Education in Washington" (50%). All of the rest of our potential objectives exhibited this kind of difference in vote choice of at least 12%, and many showed differences of 20% to 25%. Visible, but only moderate, differences of this sort appeared for objectives defined in terms of military strength, peacekeeping missions, income differences between rich and poor, pornography, affirmative action, school prayer, progressive income tax rates, capital gains, school vouchers, abortion, cutting taxes, and the balanced budget amendment. Furthermore, all of those differences in vote choice followed the expected or predicted pattern. That is, Clinton always did better among respondents who supported more liberal objectives and among respondents who opposed more conservative objectives—and Dole always did better among respondents who supported more conservative objectives and opposed more liberal objectives. As emphasized below, much remains to be done in reviewing alternative strategies for combining responses to several SGO questions in order to produce the most appropriate measures of policy-related preferences for different aspects of national life. Any reasonable strategy for item combination, however, will clearly include many of these questions concerning the appropriateness of different potential objectives.

Finally, as discussed earlier, we also expected to see substantial relationships between respondents' vote choice and their preferences concerning the federal government's priority in pursuing a variety of established objectives, where priority is measured in terms of either the level of effort that should be given to that objective (based on the fourth SGO battery) or the federal government's level of spending on that objective (based on the fifth battery). In fact, very large relationships of that sort can be seen for many of our questions concerning governmental effort and spending. Thus, differences in vote choice of over 40% can be seen between groups of respondents who preferred that more versus less (or no) effort be devoted to "protecting the environment and natural resources"(52%) and "trying to stop job discrimination against gay men and lesbians" (42%), and equally large differences can be seen concerning the level of federal spending in "providing food stamps to poor people" (46%), "maintaining a strong defense" (50%), "providing health care for poor people" (48%), "providing health care for elderly people" (41%), and "providing financial assistance to public elementary and secondary schools" (42%). Furthermore, all but one of the other questions concerning the level of governmental effort or spending produced differences in vote choice of at least 12%.

Several of these questions, however, deal with similar or related policy issues, so that some of these differences in vote choice may be due to a smaller number of more general preferences. For that reason, we have also explored the relationships between vote choice and a series of summary measures concerning broader topics or dimensions. In general, most electoral analysts are interested in these kinds of summary measures because they permit us to assess the (combined) electoral consequences of voters' attitudes concerning more general policy-related topics or aspects of national life—such as taxes, the environment, health care, racial minorities, abortion, education, aid to the disadvantaged, the federal budget deficit, homosexuality, and so forth. In other words, electoral analysts often want to summarize the impact of voter's opinions concerning particular policy-related topics and (at least temporarily) ignore the extent to which that influence is based on the seriousness of suggested problems, on conflicts about the appropriateness of specific objectives, or on disagreements about priority or emphasis.

To begin that kind of assessment, we have grouped all of the answers given by SGO96 respondents concerning each of several policy-related topics that were drafted with the questionnaire, including (for each topic) any questions that were asked about specific problems, appropriateness of objectives, and preferences concerning governmental effort or spending. In particular, we have combined all of our available questions concerning each of the following policy-related topics in order to assess their electoral relevance in 1996:

- the federal budget deficit;
- the overall level of federal taxes;
- differential tax rates for capital gains or different levels of income;
- programs for the disadvantaged;
- programs for the retired or elderly;
- other health care issues;
- environmental protection;
- business regulation;
- education;
- military strength and defense;
- foreign peacekeeping;
- crime, including punishment, drugs, and guns;
- abortion;
- racial discrimination;
- homosexuality;
- pornography;
- school prayer; and
- legal immigration.

From a variety of analyses, it is clear that most of our summary measures for these policy-related topics covered by the 1996 SGO questionnaire had substantial relationships with vote choice, and almost all of those maintained a significant relationship after we controlled for social and economic characteristics *and* partisan identification. The larger standardized regression coefficients for these measures produced by analyses with that limited set of controls appear to be based on voters' preferences concerning tax levels and differential rates (0.13 and 0.11), health care (0.22), the environment (0.10), education (0.16), defense (0.10), crime (0.15), abortion (0.17), discrimination based on race and gender (both 0.13), and homosexuality (0.17). When we add controls for all of the other summary variables that exhibited significant apparent effects, however, the resulting coefficients for most of these policy-related topics are reduced to much smaller (if not insignificant) values.

For that reason, several of these summary variables concerning specific policy-related topics have been combined into a smaller number of summary measures for somewhat broader *domains*. Standardized coefficients for those more general domains are presented in Table 7.1. From those results, it would appear that economic issues concerning health care and/or assistance to the disadvantaged were slightly more "important" in shaping individual voters' preferences than any other cluster of policy-related conflicts, based on a standardized coefficient of 0.18 after we control for social and economic characteristics, partisan identification, ideological self-designation, and the perceived state of the economy, as well as the other summary measures in this analysis. Our summary measure for policy-related opinions concerning "social" or "moral" issues came in a close second, based on a standardized coefficient of 0.13 in the same multivariate analysis. Combined preferences concerning taxes and the federal deficit, that is, fiscal policy, exhibited a smaller standardized coefficient (0.08) in this summary analysis, and all of the other coefficients failed to pass our threshold for statistical significance based on this pilot survey.

From this final analysis, we should also note that the standardized coefficient for partisan identification is 0.51, approximately the same as in parallel analyses of several surveys conducted by the National Election Studies (see below), and that the standardized coefficient for the SGO question concerning the current state of the national economy is only 0.10. A more striking aspect of this summary

TABLE 7.1   Apparent Combined Effects of Broader Policy-Related Domains on Votes (N = 416 Two-Party Voters)

General content of policy related conflicts or topic	Standardized bivariate coefficient[a]	With social and economic characteristics held constant	With party identification also held constant	With all other variables also held constant
Budget and tax topics	0.40	0.39	0.17	0.08
Disadvantaged and health care	0.49	0.43	0.23	0.18
Programs for retired/elderly	0.22	0.17	0.08	(0.02)
Environmental protection	0.30	0.25	0.10	(-0.01)
Education	0.43	0.39	0.16	(0.03)
Defense and crime/drugs/guns	0.35	0.36	0.15	(0.05)
Foreign peacekeeping	0.10	0.12	0.08	(0.05)
Racial discrimination	0.34	0.29	0.13	(0.00)
Other "social" issues (abortion, sex, gender, prayer)	0.41	0.43	0.21	0.13
For comparison:				
Party identification	0.71	0.68		0.51
Self-designated ideology	0.44	0.40	0.14	(0.00)
State of the economy	0.19	0.24	0.14	0.10

[a]Coefficient appears in parentheses if the associated p value is > 0.1.

analysis is the fact that the apparent impact of liberal versus conservative self-designation drops to 0.00 after we control for all of our summary measures for policy-related opinions in specific substantive domains. In this pilot survey, it would appear that all of the statistical "connection" between general liberal or conservative orientations and vote choice can be attributed to opinions about specific policy-related controversies, and that our instrument was quite successful in capturing those specific opinions.

Comparisons Between 1996 Analyses Based on SGO and NES Data

Many of the preceding substantive questions about the role of specific issues or topics in the 1996 presidential election can also be addressed with 1996 data from the National Election Studies. As discussed earlier, the author is also engaged in a comprehensive analysis of those materials (Shanks et al., 1999) and has compared similar kinds of results from NES and SGO concerning the apparent electoral relevance of specific issues, topics, and domains. Because of the large number of alternative measures and comparisons involved, however, this chapter provides only a few observations concerning the similarities and differences between results based on these alternative approaches to the conceptualization and measurement of electoral "issues."

Only one policy-related topic, concerning health care, showed significant total effects in both surveys, after we controlled for perceptions of the national economy, other policy-related preferences, and partisan identification, as well as social and economic characteristics. The NES measure of policy preferences concerning health care was a 7-point scale, with opposite positions defined in terms of a choice between private insurance and a government-operated plan. The SGO96 health care index included questions about the appropriateness of the federal government "making sure all Americans have health insurance" and the "seriousness" of a problem defined in terms of "the number of people who cannot afford health insurance."

There is also some agreement between the two surveys concerning the electoral relevance of one other type of issue concerning homosexuality and gay rights. A two-item NES index concerning policy preferences in this area was the only other measure concerning a current policy issue (besides health insurance) that exhibited a substantial apparent (total) effect on the vote choice, with the same set of variables held constant. In SGO96, sizable coefficients remained for homosexuality items after we controlled for partisan identification, but—possibly owing to the smaller sample size compared to NES—the total effect coefficient for that variable was not statistically significant.

Results from these two surveys were also in agreement concerning a variety of policy-related topics for which the 1996 relationship between voters' own policy preferences and their vote choice (between Dole and Clinton) was weak or nonexistent. The clearest examples of this kind of parallel (negative) results concerned school prayer and limitations on immigration. After we controlled for partisan identification, ideology, and other policy-related topics, voters' opinions about defense also seemed to have very little influence in our analyses of both 1996 surveys, making this the first presidential election in decades without some visible role for voters' defense-related preferences. Also, despite general Democratic attacks on the Republicans concerning Social Security, opinions about that topic did not seem to predict the vote in either survey.

SGO96 included questions about federal spending on Medicare and Medicaid, but NES did not. Even for this highly salient campaign theme (concerning Medicare), however, we found little evidence that voters' policy preferences concerning that specific issue had an independent impact on their choice between Dole and Clinton, over and above the influence of more general opinions about health care. The same negative results prevailed for another major campaign issue, education, regardless of whether the underlying survey questions involved the role of the federal government in that area, federal spending, or private school vouchers. The list of other topics that failed to exhibit an independent impact on vote choice in 1996 in either survey is fairly long, including opinions about environmental protection, federal spending on the disadvantaged, programs to fight racial discrimination and promote affirmative action, governmental toughness against crime and drugs, regulations on guns, and the overall budget deficit.

There were at least two major policy-related topics for which results from SGO96 and the 1996 NES survey appear to conflict. Based on results from SGO96, policy preferences concerning abortion appeared to have some independent impact on vote choice after we controlled for other policy-related preferences as well as partisan identification, economic conditions, and social and economic characteristics, but the parallel coefficient from analyses of the 1996 NES survey is very small (and insignificant). One potential explanation of this discrepancy concerns the possibility that SGO questions may have done a better job in capturing the effects of disagreements concerning the stage (or trimester) during pregnancy at which an abortion takes place. The other topic with conflicting results between the two surveys concerned taxes, where SGO results showed a significant total effect, whereas a simple replication of the analytic procedures used in *The New American Voter* did not. This discrepancy may also have occurred because SGO questions about taxes were more clearly linked to differences between the candidates in their approaches to that topic, but such differences may also have arisen because of other differences (between the two surveys) in the other variables being controlled, or in the socioeconomic composition of the samples.

We should note that most of our analyses of the 1996 NES data have been structured to facilitate comparisons with parallel results from the 1992 election discussed in *The New American Voter* (Miller and Shanks, 1996), and that the analytic categories used to define and select specific measures explanatory variables for those NES analyses are not strictly comparable to those used in the 1996 Survey of Governmental Objectives. Furthermore, the summary measures used in the foregoing SGO96 analyses were not based on any kind of item combination that concentrates on the "best" predictors of the vote, or that discards items with only weak relationships with vote choice (as was the case with the NES analyses). For these reasons, all of the preceding comparisons between results based on the SGO and NES surveys should be regarded as suggestive, instead of definitive. It does seem clear, however, that the apparent electoral relevance of some policy-related topics depends on the way in which specific issues are defined and measured.

Major Candidates' Positions on Specific Policy-Related Issues

A major advantage of the SGO96 batteries is their ability to cover a substantial number of questions about different governmental objectives with a common frame of reference or perspective. The same approach can also be used to fairly quickly obtain respondents' impressions of the "positions" of a given candidate on several issues, using the same response categories that were used to record the respondents' own views. To test that possibility, the 1996 SGO asked half of all respondents to describe Bob Dole's and Bill Clinton's positions concerning the most appropriate level of governmental effort or financing of several objectives, and the other (randomly selected) half of the sample was asked to "place" both candidates concerning their positions on spending on several objectives. Several SGO96 participants were interested in this alternative approach to candidate "placements," but no definitive conclusions have emerged from analyses that take advantage of those measures.

Utilization of SGO Batteries in Future Surveys

In future presidential elections, SGO-affiliated researchers will recommend that the U.S. National Election Studies adopt some of the SGO batteries concerning voters' perceptions of current national conditions, their assessments of the seriousness of various problems, their views concerning the appropriateness of potential objectives, and their preferences concerning the relative priority of current objectives (in terms of effort, as well as the continuing NES battery concerning federal spending). If (or when) enough analysts request these question formats (or batteries), that kind of change in the NES interview schedule may eventually be made, but such a shift would clearly involve some difficult choices. Because of their comprehensive nature, the SGO batteries require a substantial amount of interview time, and all of the new questions involved must compete with a large number of continuing NES questions that serve many different analytic purposes, including questions that have been asked for several previous elections, and some with an unbroken time series since the 1960s.

In recent years, several recommendations have been submitted to the NES Board of Overseers concerning the desirability of comprehensive batteries of questions like those discussed in this chapter. These recommendations for change have been difficult to evaluate, because the analyses that could resolve these completing claims on the NES interview schedule would require that new questions about each topic be asked of a substantial subset of respondents who have also answered the established or traditional NES questions about the same "issues"—and no existing survey includes all of those questions. Given that difficulty, we believe that much more evidence from other surveys will be needed before these batteries are likely to be adopted for the full range of potential governmental objectives in future NES surveys.

Alternative Strategies and Designs

In addition to their potential utilization in future NES surveys, these kinds of questions would be more useful for a variety of analytic purposes if they were administered frequently over time, and if respondents from earlier points in time were reinterviewed after the next national election. Postelection reinterviews with respondents who had answered questions about alternative objectives many months before the campaign can provide direct evidence concerning the degree to which apparent effects based on more proximate pre-election interviews are subject to persuasion effects or other forms of "endogeneity bias." For that reason, we intend to initiate a continuing version of the Survey of Governmental Objectives that uses a "continuous monitoring" design like the one used in the 1984 U.S. NES and in two recent Canadian election studies (Johnston et al., 1992). A similar, but much larger, version of that design is also being used for the presidential election study being conducted in 2000 by the Annenberg School for Communication—a project that initiated the colloquium on which this book is based. Since that seminar, the Annenberg 2000 survey has decided to use many of the preceding SGO-type questions, but the interview time required for other measurement objectives in that project has led to an initial set of batteries that do not "cover" all of the alternative (specific) issues concerning each potentially relevant topic.

Implications for the 2000 Election

These very general questions about electoral behavior and survey design have always taken on a more immediate and specific form as electoral researchers prepared for the next national election. Such questions are certain to arise in both popular and scientific interpretations of voters' evaluations of specific candidates (and final choices) in the 2000 election. In particular, it seems inevitable that analyses of survey data collected before and after the 2000 election will focus on the following kinds of questions:

1. Which policy-related *topics* played a visible role in shaping voters' choices, in the sense that voters' own attitudes toward some aspect(s) of these topics influenced their evaluation of the Republican or Democratic candidate? For example, did voters' attitudes toward some aspects of taxes really make a difference? How about health care? School vouchers or some other aspect of education? Abortion? Homosexuality? Campaign finance reform? Gun control or some other aspect of crime? Affirmative action or some other aspect of race, or immigration? Issues concerning defense or foreign policy? The environment? Or some other topic?

2. For each of these potentially important topics, post-election analysts will also suggest somewhat different interpretations of the way in which that general topic influenced electoral decisions because they are based on different *specific issues* concerning that topic—or on different *aspects* of that topic. For example, analysts will not be satisfied to conclude that voters' attitudes toward "health care" played

some role in shaping their ultimate choice for president. Social scientists and politicians will want to know which aspects of that topic were involved—or which *specific* policy-related issues. Should we primarily describe the influence of this topic in terms of voters' opinions concerning the seriousness of the "problem" defined in terms of the number of Americans without health insurance? Or their views concerning the appropriateness (or inappropriateness) of particular governmental objectives in this area? Or their preferences for more or less federal spending on specific health-related programs? Or their attitudes toward a change in federal regulation, of insurance plans or HMOs?

3. In addition to potential disagreements concerning the specific issues that are important within each policy-related topic, electoral researchers will also disagree about the most appropriate *level* of generality (or specificity) in describing the influence of voters' policy-related attitudes. Should we concentrate on improving our estimates for the combined influence of all policy-related attitudes on vote choice? Or should our major efforts be devoted to assessing the combined influence of attitudes toward a small number of general substantive domains, such as "economic equality" or "morality"? Alternatively, should our explanatory effort focus on particular policy-related topics within those domains, such as taxes, health care, or aid to the poor (within the broad collection of concern about inequality)?

None of these questions will be "resolved" in the near future. These kinds of disagreements are likely to persist for quite some time, even if all parties to such controversies had access to the same comprehensive collection of survey-based measures and designs, so that they could compare results based on different perspectives. In short, there is a lot of work to be done in developing better measures (at different levels of generality), in testing alternative designs to test different ideas about causation and change, and in trying to make sense of all the resulting data. Together, these unresolved questions represent a major challenge to the electoral field. They should lead to a variety of parallel inquiries, rather than a single or dominant approach.

Concluding Observations

On the basis of the perspective outlined here, this chapter has argued that electoral analysts need to know which controversies about current or potential governmental objectives do play some kind of role in shaping voters' evaluations of the major candidates before any given election—and which such controversies do not. In most elections, each of the potential issues is defined in terms of some aspect of one or more governmental objectives that have been advocated or emphasized by the candidates. From this perspective, the best (and perhaps the only) way to identify the specific issues that play some role in shaping voters' choices is to ask survey respondents a comprehensive set of questions about the explicit or implicit objectives involved—each of which may be defined in terms of current conditions, potential problems, the appropriateness of governmental responsibility, or relative priorities.

In other words, electoral researchers may have no satisfactory alternative other than trying to produce a fairly comprehensive description of voters' opinions about potential issues by asking questions about many different topics within a series of common formats (or batteries). This approach is designed to provide a "survey" of alternative or potential governmental objectives as well as a representative sample of the American electorate. Those of us who are pursuing the SGO-based approach concerning alternative government objectives look forward to discussing any alternative approach suggested by researchers who share our interest in comprehensive issue-related measurement.

Notes

1. An earlier presentation of these results appeared in Shanks and Strand (1998) and Shanks (1999).

References

Abramowitz, Alan I. 1995. "It's Abortion Stupid: Policy Voting in the 1992 Presidential Election." *Journal of Politics* 57: 176–186.

Alvarez, R. Michael, and Jonathan Nagler. 1998. "Economics, Entitlements, and Social Issues: Voter Choice in the 1996 Presidential Election." *American Journal of Political Science* 42: 1348–1363.

Asher, Herbert B. 1992. *Presidential Elections and American Politics,* 5th ed. Belmont, Calif.: Wadsworth.

Brody, Richard A., and Benjamin I. Page. 1972. "Comment: The Assessment of Policy Voting." *American Political Science Review* 66: 450–458.

Campbell, Angus, Gerald Gurin, and Warren E. Miller. 1954. *The Voter Decides.* Evanston, Ill.: Row Peterson.

Campbell, Angus, Phillip E. Converse, Warren E. Miller, and Donald E. Stokes. 1960. *The American Voter*. Chicago: University of Chicago Press.

Carmines, Edward G., and James A. Stimson. 1980. "The Two Faces of Issue Voting." *American Political Science Review* 74: 78–91.

Converse, Philip. E. 1964. "The Nature of Belief Systems in Mass Publics." In *Ideology and Discontent*, David E. Apter, ed., pp. 206–261. London: The Free Press of Glencoe.

Feldman, Stanley. 1983. *Report on Values in the 1983 NES Pilot Survey*. National Election Studies.

Fiorina, Morris. 1981. *Retrospective Voting in American National Elections*. New Haven: Yale University Press.

Franklin, Charles H., and John E. Jackson. 1983. "The Dynamics of Party Identification." *American Political Science Review* 77: 957–973.

Funk, Carolyn L. 1997. Candidate-Based Voting Behavior: Understanding Images of U.S. Presidents. Paper presented at the Annual Meeting of the American Political Science Association, August 1997, Washington, D.C.

Jackson, John E. 1975. "Issues, Party Choices, and Presidential Votes." *American Journal of Political Science* 19: 161–185.

Johnston, Richard, Andre Blais, Henry Brady, and Jean Crete. 1992. *Letting the People Decide: Dynamics of a Canadian Election*. McGill-Queen's University Press.

Kelley, Stanley, Jr. 1983. *Interpreting Elections*. Princeton: Princeton University Press.

Kinder, Donald R., and Lynn M. Sanders. 1996. *Divided by Color: Racial Politics and Democratic Ideals*. Chicago: University of Chicago Press.

Kinder, Donald R, Mark D. Peters, Robert P. Abelson, and Susan T. Fiske. 1980. "Presidential Prototypes." *Political Behavior* 2: 315–338.

Lodge, Milton, Kathleen McGraw, and Patrick Stroh. 1989. "An Impression-Driven Model of Candidate Evaluation." *American Political Science Review* 83: 399–420.

Luskin, Robert C. 1987. "Measuring Political Sophistication." *American Journal of Political Science* 31: 856–899.

Marcus, Gregory B. 1992. "The Impact of Personal and National Economic Conditions on Presidential Voting, 1954–1988." *American Journal of Political Science* 36: 829–834.

Miller, Arthur H., and Warren E. Miller. 1976. "A Majority Party in Disarray." *American Political Science Review* 70: 753–778.

Miller, Warren E., and J. Merrill Shanks. 1996. *The New American Voter*. Cambridge, Mass.: Harvard University Press.

Nisbett, R. E., and T. D. Wilson. 1977. "Telling More Than We Know: Verbal Reports of Mental Processes." *Psychological Review* 84: 231–259.

Page, Benjamin, and Calvin Jones. 1979. "Reciprocal Effects of Policy Preferences, Party Loyalties, and the Vote." *American Political Science Review* 66: 979–985.

Page, Benjamin I., and Richard A. Brody. 1972. "Policy Voting and the Electoral Process: The Vietnam War Issue." *American Political Science Review* 66: 979–995.

Shanks, J. Merrill. 1999. "Political Agendas." In *Measures of Political Attitudes*, John P. Robinson, Phillip R. Shaver, and Lawrence S. Wrightsman, eds., pp. 641–680. New York: Academic Press.

Shanks, J. Merrill, and Douglas Alan Strand. 1998. Understanding Issue Voting in Presidential Elections: Results from the 1996 Survey of Governmental Objectives. Paper presented at the Annual Meeting of the American Association of Public Opinion Research, May 14–17, 1998, St. Louis.

Shanks, J. Merrill, Douglas A. Strand, and Warren E. Miller. 1999. The Electoral Relevance of General Policy-Related Predispositions and Specific Issues: Conflicting Interpretations of the 1996 Presidential Election. Paper presented at the Annual Meeting of the American Political Science Association, September 2–5, 1999.

Smith, Eric R. A. N. 1989. *The Unchanging American Voter*. Berkeley: University of California Press.

Wattenberg, Martin P. 1991. *The Rise of Candidate-Centered Politics*. Cambridge, Mass.: Harvard University Press.

Zaller, John R. 1992. *The Nature and Origins of Mass Opinions*. Cambridge, England: Cambridge University Press.

8

POLITICAL COMMUNICATION SCHOLARSHIP: THE USES OF ELECTION RESEARCH

JAY G. BLUMLER AND DENIS MCQUAIL

Democratic elections are culled for data by political scientists and communication researchers, rather like terrain regularly visited by two swarms of locusts, each intent on stripping them of all available nutrients. Of course their interests overlap to some degree: many communication scholars expect the factors they study to have political consequences, while many political scientists appreciate the central roles of communication in campaigning and government. Nevertheless, their goals also diverge, since for political scientists elections matter chiefly for their impact on political institutions and processes or as sources of data for explaining voting behavior, whereas media scholars regard them as occasions when institutions and citizens disclose much about how they produce, process, and receive communications within a political context. Taking the latter perspective, the aim of this chapter differs from that of most other chapters in this volume. It is to review and assess the contributions of election campaign research to *communication* studies and especially to the development of political communications as an increasingly specialist and self-confident field within it.[1]

Assessments of how the political communications field has been influenced by the long-standing prominence of election research are surprisingly rare in the literature. Lacking a strand of such audits to build on, we can therefore offer little more than an initial stocktaking, the perspective of which is influenced partly by our own experience in designing and publishing a British election campaign study in the 1960s (Blumler and McQuail, 1968/1969).

Of course elections are just one of a much larger category of events in which communication processes are central. But certain properties explain their attraction as a repeated object of study. They have been chosen partly because of the volume and intensity of competing communication flows that they generate, promising thereby to reveal something about the working of political institutions in their communication aspects and of media institutions in their political aspects. They also reveal something of the behavior of audience members in their roles as citizens, and of the forces that shape interrelations and interactions across the different levels. The presumed salience of campaigns for learning and decisionmaking has been a factor as well. Elections have also been favored because they constitute more or less ideal "field experiments," in which causal influences can be studied under natural conditions and for which fieldwork can be prepared well in advance. Not unimportant, finally, is the public significance of elections, which makes it easier to find funding for research.

Quantitatively, then, election communication research undoubtedly flourishes. Many scholars engage in it, and numerous monographs, texts, readers, and articles continually emerge from it. Thus a special issue of *American Behavioral Scientist* reported empirical findings from 20 studies carried out during the U.S. presidential campaign of 1996 by 28 communication scholars (Payne, 1997). The same event was also investigated by 29 members of a National Election Research Team, whose results from data gathered in 17 states appear in a 25-chapter monograph (Kaid and Bystrom, 1999). Similarly, a book on political communications in Britain's general election of 1997 (the latest in a series of such volumes going back to the 1979 election) comprises 18 chapters (Crewe et al., 1998).

A relative measure of the importance of election research to the political communications field can be calculated by considering the focus of articles published in its two leading journals. In both cases election campaigns have been far and away the most important site of the enquiries reported. Out of 68 main articles printed in *Press/Politics* since its inauguration in 1996, 28 or 41 percent centered on election campaign data and analyses (rising to 47 percent if four articles that referred less comprehensively to such material are also included). Of 166 articles that appeared in *Political Communication* since its relaunch in 1993 as a joint organ of the International Communication Association and the Political Communication Division of the American Political Science Association, 55 or 33 percent were based on election campaigns (rising to 40 percent when 13 other articles that also included election references are added).

Such quantitative indicators, however, provoke some issues of justification. Has the devotion of heavy financial, intellectual, and publishing resources to this enterprise been worth it? What exactly are its main advantages and limitations? What may be its future in the emerging more complex political communication system of present-day media abundance? In the following sections we consider the place of election research in political communication scholarship from three standpoints: historically, analytically, and prescriptively.

Elections in Political Communication Research: A Historical Overview

The story of cumulative political communication scholarship starts with election studies in the United States in the 1940s and has unfolded ever since in line with key developments in campaign-based research. According to Nimmo and Swanson (1990: 8), communication in election campaigning has been a main source of "the field's rough-and-ready identity." Writing specifically about the United States, Chaffee and Jamieson (1994: 261) state that "Presidential election campaigns have provided the setting for innovative research on communication processes for more than half a century." We understand, having ourselves experienced it, their stress on elections as goads to innovation. When scholars contemplate researching such a periodically recurrent and much-studied event as a campaign, they may be challenged to advance understandings by doing it somewhat differently than before.

Before fleshing out the story, however, it may be useful to summarize the leading trends in election research relating to the political communications field in the postwar period. In roughly the first two decades, much campaign research was conducted within what has been called "the voter persuasion paradigm" (McQuail, 1977; Nimmo and Swanson, 1990), which sought primarily to understand media influences on political attitudes and voting decisions. But when its outcomes were authoritatively summarized by Klapper (1960), they showed so little scope for communication factors that there seemed little point in persevering with the paradigm itself. This was something of a polarizing watershed. An increasingly insurgent school of critical thinkers turned their backs on campaign research, objecting that election choices are essentially slight and spurious and that the role of communication in upholding social and political power must be sought elsewhere, namely, in media-propagated ideologies supportive of the institutional status quo. The more empirically minded scholars persisted with campaign research but took much of it in fresh directions, principally advancing down three avenues: cognitive, systemic, and normative. Highly influential in each of these was a widely shared perception of the increasing importance of television news as a prime source of the public's awareness of politics. This encouraged scholarly attention to (1) how people process audiovisual information, (2) politician–journalist relations, including how politicians adapt to news imperatives and seek to bend them to their needs, as well as how journalists react to such attempts at news management, and (3) whether what emerges in the media satisfies appropriate requirements of informed and involved citizenship.

The Classic Foundations

A connection between the field of communication research and political science was forged rather fortuitously by the example and influence of Lazarsfeld et al. (1944) in their research on the 1940 U.S. presidential election. The main aim of that research was to shed light on the process of the development of public opinion and the influences on this process. In retrospect, it may not be going too far to suggest that it is the phenomenon of public opinion that explains much of the sharing of interests of political scientists and communication researchers. For the former, public opinion matters because it can be transformed via voting in particular into political power. For the latter, public opinion in itself accounts for a large share of the potential consequences of communication, and voting is mainly of interest as an outcome that is reliably measurable. Even before 1940, public opinion was well established as an object of study for communication research.

The experiences of the war years led to heightened expectations about the possibility of applying the mass media to influence opinion and behavior for policy purposes. In the preface to the 1948 edition of *The People's Choice*, the authors write that "If their [social scientists'] work is to yield useful and usable knowledge, they must focus their attention on areas of central significance, and they must, at the same time, approach their problems through techniques which lead to empirical facts" (p. viii). In these remarks we can find some clues to underlying features of the foundation years of the election research tradition. These features included a strong emphasis on policy relevance, on studying "significant" events (i.e., elections), and on producing useful, factually grounded knowledge. In practice, "useful" tended to be translated as useful to those who wanted to persuade the public, and the main emphasis in campaign research was on *effectiveness* from the communicator's point of view.

In any case, the postwar renewal (and in most of Europe, the foundation) of communication research was strongly under the influence of these tendencies, especially evident in election campaign research. *The People's Choice* was pored over for clues to the power of the mass media and also as a methodological model for the conduct of research situated within the "voter persuasion paradigm." It should have made somewhat sobering reading, since it demonstrated a very limited degree of change in political choices and also a limited scope for direct media effects. According to a widely circulated and highly influential formulation in chapter IX of Lazarsfeld et al. (1944: 87), for the largest number of voters "political communications served the important purpose of preserving prior decisions instead of initiating new decisions . . . It had the effect of *reinforcing* the original vote decisions" [emphasis added].

However, the study also opened up new pathways for research by highlighting the importance of *interest* (and its social and demographic antecedents) in determining the extent of participation and the use of media. The latter was characterized by selective exposure and varying involvement. It also pointed to the indirect effects produced by way of informal "opinion leaders" (positioned on top of the ladder of "interest") and in general the importance of the immediate social environment. Furthermore, the study directed attention to media influences on political knowledge and attitudes as well as on voting. All in all a rich spectrum of possibilities was opened up, and these were eagerly pursued in a sequence of studies of U.S. presidential elections (e.g., Berelson et al., 1954).

Despite the expectations, the resources applied, and the impressive methodologies developed, the results of this early phase of election communication research did not go much further, when expressed in general terms, than the findings of Lazarsfeld et al. But they did provide a good base of ideas, concepts, and methods. The significance of a person's prior social commitments, attitudes, and identifications for response to attempted persuasion was further underlined and clarified, at the same time setting clear limits to what persuasion can be expected to achieve. Communication flows were revealed to follow complex and indirect paths rather than in unmediated ways from medium to mass audience. Important distinctions between types of effects were introduced, with special emphasis on the interplay between cognitive and affective elements. Among cognitive matters, the links between the "issues" around which opinion formed and the policy proposals and issue identification of parties were explored. The complexity of individual movements to and fro over a period of time was revealed, challenging the idea that campaigns cause little change. Some doubts were also cast (especially in the concluding chapter of Berelson et al., 1954) on the knowledgeability, principled thoughtfulness, zest to participate, and "rationality" of the typical voter, showing that he "was not all what the theory of democracy required of him," and raising fundamental questions about political communication, democracy, and citizenship.

What research of the early classic period did not seem able to do was to actually account for the contribution of media to the result of any given election or to provide practical lessons for future campaigning strategy and tactics. In this respect, election research certainly contributed to the sense of disillusion about communication research itself that was expressed by some participants at the time (e.g., by Berelson, 1959) and is now written into the history of the field. This "disillusion" can better be understood as the end of illusions about the amount of difference that media can make to such complex events as elections. This applied not only to elections, but also to the study of persuasion effects more generally. From the early 1960s there was a search for alternative lines of communication research and for new approaches to old problems (even that of "persuasion" in a somewhat different guise).

From the perspective of communication research, the apparent paucity of significant findings about the influence of mass media in election campaigns is not too difficult to account for, quite apart from the power of methods available, especially with the benefit of hindsight. Early expectations about the role of the media were often naive or misplaced, reflecting more the optimism of candidates or the oversell of the communication industries. It was unrealistic to expect fundamental political allegiances rooted in experience to respond to short-term and fleeting exposure to party propaganda. Even now, when allegiances are generally looser, the chances are not great. It was generally mistaken to expect that an election outcome could be "explained" with any certainty. The tendency to try to do so still persists to judge from the subtitle of a recent British study, *Why Labour Won the General Election of 1997* (Crewe et al., 1998). Second, too much faith was (and still is) placed in the power of computers to extract answers from the vast volumes of (in themselves reliable) data that are generated during a campaign. Third, the attention paid to elections was often at the expense of attention to long-term processes of political communication and change. The "critical events" that influence opinion do not usually occur during campaigns, and in fact sitting administrations generally do their very best not to permit such events, given their unpredictable outcomes.

There have also been theoretical reasons why communication research distanced itself somewhat from the election as an attractive option for research into voting and persuasion effects. Early communication research (including the study of election campaigns) had been fitted into what has been called a "transmission model" (Carey, 1975), according to which the key communication problem is how efficiently a given "message" can be transported from a sender to a receiver, without distortion of meaning and with the consequences as intended by the sender. This model has for long been considered inadequate. Three main criticisms have been made. First, we have to consider communication not so much as a process of transmission but as one of collective sharing and expression. An election campaign is a good example of a prominent public event that is also a societywide manifestation, celebration, and reinforcement of democratic values and practices, whatever the outcome. The main condition of communication "success," from this point of view, is that citizens participate and become involved and aware.

Second, even in terms of persuasive effectiveness, the transmission model privileges the sender and leaves out of account or undervalues the role of the receiver. Informing and persuading are not one-way processes but necessarily interactive and intersubjective if they are to succeed. Third, and not inconsistently with either of these perspectives, elections can be seen as exercises in hegemonic communication. They are events that express the dominant ideology and implicitly reaffirm the status quo. They usually offer a limited range of acceptable alternatives of political choice and implicitly delegitimate the voices that are excluded for one reason or another, usually because they do not have large followings or resources to buy into the campaign (unlike Ross Perot in the United States in 1992, Silvio Berlusconi in Italy in 1994, and James Goldsmith in the United Kingdom in 1997). This objection was probably more valid in the 1970s than today, but it still carries some weight.

An Alternative Approach to Campaign
Effects Research: Taking the Receiver's View

The British case study described in this section (Blumler and Mc-Quail, 1968/1969) was one response to the relative disillusion with the prevailing "voter persuasion paradigm." Looking back, one can perhaps regard it as having been on the cusp of change from the classic model of effects research to a period of new directions and questions in the study of political communications. Its immediate stimulus was a previous investigation of the 1959 general election in Britain, in which television played a major role for the first time (Trenaman and McQuail, 1961), but which failed to show a direct relation between media exposure and changes in attitudes or voting intentions. Research into the 1964 general election was designed to explore the paradox of high exposure to campaign communication coupled with low propensity to change. The focus was on the perception of the campaign by voters and on their motivations for viewing political television. A guiding idea was that the influence of campaign communication might turn not so much on its volume but on how and why it is received by its intended or unintended audience.

This approach had theoretical support in contemporary communication theory that emphasized the disposition of recipients in selecting and responding and the different uses to which incoming information might be put (e.g., Katz, 1959). In their overview of research into the 1960 Kennedy–Nixon television debates, Katz and Feldman (1962: 216) had already raised the question of why the audience might be watching the debates at all: "Was this entertainment or education or politics or what?" The new approach was intended not only to provide a consumer's view of election television but also to see whether including variables of amount and type of motivation might not reveal otherwise concealed media influences.

The circumstances of the 1964 election in Britain were such as to potentially enhance the role of television. The medium enjoyed a 90 percent reach and hosted an unprecedented volume of election coverage. Moreover, party programs were required to be shown simultaneously on all national channels at peak viewing times, leading not only to large audiences, but also to much unselective exposure to the views of political opponents as well as to inadvertent exposure to politics in general. As far as the "involuntary" audience was concerned, two main, but opposed, expectations were formulated. Either they would be protected from any influence by their lack of interest and information, or they would have an above-average susceptibility to influence owing to their tabula rasa condition. As it turned out, it was not a question of either one or the other, since both kinds of effects were found.

To account for the relative motivation of voters to follow the election campaign on television, a good deal of work was required to develop suitable instruments. The design of questions was based on exploratory interviews, and from the resulting materials a small number of statements about motivation were distilled. One set expressed reasons for watching politics on television and another some reasons for avoiding it. This approach reflected the clear evidence from exploratory research that electors were highly ambivalent about political "propaganda"—both appreciating its necessity and disliking several of its characteristic features. The aim in developing a measure of motivation along these lines was to eventually be able to classify each respondent in terms of both *degree* and *type* of motivation.

The chosen items were included in a question about viewing and nonviewing of party programs asked in the first round of a three-stage panel, approximately four months before the election took place. The second round of the panel was carried out immediately before the opening of the official campaign period of three weeks, while the third round immediately followed voting. The results of the motivation question were used in the eventual analysis in two main ways. First, they provided an overall measure of degree of motivation to follow the campaign (using an index based on the ratio of positive to negative items). This measure had the advantage of incorporating the ambivalence referred to above. For the average citizen, elections, then as now, tended to provoke a mixture of civic duty, interest, boredom, and distrust.

Second, we obtained an index of the *type* of motivation for following the campaign, using the eight positive attitude items (reasons for watching). A cluster analysis applied to the matrix of responses indicated a fairly clear pattern. The main axis of motivation lay between one pole that could be labeled "surveillance" and another "contest-excitement." The first included the ideas of keeping up with the issues, learning what the parties might do if elected, and judging what the leaders are like. The opposite pole stressed the excitement of the race, an interest in spotting winners, and the use of materials in political arguments. Unaccounted for by this general dimension are two other rather specifically "political" motives: looking for reinforcement of existing beliefs (reminders of one's party's strong points) and looking for guidance in voting (help in making up one's mind).

This material lent itself to various uses in the overall analysis. It differentiated between the more and the less "politically" motivated and, among the former, between those who might be more disposed to change (looking for guidance) and those less likely to change (the "reinforcement seekers"). Attention to motivational factors opened several possibilities for examining potential media effects that would not otherwise be available. Respondents were also asked to evaluate different television formats for political programming and to give an overall assessment of the campaign on television after the event.

All told, much material was made available for answering the question "Why do people watch political television?" and for testing the relevance of this to campaign effects. On the first issue, it was at least apparent that attention to campaign communication has an underlying rationality. Despite the fact that in this particular case there was a high degree of unintentional exposure, viewers made sense of the experience in terms broadly relevant to their role as citizens as well as consumers of television. The findings also served to put reinforcement-seeking as a voter orientation in its place as a minority concern, largely confined to the more partisan members of the audience. They singled out surveillance of the political environment as most important among the gratifications that people sought to satisfy when following a campaign. And they disclosed that many sample members expected more challenging forms of political television (such as debates and interviews with politicians) to help resolve some of their campaign tensions and problems. These included the need to distinguish between promises that were reasonable to count on and ones that were extravagant or impractical, or to assess leaders' trustworthiness for themselves. It was as if, through viewer-voters' eyes, the British campaign communication system comprised a mixture of pitfalls and handholds. The former were mainly associated with how politicians campaigned and the latter with what television could offer.

The evidence relating to mediation in the effects process was more complex, but an overall conclusion is that motivational distinctions did help in locating certain small and fluctuating groups within any "target audience" for political campaigning.

The following indications of the part played by motivation can be mentioned. The particular motivation of seeking reinforcement was associated with increased awareness of the central issues of the campaign. Second, those looking for guidance in a voting choice appeared to learn more from the campaign than others, although independently of their degree of exposure to television. Third, the amount of exposure to television did make some contribution to acquiring information about issues, but beyond a certain ceiling of this effect, the degree of motivation was an additional predictor of learning. Fourth, while the overall campaign trend of attitudes was favorable to Labour, in itself unrelated to television exposure, there was an association between television viewing and a weaker pro-Labour trend among the more highly motivated sector of the electorate. This suggested that exposure without positive motivation could produce more susceptibility to following current trends. On the other hand, a countertrend affected attitude movements toward the Conservative Party leader, Sir Alec Douglas-Home. Here exposure to television coupled with higher motivation seemed to hold back the general trend of criticism of Douglas-Home.

Perhaps the strongest piece of evidence was the indication that the third party (the Liberals) did benefit from its high exposure on television among the generally less motivated sector of the electorate. This showed the potential advantage offered by television (at that time at least) of reaching a large and relatively uninformed body of voters with a relatively novel message. Blumler and McQuail (1968/1969: 218) commented that "In a situation where much television viewing arises from habit, and where the political content of the medium is suddenly enlarged by the launching of an election campaign, the group most likely to undergo a substantial increase in exposure to political communication will consist of those individuals who would not normally seek out political programmes but who are unwilling to give up viewing television during an election."

The general lesson of this finding was that "propaganda" works best where defenses are not erected in advance and where attention is casual rather than motivated. However, taking the findings as a whole, there is support for a number of other propositions about the influence of planned communication on specific subgroups. A number of effects go in quite different directions and are obscured if one only looks at net changes. One might also add that this study disclosed a general effect that was not anticipated and not usually associated with election campaigns, namely, an increased consensus across the electorate. The less habitually politically inclined were "brought into line" in informational and even attitude terms with trends affecting the majority. This applied to perceptions of parties and leaders as well as to matters of information and opinion about issues. Such an effect is close to that later dubbed by Gerbner et al. (1980) as "mainstreaming."

Did this election study affect the subsequent development of communication research in any way? Perhaps four contributions to the field flowed from it (albeit in conjunction with other influences).

First, it strengthened interest in the uses and gratifications approach to media audiences generally, and, in demonstrating that its variables could be measured, validated, and related to other receiver variables, helped to shift that approach from predominantly qualitative to more quantitative work. Second, it stimulated several other studies of audience uses of political materials, the most substantial of which was Mendelsohn and O'Keefe's (1976) survey of U.S. voters' orientations to the presidential campaign of 1972.[2] One mid-1970s study treated Belgian, British, and French audience members' expectations of campaign messages, and their evaluations of diverse media for satisfying them, as a comparative point of entry into the analysis of national political communication systems (Blumler et al., 1978).

Third, the study's results were interpreted (especially by U.S. scholars) as challenging the "limited effects" model of political communication impact, which had emerged from much campaign research of the classic period. A search for media effects, it seemed to them, could still be meaningful provided that the earlier almost exclusive concern of political communication research with persuasion through attitude change was replaced by "consideration of other more likely ... dependent variables as effects" (Blumler and McLeod, 1974: 268). This resonated with Elisabeth Noelle-Neumann's (1973) call for "a return to powerful mass media" (itself an outcome of her work on German elections). Fourth, it added support to the emerging "transactional model" of communication effects, which held that they should be investigated "by combining knowledge of message characteristics, the level of exposure given them, and *orientations* of the audience members to those messages" (McLeod and Becker, 1981: 72).

Postclassic Election Research

There followed a more general reassessment of priorities and strategies for research into election communication (see especially Kraus and Davis, 1976, and Chaffee, 1975, for typical statements). Although attempts still persisted to check whether particular campaigns, media, or messages had affected voting decisions, partisan support, or other political attitudes—especially now among undecided electors—the "voter persuasion paradigm" no longer dominated. As Blumler and McLeod (1974: 309) summed up:

> ... The climate of political communication research is distinctly different today from that which prevailed a few years ago. The critique of the "limited effects" model has become more wide-ranging and insistent ... That model is being displaced by other perspectives as a source of research guidance. And empirically minded investigators are devising new measures of political communication effects that do not involve a reversion to outdated mass persuasion models of media influence.

Two factors were probably most influential in paving the way for fresh research perspectives. One was sensitivity to new currents of sociopolitical change. Interpretations of the classic election research findings usually put more stress on the underlying stability of the world of politics than its flux. But the 1960s onward were a time of widespread dissent, questioning, and even social upheaval in many countries. This was most obvious in the United States as a result of the Vietnam War, the civil rights and feminist movements, and the promotion of new, more liberated lifestyles, but similar tendencies were apparent in Europe, which was affected by economic crisis as well as social change.

In Europe these developments coincided with the rise of critical and neo-Marxist theory concerning dominant ideologies and repressive tolerance and generally more radical thinking. This combination of circumstances tended to sideline routine electoral politics and to focus attention on the ideological implications of media coverage of the big issues of the moment (as in Glasgow University Media Group, 1976). Consequently, a burgeoning literature strongly criticized news professionals' pretensions to objectivity and emphasized the artificially "constructed" nature of news portrayals of political realities in support of dominant institutional interests.

Other less radical scholars, however, to whom election campaigns still presented meaningful opportunities for research, tended to respond to a different source of sociopolitical change. They noticed that the hitherto relatively solid props of social support for traditional party allegiances were weakening and that electoral volatility was on the increase. This seemed to create new potentials for short-term information flows, reaching people through the news media, to affect their political outlooks in various ways.

The second influential factor was the arrival of television, which by the late 1960s had become not just a source of entertainment but a main and most trusted source of news. This hammered yet another nail into the classic model's coffin, since a medium of even-handed news, several-sided discussion, and free slots for most parties (paid commercials in the United States) afforded less scope for viewers to tune in consistently and selectively to their own side of the argument. It also enlarged the audience for political communication by penetrating a sector of the electorate that was previously more difficult to reach and less heavily exposed to political message flows. And if long-term influences on political outlook, such as party identification and early socialization, were really starting to give way to more short-term ones, then a crucial channel of such impact must (it was thought) be television news with its reports on current news events, governments' main successes and failures, and opposition lines of attack. Hence, television's values and formats had an increasingly far-reaching impact on parties' and leaders' attempts to reach the mass electorate, for example, in the scheduling of political events (timed to major news programs), the language of politics (through the crafting of sound bites and cultivation of more intimate styles of address), and the personalization of its presentation (with a sharper focus on top leaders).

In these conditions, election research proliferated, addressing a wider range of topics than can be dealt with here. Amid a wealth of studies and findings, however, three main lines of continuous enquiry were most formative in shaping postclassic political communication research.

The first was a greater appreciation of the role of all matters cognitive in political communication—not only news itself, but also the processing of news by newsmakers and audiences. If people follow politics mainly through news of its events, conflicts, and personalities, then scholars should investigate potential relationships between characteristic practices of journalism and the categories and frameworks through which audience members perceive and think about sociopolitical reality. Hence, election campaigns were approached as affording opportunities to explore such connections through a number of key concepts.

The most central of these was emphasis on the "agenda-setting function" of the mass media. This approach emerged from research by McCombs and Shaw (1972), which found close parallels between the issues covered most often by the U.S. media during the 1968 presidential election and those thought most important by undecided voters. Simply put, then, the theory proposed that whatever issues are most salient in news media (given most space, time, and prominence) will largely determine what the public thinks to be most important. For competing party politicians a key objective is to fight an election on issues that are most likely to favor them. The problem is that in the end only the public can determine what are the main issues. This is where the media, and especially the news, can make a decisive difference according to agenda-setting theory. The hypothesis has been much tested and contested, and Weaver (1996: 37) notes that since McCombs and Shaw (1972), there have been "scores of similar studies of agenda-setting . . . most conducted during election years, especially the presidential election years of 1976, 1980, 1984 and 1988." In fact, the 1976 study (Weaver et al., 1981) centered entirely on agenda setting, stretching it beyond its original focus on issue priorities to other political qualities that could be ranked, such as the personality traits regarded as most desirable in political leaders.[3]

Another cognitive concept in the literature, namely, priming, follows from the agenda-setting perspective. This presumes that whenever media content activates a concept in people's minds, they will tend to use it in other relevant contexts. If through agenda setting, then, a certain issue has become important to them, they will tend to judge politicians by their stands on that issue or by how effectively they seem to have handled it. In American experiments, for example, when people were primed by stories based on national defense, they gave considerable weight to impressions of how well the president had looked after defense when rating his overall performance (Iyengar and Kinder, 1987). Of course situations of electoral choice are natural loci for such priming research and have dominated it to date.

Finally, no issue is usually presented "bare" in the news. It is typically dressed—or "framed"—in material that suggests how it has arisen, why it is important, and the implications of tackling it in certain ways rather than others. Latterly, then, there has been interest in the more complex idea of political communication as "framing." The concept originated in the work of Erving Goffman (1974), but in a political context Entman (1993: 52) defines it as follows: "To frame is to select some aspects of perceived reality and make them salient in a communicating context, in such a way as to promote a particular problem definition, causal interpretation, moral evaluation, and or treatment/recommendation." This notion can be applied to a wide range of news events and stories. In election research it has been fruitfully used to distinguish reports framed by campaign "issues" from those framed by campaign "strategies." For example, after analyzing U.S. network coverage of presidential candidates' speeches in three recent elections, Devitt (1997) found that the evidence they used to support their arguments was far more likely to be presented in "issue" than "strategy" stories. Influences of these frames on audience perceptions of what electioneering is about and (of the strategy focus) on public cynicism have also been detected in other research. For Entman (1993: 55), framing "plays a major role in the exertion of political power." In part, this is because it sets the "boundaries of discourse over an issue," wherein news texts can exhibit homogeneous or competing frameworks.[4] But in part, it is also because "politicians seeking support are . . . compelled to compete with each other and with journalists over news frames."

This *systemic* comment conveniently introduces the second main line of more or less continuous political communication enquiry that election research has promoted in the postclassic period. Whereas, according to Nimmo and Swanson (1990: 23), "early generations of voting studies . . . offered . . . political institutions . . . short shrift," today they pay far more attention to how parties and candidates organize themselves to address (and, if possible, master) the news media, to how journalistic institutions organize for political and especially campaign coverage, and to the modes of accommodation and conflict that often arise between these camps. Main examples of such systemically oriented election communication research include: many studies of the professionalization of party publicity (Kavanagh, 1995; Mayhew, 1997; Mancini, 1999); equally numerous (and conceptually increasingly elaborate) studies of political marketing (Scammell, 1999); a series of observation studies (based at BBC newsrooms during the British election campaigns of 1966, 1979, 1982, 1987, 1992, and 1997) of journalists' orientations to campaigning politicians (Gurevitch and Blumler, 1993; Blumler and Gurevitch, 1998); comparative analysis of party and media influences on campaign agendas in British and U.S. elections (Semetko et al., 1991); and a comparative analysis across eleven democracies of global trends and nationally specific features of innovations in modern election campaigning (Swanson and Mancini, 1996).

Swanson (1997: 1270) dryly notes that "the quality of political communication as it is shaped by the institutional needs and goals that interact within the political-media complex has received little praise and frequent condemnation." This *normative* comment introduces the third main trend in latter-day political communication analysis, to which election research has heavily contributed, namely, an increasing tendency to evaluate the political output offered citizens through the mass media.

Space does not permit a comprehensive review of such work, but its main features may be summarized as follows:

1. The large amount of time or space in news devoted to what is now called the "horse race" or "strategic" reporting at the expense of substantive issues and policy proposals (Patterson and McLure, 1976; Patterson, 1980; Robinson and Sheehan, 1983; Cappella and Jamieson, 1997).

2. The increased "mediation" of political and campaign coverage, in which contributions from reporters exceed those from politicians, whose "sound bites" have measurably become progressively shorter in recent decades, while journalistic commentary has become increasingly interpretative (Hallin, 1992; Patterson, 1993; Kendall, 1997).

3. The increasing negativity of both campaign commercials and news coverage of politicians' statements and activities (Jamieson, 1992).

It is obvious from this list of documented trends why so much academic writing on present-day political communication is critical. The itemized features support charges (1) that citizens are being fed a starvation diet of political information, (2) that access to them by their would-be representatives is impeded and distorted by over-mighty journalists, and (3) that the coverage is tailor-made to foster cynicism, loss of confidence in public institutions, and disappointment with the political process. Unsurprising, therefore, is Joslyn's (1990: 89) claim that "campaign news coverage actually prevents rather than promotes civic education"; Payne's (1997: 987) complaint that "what is lacking are meaningful messages in our expanding web of communication"; and Blumler and Gurevitch's (1995) proclamation of a building "crisis of public communication."

The normative strand of election-based political communication analysis is not all doom and gloom, however. Studies of televised debates have highlighted their massive audiences, predominant policy focus, and potential for civic learning (Kraus, 1962, 1979). Doris Graber (1993) has been a fertile source of suggestions for making campaign news more "user friendly," based on her earlier research into how people process audiovisual information. And a small but perhaps growing number of scholars are seeking evidence and giving reasons for supposing that alarmism over media-and-citizenship is not entirely warranted (Brants, 1998; Norris, 2000; Zaller, 2000).

The Uses of Election Communication Research: An Analytical Overview

From the foregoing account (plus other campaign studies in the literature), the following summary of six important uses of election communication research can be compiled:

1. *Being occasions when the levers of political power either stay in place or are passed on to other hands, elections are spurs to continual innovation and development in the strategic organization and conduct of political communication by competing parties, leaders, and candidates.* This has been a stimulus to the emergence of two substantial and revealing literatures (1) on the professionalization of

campaigning, news management, and spin-doctoring (including its impact on relations between politicians and journalists) and (2) on the spread of political marketing, including its impact on relations between leaders, parties, and voters.[5] Of course politicians' concern to fare as well as possible at the next election is not the only source of these developments. They also spring from and take account of changes in communication technology, media organization, politically relevant social structures, and public attitudes. With the onset of the "permanent campaign," what Mayhew (1997) has termed "the instrumental rationalization of persuasion" is no longer limited to the temporal bounds of official campaign periods. It is increasingly being regarded, by politicians and academics alike, as integral to effective government itself.

2. *Elections are highly convenient benchmarks for charting trends over time in political communication content in the media.* Recent examples include:

(a) Measures of the amount and prominence of political news in the media (as in Goddard et al., 1998).

(b) Indices of politics presented as a forum of policy debate versus its presentation as an arena of power maneuvering (as discussed in the passage in the previous section on issue and strategy frames).

(c) Measures of negativity in attack campaigning by politicians and in pejorative coverage by journalists (as in Patterson, 1993, and Lichter and Smith, 1996).

(d) Measures of broadcasters' reliance on "infotainment" formats (see Brants and Neijens, 1995, for such research on Dutch campaigns).

(e) Measures of trends in styles of political rhetoric, revelatory of changes in the constraints to which politicians adapt when tailoring their messages to media and electorates (as in an analysis by Hart and Jarvis, 1997, of discourse in U.S. candidate debates from 1960 to 1996).

3. *Elections provide opportunities to study the roles in political communication of major innovations in media formats.* Examples that have prompted a considerable amount of research and academic commentary include: candidate debates (from Kraus, 1962, onward); public journalism (e.g., Glasser, 1999); talk shows (much examined for their redemptive potential in the 1992 presidential election by, among others, Ratzan, 1993; Ridout, 1993; Graber, 1994; Newhagen, 1994; and Weaver, 1994); "adwatches" (Pfau and

Louden, 1994; Capella and Jamieson, 1994); and, latterly, the Internet (Delli Carpini, 1996; Jacques and Ratzan, 1997; Whillock, 1997; Ward and Gibson, 1998).

4. *Election campaigns are highly amenable to cross-national political communication comparisons* (as in Blumler, 1983; Kaid et al., 1991; Swanson and Mancini, 1996). Such comparisons are indispensable if the often alleged trends of Americanization and globalization of political communication arrangements are to be properly traced and clarified.

5. *Key concepts in political communication theory can be pioneered and tested in election campaign conditions*—as has been the case with notions of agenda setting, priming, framing, and the "spiral of silence."

6. *Data from election campaign surveys have contributed significantly to the ongoing debate about the validity and viability of diverse notions of citizenship* (from Berelson et al., 1954, to Zaller, 2000).

In endorsing the uses outlined here, we have no wish to overstate the value of election research for communication studies. Most of the avenues mentioned can—and should—be pursued in out-of-election research as well. Nevertheless, campaigns are distinctive for two qualities that justify their continuing occupancy of a special place in political communication research. First, an election is a universal event, testing the commitment and involvement of all political communication senders and recipients. Second, an election is a relatively holistic event, enabling processes and interrelations operative within a political communication system to be highlighted "in the round."[6]

A Postmodern Prescriptive Postscript

Nevertheless, we regret a continuing imbalance in much election communication research. Despite frequent lip service to the idea that audiences and citizens are "active," scholars still tend to approach campaigns from the perspective of the primary producers of political communication, to whom the mass of receivers are seen chiefly as reacting. It is intriguing to recall therefore that one aim of our 1964 election study was to counter just such a bias. In our words, an "element which has so far been noticeably absent from characterizations of the [electoral] audience is an understanding of how the individual sees his own situation and how he perceives those who address him" (Blumler and McQuail, 1970: 478).

The case for revisiting those perceptions in present-day conditions of mediated politics is strong. Democratic political communication systems have been transformed since the mid-1960s by a host of developments. Campaigns were already centrally organized to some degree, but much more was left to local initiative and the present-day professionalization of party and candidate publicity was at a prototypical stage. Currently, this involves continuous and extensive efforts at news management, orientation to the content and timing requirements of news media, image projection coordinated with public opinion research, central control of the "message," and reliance on communication experts for all of this. Not surprisingly, these efforts have become familiar to the public along with the specialist vocabulary of spin-doctoring and political marketing, as well as the names of key public relations advisors.

Political news itself is a conduit for much of this perspective on campaigning activity and also for blow-by-blow accounts of strategy, tactics, and political skirmishes. In carrying out this new or enhanced role, the news has arguably become more conflict-oriented and more negative toward politics, as well as relatively less nourishing in political substance. Nevertheless, a greater sensitivity to audience interests and tastes also pervades much public communication today, including more emphasis on the accessibility of news reports and cultivation of a popular touch by politicians, more appearances of ordinary citizens in the news, and more talk shows and discussion programs built around the views of ordinary people.

In sum, compared with the situation three decades ago, the modern political communication system seems more elaborate and complex, more professionalized, more imbued with journalistic values, more power oriented, and more tinged with skepticism—but also more "populist." Yet empirically based insights into voters' responses to all this are in remarkably short supply. Too much of what we "know" about them comes from insistent media references to the public's disenchantment with its leaders and institutions.

Research to put this right and ascertain people's views on the present state of campaign communication might be designed to answer questions in two main areas:

Awareness. What impressions of how campaign communications are shaped nowadays are uppermost in people's minds? Do the features they notice tally with some or all of those mentioned in the paragraphs above? Or would a popular sample come up with a different list?

Evaluation. How do people evaluate those features of political communication of which they are most aware? Are they helpful or not in following politics? Do they make for more involvement or greater distance? Does the campaign communication system still seem to offer a more or less balanced mixture of pitfalls and hand-holds even if the precise elements have changed? Does professionalized campaigning make it easier or harder to make sense of the alternatives posed? Do people appreciate the increased chance of finding political materials suited to their levels of understanding somewhere in the more abundant media system and by more opportunities to hear other voters express their views and concerns? Is the system working for or against democracy? Is it spectator sport rather than serious debate?

A return to research into the "worm's-eye view" would require scholars (and provide the opportunity) to expose and reexamine a number of assumptions about media and democracy that still lurk in much thinking about political campaigning. The assumptions in question can have either an empirical or a normative character, sometimes both at the same time. They include the notion that there is a mass audience for politics waiting to be informed and that people need large amounts of information in order to participate; that information is more important than feelings and values; that people have a civic duty to pay attention to campaigning politicians; and that certain channels, sources, and formats are superior to others.

There are also assumptions for reconsideration about the nature of the political and about the definition and relative significance of what should count as political issues. The privileged definition of an election as a rare opportunity for making rational and informed choices between policy alternatives and candidates is itself due for reassessment. Many of these problematic points lend themselves for examination through the eyes of "ordinary citizens," even if the obstacles to productive questioning are considerable. It is arguable that political communication research and theory has over the five decades covered by this review accumulated a rich assortment of viable ideas and methods that are still too constrained by the strait-ʳket of "high modernist" models of politics (see Blumler and Ka-ᵗh, 1999), elections, and campaigning. The time has come to the limbs of the creature so confined.

Notes

1. Our review is largely based on U.S. and U.K. election studies. Other countries' rich literatures of campaign research also deserve attention from this standpoint, as the bibliographical essays of Schulz (1997) for Germany and Cayrol and Mercier (1998) for France suggest.

2. McLeod and Becker (1981) may be consulted for a review and assessment of other work of this kind.

3. Even more ambitious extensions of the theory are proposed in McCombs et al. (1997).

4. This idea may be associated with Bennett's (1990) theory of indexing, according to which the bounds of political controversy reported in the news media are likely to depend on the degree of elite consensus or dissensus that prevails over an issue.

5. See Scammell (1999) for a substantial review of a voluminous literature on political marketing.

6. Illustrative of this point is the Norris et al. (1999) study of the organization, content, and reception of campaign communication in the British general election of 1997.

References

Bennett, W. Lance. 1990. "Toward a Theory of Press–State Relations in the United States." *Journal of Communication* **40**(2): 103–125.

Berelson, Bernard R. 1959. "The State of Communication Research." *Public Opinion Quarterly* **23**(1): 1–6.

Berelson, Bernard R., Paul F. Lazarsfeld, and William N. McPhee. 1954. *Voting: A Study of Opinion Formation in a Presidential Campaign*. Chicago: University of Chicago Press.

Blumler, Jay G., ed. 1983. *Communicating to Voters: Television in the First European Parliamentary Elections*. London/Beverly Hills, Calif./New Delhi: Sage.

Blumler, Jay G., and Michael Gurevitch. 1995. *The Crisis of Public Communication*. London/New York: Routledge.

Blumler, Jay G., and Michael Gurevitch. 1998. "Change in the Air: Campaign Journalism at the BBC, 1997." In *Political Communications: Why Labour Won the General Election of 1997*, Ivor Crewe, Brian Gosschalk, and John Bartle, eds., pp. 176–194. London/Portland: Frank Cass.

Blumler, Jay G., and Dennis Kavanagh. 1999. "The Third Age of Political Communication: Influences and Features." *Political Communication* **16**(3): 209–230.

Blumler, Jay G., and Jack M. McLeod. 1974. "Communication and Voter Turnout in Britain." In *Sociological Theory and Survey Research: Institutional Change and Social Policy in Britain*, Timothy Leggatt, ed., pp. 265–312. London/Beverly Hills, Calif.: Sage.

Blumler, Jay G., and Denis McQuail. 1968/1969. *Television in Politics: Its Uses and Influence*. London: Faber & Faber, and Chicago: University of Chicago Press.

Blumler, Jay G., and Denis McQuail. 1970. "The Audience for Election Television." In *Media Sociology: A Reader,* Jeremy Tunstall, ed., pp. 452–478. London: Constable.

Blumler, Jay G., Roland Cayrol, Claude Geerts, and Gabriel Thoveron. 1978. "A Three-Nation Analysis of Voters' Attitudes to Election Communication." *European Journal of Political Research* 6(1): 127–156.

Brants, Kees. 1998. "Who's Afraid of Infotainment?" *European Journal of Communication* 13(3): 315–335.

Brants, Kees, and P. Neijens. 1995. "The Infotainment of Politics." *Political Communication* 15(2): 149–165.

Cappella, Joseph N., and Kathleen Hall Jamieson. 1994. "Broadcast Adwatch Effects: A Field Experiment." *Communication Research* 21(3): 342–365.

Cappella, Joseph N., and Kathleen Hall Jamieson. 1997. *The Spiral of Cynicism: The Press and the Public Good.* New York/Oxford: Oxford University Press.

Carey, James. 1975. "A Cultural Approach to Communication." *Communication* 2(1): 1–22.

Cayrol, Roland, and Arnaud Mercier. 1998. "Political Communication and Scholarship in France." *Political Communication* 15(3): 383–412.

Chaffee, Steven H., ed. 1975. *Political Communication: Issues and Strategies for Research.* Beverly Hills, Calif./London: Sage.

Chaffee, Steven H., and Kathleen Hall Jamieson. 1994. "Studies of the 1992 U.S. Election Campaign: An Overview." *Communication Research* 21(3): 261–263.

Crewe, Ivor, Brian Gosschalk, and John Bartle, eds. 1998. *Political Communications: Why Labour Won the General Election of 1997.* London/Portland: Frank Cass.

Delli Carpini, Michael X. 1996. "Voters, Candidates and Campaigns in the New Information Age." *Harvard International Journal of Press Politics* 1(4): 36–56.

Devitt, James. 1997. "Framing Politicians." *American Behavioral Scientist* 40(8): 1139–1160.

Entman, Robert M. 1993. "Framing: Toward Clarification of a Fractured Paradigm." *Journal of Communication* 43(4): 51–58.

Gerbner, George, Larry Gross, M. Morgan, and Nancy Signorelli. 1980. "The Mainstreaming of America: Violence Profile No. 11." *Journal of Communication* 30(1): 10–27.

Glasgow University Media Group. 1976. *Bad News.* London: Routledge and Kegan Paul.

Glasser, Thomas L. 1999. *The Idea of Public Journalism.* New York: Guilford Press.

Goddard, Peter, Margaret Scammell, and Holli A. Semetko. 1998. "Too Much of a Good Thing? Television in the 1997 Election Campaign." In *Political Communications: Why Labour Won the General Election of 1997,* Ivor Crewe, Brian Gosschalk, and John Bartle, eds., pp. 149–175. London/Portland: Frank Cass.

Goffman, Ernest. 1974. *Frame Analysis.* New York: Harper & Row.

Graber, Doris A. 1993. "Making Campaign News User Friendly: The Lessons of 1992 and Beyond." *American Behavioral Scientist* 37(2): 328–336.

Graber, Doris A. 1994. "Why Voters Fail Information Tests: Can the Hurdles Be Overcome?" *Political Communication* 11(4): 331–346.

Gurevitch, Michael, and Jay G. Blumler. 1993. "Longitudinal Analysis of an Election Communication System: Newsroom Observation at the BBC, 1992–1996." *Osterreichische Zeitschrift fur Politikwissenschaft* 4: 427–444.

Hallin, Daniel C. 1992. "Soundbite News: Television Coverage of Elections, 1968–1988." *Journal of Communication* 42(1): 5–24.

Hart, Roderick P., and Sharon E. Jarvis. 1997. "Political Debate: Forms, Styles and Media." *American Behavioral Scientist* 40(8): 1095–1122.

Iyengar, S., and D. R. Kinder. 1987. *News That Matters: Television and American Opinion*. Chicago: University of Chicago Press.

Jacques, Wayne W., and Scott C. Ratzan. 1997. "The Internet's World Wide Web and Political Accountability." *American Behavioral Scientist* 40(8): 1226–1237.

Jamieson, Kathleen Hall. 1992. *Dirty Politics: Deception, Distraction and Democracy*. New York/Oxford: Oxford University Press.

Joslyn, Richard A. 1990. "Election Campaigns as Occasions for Civic Education." In *New Directions in Political Communication: A Resource Book*, David L. Swanson and Dan Nimmo, eds., pp. 86–119. Newbury Park/London/New Delhi: Sage.

Kaid, Linda Lee, and Dianne Bystrom. 1999. *The Electronic Election: Perspectives on the 1996 Campaign Communication*. Hillsdale, N.J.: Lawrence Erlbaum.

Kaid, Linda Lee, Jacques Gerstle, and Keith R. Sanders. 1991. *Mediated Politics in Two Cultures: Presidential Campaigning in the United States and France*. New York: Praeger.

Katz, Elihu. 1959. "Mass Communication Research and the Study of Popular Culture." *Studies in Public Communication* 2(1): 1–6.

Katz, Elihu, and Jacob J. Feldman. 1962. "The Debates in the Light of Research: A Survey of Surveys." In *The Great Debates: Background, Perspective, Effects*, Sidney Kraus, ed., pp. 173–223. Bloomington: Indiana University Press.

Kavanagh, Dennis. 1995. *Election Campaigning: The New Marketing of Politics*. Oxford: Blackwells.

Kendall, Kathleen E. 1997. "Presidential Debates through Media Eyes." *American Behavioral Scientist* 40(8): 1193–1207.

Klapper, Joseph. 1960. *The Effects of Mass Communication*. New York: Free Press.

Kraus, Sidney, ed. 1962. *The Great Debates: Background, Perspective, Effects*. Bloomington: Indiana University Press.

Kraus, Sidney, ed. 1979. *The Great Debates: Carter vs. Ford 1976*. Bloomington: Indiana University Press.

Kraus, Sidney, and Dennis K. Davis. 1976. *The Effects of Mass Communication on Political Behavior*. University Park: University of Pennsylvania Press.

Lazarsfeld, Paul F., Bernard Berelson, and Hazel Gaudet. 1944/1948. *The People's Choice*. New York: Columbia University Press.

Lichter, Robert, and T. Smith. 1996. "Why Elections Are Bad News: Media and Candidate Discourse in the 1966 Presidential Primaries." *Harvard International Journal of Press/Politics* 1(1): 15–35.

Mancini, Paolo. 1999. "New Frontiers in Political Professionalism." *Political Communication* 16(3): 231–246.

Mayhew, Leon H. 1997. *The New Public: Professional Communication and the Means of Social Influence*. Cambridge, England/New York: Cambridge University Press.

McCombs, Maxwell E., and Donald L. Shaw. 1972. "The Agenda-Setting Function of Mass Media." *Public Opinion Quarterly* 36(2): 176–187.

McCombs, Maxwell, Donald L. Shaw, and David Weaver, eds. 1997. *Communication and Democracy: Exploring the Intellectual Frontiers in Agenda-Setting Theory.* Mahwah, N.J.: Lawrence Erlbaum.

McLeod, Jack M., and Lee B. Becker. 1981. "The Uses and Gratifications Approach." In *Handbook of Political Communication,* Dan D. Nimmo and Keith R. Sanders, eds., pp. 67–99. Beverly Hills, Calif./London: Sage.

McQuail, Denis. 1977. "The Influence and Effects of Mass Media." In *Mass Communication and Society,* James Curran, Michael Gurevitch, and Janet Woollacott, eds., pp. 70–94. London: Edward Arnold.

Mendelsohn, Harold, and Garrett J. O'Keefe. 1976. *The People Choose a President.* New York: Praeger.

Newhagen, John E. 1994. "Self-Efficacy and Call-in Political Television Show Use." *Communication Research* 21(3): 366–379.

Nimmo, Dan, and David L. Swanson. 1990. "The Field of Political Communication: Beyond the Voter Persuasion Paradigm." In *New Directions in Political Communication: A Resource Book,* David L. Swanson and Dan Nimmo, eds., pp. 7–47. Newbury Park/London/New Delhi: Sage.

Noelle-Neumann, Elisabeth. 1973. "Return to the Concept of Powerful Mass Media." *Studies of Broadcasting* 9: 66–112.

Norris, Pippa. 2000. *A Virtuous Circle: Political Communications in Post-Industrial Democracies.* Cambridge, England/New York: Cambridge University Press.

Norris, Pippa, John Curtice, David Sanders, Margaret Scammell, and Holli A. Semetko. 1999. *On Message: Communicating the Campaign.* London/Newbury Park/New Delhi: Sage.

Patterson, Thomas E. 1980. *The Mass Media Election: How Americans Choose Their President.* New York: Praeger.

Patterson, Thomas E. 1993. *Out of Order.* New York: Alfred A. Knopf.

Patterson, Thomas E., and Robert D. McLure. 1976. *The Unseeing Eye: The Myth of Television Power in Election Campaigns.* New York: Putnam.

Payne, J. Gregory. 1997. "Campaign '96: Messages for the New Millennium." *American Behavioral Scientist* 40(8): 987–993.

Pfau, Michael, and Allan Louden. 1994. "Effectiveness of Adwatch Formats in Deflecting Political Attack Ads." *Communication Research* 21(3): 325–341.

Ratzan, Scott C. 1993. "Political Communication as Negotiation: Breathing New Life into Government." *American Behavioral Scientist* 37(2): 194–199.

Ridout, C. F. 1993. "News Coverage and Talk Shows in the 1992 Presidential Campaign." PS: *Political Science and Politics* 26(4): 712–716.

Robinson, Michael, and Margaret Sheehan. 1983. *Over the Wire and on TV.* New York: Sage.

Scammell, Margaret. 1999. "Political Marketing: Lessons for Political Science." *Political Studies* 47(4): 718–739.

Schulz, Winfried. 1997. "Political Communication Scholarship in Germany." *Political Communication* 14(1): 113–146.

Semetko, Holli A., Jay G. Blumler, Michael Gurevitch, and David H. Weaver. 1991. *The Formation of Campaign Agendas: A Comparative Analysis of Party and Me-*

dia Roles in Recent American and British Elections. Hillsdale, N.J.: Lawrence Erlbaum.

Swanson, David L. 1997. "The Political–Media Complex at 50: Putting the 1996 Presidential Campaign in Context." *American Behavioral Scientist* 40(8): 1264–1282.

Swanson, David L., and Paolo Mancini, eds. 1996. *Politics, Media and Modern Democracy: An International Study of Innovations in Electoral Campaigning and Their Consequences.* Westport, Conn.: Praeger.

Trenaman, Joseph, and Denis McQuail. 1961. *Television and the Political Image.* London: Methuen.

Ward, Stephen, and Rachel Gibson. 1998. "The First Internet Election? UK Political Parties and Campaigning in Cyberspace." In *Political Communications: Why Labour Won the General Election of 1997,* Ivor Crewe, Brian Gosschalk, and John Bartle, eds., pp. 93–112. London/Portland: Frank Cass.

Weaver, David H. 1994. "Media Agenda Setting and Elections: Voter Involvement or Alienation?" *Political Communication* 11(4): 347–356.

Weaver, David H. 1996. "What Voters Learn from Media." *The Annals of the American Academy of Political and Social Science* 546: 34–47.

Weaver, David H., Doris A. Graber, Maxwell E. McCombs, and C. H. Eyal. 1981. *Agenda-Setting in a Presidential Election: Issues, Images and Interest.* New York: Praeger.

Whillock, Rita Kirk. 1997. "Cyber-Politics: The Online Strategies of '96." *American Behavioral Scientist* 40(8): 1208–1225.

Zaller, John. 2000. "The Politics of Substance." In *Mediated Politics: Communication in the Future of Democracy,* W. Lance Bennett and Robert Entman, eds. Cambridge, England/New York: Cambridge University Press.

9

THE RULE OF PRODUCT SUBSTITUTION IN PRESIDENTIAL CAMPAIGN NEWS

JOHN ZALLER

University of California at Los Angeles

Flag sales are doing well and America is doing well and we should understand that and we should appreciate that." So declared presidential candidate George Bush in 1988 from a flag-festooned podium at a New Jersey flag factory. Although Bush gave another address that day, it mostly repeated ideas from earlier speeches. As a result, the rally at the flag factory became the centerpiece of television news reports on that day's Republican campaign.

This, of course, is what the Bush campaign intended. In serving up a visually attractive backdrop, a sound bite to fit it, and an otherwise light schedule, campaign strategists sought to compel the media to present Bush in a patriotic vein. Bush's rally at the New Jersey flag factory was one of the signature events of the 1988 presidential campaign. But what I have related so far is only half the story. Professional reporters loathe running politicians' press releases, and events like the Bush rally at the flag factory are, in effect, visual press releases. Reporters therefore rewrote the script. On NBC, Tom Brokaw announced that "the vice president wrapped himself in the flag again." Dan Rather said on CBS that "George Bush gives his 'my patriotism is better than yours' the hard sell." ABC's Brit Hume reminded viewers of an event a week earlier in which the vice president had used the word "America" 31 times in 15 minutes, for an average of twice a minute (Grove 1988). NBC's Lisa Myers added that Bush's use of national symbols "lead some to quote Samuel Johnson that patriotism is the last refuge of scoundrels" (quoted in Siegel 1988).

Thus, although all three networks carried Bush's rally at the flag factory, the coverage may not have won many votes for Bush. "That," as campaign manager Lee Atwater said afterward, "was one flag factory too many" (quoted in Germond and Witcover 1989, 408).

If attempts by campaign strategists to influence what journalists report are a staple of modern election campaigns, so are attempts by reporters to resist. Hence the central argument of this chapter: the harder presidential campaigns try to control what journalists report about their candidate, the harder journalists try to report something else instead. I call this the rule of product substitution. The first section of this chapter proposes a theory of media politics to explain why this sort of product substitution occurs, the second section discusses political product substitution itself, and the third section reports on an empirical test of the rule.

A Theory of Media Politics

With the weakening of traditional parties, candidates must reach and persuade voters on their own. Political advertising is one way of doing this. Getting out on the campaign trail and creating events that a nonpartisan media will see fit to report as news is another. The goal of such campaigning is to use journalists to get the candidate's story out.

The techniques by which politicians try to create favorable news are well known. On one hand, they take actions and stage events that promote their campaign agenda and that are so compelling that reporters will feel obliged to report them as news. On the other hand, they attempt to avoid situations, such as news conferences, that make it difficult for them to control the kind of news that gets made.

Both elements were present in the flag factory rally discussed earlier. The Bush campaign calculated that journalists would be unable to resist the visual appeal of the patriotic setting, even if what the vice president said was somewhat vacuous. Also, campaign managers kept Bush physically separated from reporters on that day, so as to prevent journalists from asking Bush to address questions that would distract from his primary message of patriotism.

All of this smacks of manipulation, but when politics is conducted by means of mass communication, politicians must approach communication strategically. Candidates who fail to be strategic will be beaten by—that is, judged by voters to be less attractive than—candidates who do handle communication strategically.

But if candidates are constrained to approach communication strategically, journalists are not constrained to like it, and most do not. Yet it is not immediately obvious why they do not. Why could journalists not sell as many newspapers, or get as many audience rating points, by providing straight reports of campaign events? Why do journalists so often feel compelled to make sarcastic or other negative comments when, as in the case of the flag factory rally, the candidates do such a good job of appealing to the production values of journalists? Why not just cooperate with politicians rather than treat them as adversaries? In this chapter I can only sketch answers to these questions (see Zaller, forthcoming, for a fuller argument). I also limit discussion to elite journalists, that is, those who work for television network news or prestigious national publications.

Let me begin with a commonly given argument that I consider unsatisfactory: the reason reporters take an adversarial stance toward politicians is that they distrust and dislike them. An alternative argument, essentially the same, is that reporters' values lead them to distrust politicians.

I consider such arguments unsatisfactory for two reasons. First, there are numerous cases in which journalists cooperate closely with politicians, including, most notably, foreign policy coverage (Zaller with Chiu 1996). According to Kernell (1997), even the relationship between the presidential press corps and the president was once very cooperative. Second, and more fundamentally, the argument that reporters adopt an adversarial stance toward politicians because their values lead them to do so is like arguing that they do it because they want to do it. It is hardly an explanation at all.

The explanation I shall propose is that reporters adopt an adversarial posture toward their sources because it is in their self-interest to do so. I reach this conclusion through the following logic. Like other professional groups—lawyers, doctors, architects, and university professors—journalists value autonomy both as an end in itself and as a means to creating the kind of product they wish to create. The kind of product they wish to create is one that requires as much personal skill and expertise as possible. The exercise of skill and expertise is not only inherently satisfying; it also leads to higher pay and higher status.

Consider, as a parallel, the case of architecture. If an architect had a choice between designing a no-frills box of a building according to someone else's instructions or an irregularly shaped and elaborately styled structure of her own design, which would she choose? The latter, of course, since architects get higher fees, more intellectual satisfaction, and greater peer recognition for producing the latter type of building. The major constraint on this preference is the consumer, who might want just a box, or at least something that costs what a box costs.

It is much the same for journalists. Journalists have an occupational interest in a relatively activist and autonomous conception of journalism, one that offers more than stenographic transcription of what others have said and that has appeal beyond the lowest common denominator of the mass market. Journalists want to be members of a profession that adds something to the news—a profession that not only reports, but also digs, selects, frames, investigates, interprets, and regulates the flow of political communication.

If journalists allowed themselves to become a mere transmission belt for the communication of politicians—if, that is, they ceded politicians control over the content of the news by simply reporting the information that politicians give them to report—their professional standing would erode. They would gradually lose status, the opportunity for interesting work, and perhaps even pay. They would come to resemble the glittering personalities of happy-talk television news—widely seen but not widely admired.

What journalists want, then, is to be in charge of political communication. They want to control their turf in the same way that elite architects, doctors, lawyers, and professors control their turf, and to use this control to create and sell a product that shows off their special knowledge and skill.[1] Summarizing this general argument in a form specific to journalism, I propose that, acting from occupational interest, journalists seek to control the content of the news and to use this control to maximize their independent and distinctive voice in the news.

This occupational interest brings journalists into regular conflict with politicians, who, as noted earlier, also have a clear occupational interest in controlling the content of the news. In the first half of the twentieth century, journalists fought for and largely won the autonomy to report the news as they saw it rather than as their publishers saw it (Halberstam 1978); in the second half of the twentieth century, they are fighting to keep politicians from dominating the news product. This basic conflict of interest, rather than the values or personal dislikes of journalists, explains the conflictual relationship that exists between politicians and journalists.

One might suppose that, inasmuch as journalists make final decisions about what counts as news, they would be able to control news content without any special effort. But it is not so simple. For one thing, politicians, with their armies of media consultants, determine most of the day-to-day content of campaigns, which are the raw material of news. If, as campaign managers try to ensure, journalists can find nothing more interesting to report, they are constrained to report what the candidates give them.

The other factor is the constraining influence of the mass audience, which critically affects the power balance between politicians and journalists. Citizen consumers of news have no rational interest in permitting either politicians or journalists to dominate the flow of political communication. Their interest, rather, is in having the two groups share control, as actually occurs in practice most of the time.

Since this latter point is a key proposition for which there is no direct evidence, I shall develop an a priori argument from first principles. To begin with, each individual voter is more likely to be mugged on the way to the polls than to affect an election outcome through voting.[2] Thus an individual citizen could devote his entire lifetime to studying how to cast wise votes in elections and be no better off than if he had spent no time studying politics at all—and quite possibly worse off for having wasted time on politics. As Anthony Downs (1957) argued in *An Economic Theory of Democracy,* it is therefore individually rational for most citizens to be largely ignorant of politics.

Most citizens behave as if they had been raised from infancy on this book of Downs. Americans sometimes say they are interested in politics, but in practice few are. As Doris Graber (1984, 105) found in her study of news consumption habits:

[Citizens] grumbled frequently about the oversimplified treatment of all news, including elections news, on television. Yet when the debates and other special news programs and newspaper features presented a small opportunity for more extensive exposure to issues, they were unwilling to seize it. For the most part, the [study subjects] would not read and study carefully the more extensive versions of election and other news in newspapers and news magazines. Masses of specific facts and statistics were uniformly characterized as dull, confusing, and unduly detailed.

Over the years, journalists have tried different schemes to increase the attention that citizens pay to news, mostly without success. As Lance Bennett (1996, 22–23) reports, editors and marketers have concluded that efforts "to improve election issue coverage and offer more in-depth political reporting are up against a basic obstacle: People really do not want more serious news, even when they say they do." Yet citizens do consume some political news. What do they want from this small amount of news?

To whatever (modest) extent that rational voters seek information whose purpose is to help them form informed opinions or cast wise votes, they will look for time-saving ways to minimize their effort. Party attachment and peer group opinion are, as Downs pointed out, two such aids. Another obvious time-saving device is to focus on points of political controversy. When elites achieve a consensus on a policy, there is no reason for each voter to trouble to figure out which side is best and how the parties line up. If, on the other hand, elites disagree, citizens may wish to prepare themselves to express an opinion on it. By this reasoning I reach the conclusion that the rational voter is engaged by news of political conflict and bored by news of political consensus. Consistent with the argument that citizens want news about conflict, Cook (1998, 101) remarks that "conflict may be one of the few cross-cultural characteristics of news." [3]

When elites engage in public disagreement, each side works hard to advance the best arguments for its position and to expose the weaknesses of the other side. By monitoring such disagreements, citizens can often get incisive information for little effort. Of course, even a little bit of effort may be more than many citizens want to make. But, even so, rational citizens want the option of paying attention in case a really important issue comes up. Also, they know that some of their fellow citizens are paying attention, and they want this minority of politics junkies to be able to see what is going on.

For these reasons, rational citizens do not want major conflict swept under the carpet, away from public view; nor do they want any group—politicians or journalists or corporate owners—to monopolize public discourse with its own point of view. Rather, when political elites disagree, rational citizens want exposure to both sides of the argument, and under no circumstances do they want to see one side monopolize public discussion.

I do not claim that citizens are consciously aware of any of these principles. In the same way, however, that many citizens vote their class interest without thinking consciously of either class or interest, I propose that citizens tend to make habitual news choices that reflect their actual interests.

Returning to my main line of argument, I claim that conflict between politicians and journalists is played out within this set of audience constraints. Citizens want some original exposure to what politicians are saying, and they would be indignant if journalists were, for any reason, to refuse to provide it routinely. Even though a witty exchange between Sam Donaldson and Cokie Roberts would be at least as interesting as any politician's speech, the public wants to hear the speech anyway, or *thinks* it does. This attitude strengthens the hand of politicians in their turf war with journalists. Yet the public also remains both easily bored by politicians and suspicious of them and so is willing to cede journalists wide leeway to criticize and dig up dirt on politicians. This strengthens the hand of journalists against politicians.

This three-cornered contest—politicians and journalists struggling to control news content within constraints set by the mass audience—is at the heart of media politics. In the next section, I show how this general conflict works out in the context of presidential campaigning.

The Rule of Product Substitution

All presidential candidates behave in ways designed to attract good news coverage, but their approaches vary. Two idealized approaches may be identified. The first is to engage in aggressive news management, the essential feature of which is, in the context of presidential campaigns, to control what journalists can report by serving up a limited number of carefully crafted and controlled events. Politicians who follow this strategy tend, for example, to campaign in friendly territory, where chances of unplanned occurrences are minimal, and to hold events in closed settings, such as indoor arenas, where attendance can be limited to loyalists. In addition, since the candidate's utterances are most important of all, they avoid any unscripted exchanges, with either journalists or ordinary citizens. Even simple visual access of journalists to the candidate is routinely controlled, as illustrated by an incident from Nixon's 1968 campaign in which reporters were denied permission to come into a television studio to watch the candidate respond to questions from a panel of local denizens. Instead, the national press was forced to watch on television monitors in an adjacent room. The reporters demanded to know why they were not allowed inside the studio. Because, a campaign official told them, "if that happens you're going to write about the lights, the cameras and that sort of thing and you're not going to understand what happens in the living rooms across America" (quoted in Jamieson 1996, 260).

The second of the two idealized approaches is an open-news style: candidates mount relatively free-wheeling campaigns in which there are multiple, somewhat loosely scripted events each day, including regular opportunity for citizens and reporters to quiz the candidate. Such campaigns can create a sense of energy and spontaneity that makes for naturally good news coverage.

The famous Truman "give 'em hell" whistle-stop campaign of 1948 adhered to the open-news strategy, as did the Kennedy and Nixon campaigns of 1960. Among recent campaigns, Michael Dukakis's 1988 campaign was relatively open. Ronald Reagan's 1984 campaign, by contrast, nearly matched the idealized account of aggressive news management.

The closed-news strategy of aggressive news management attempts to force journalists into a role they detest, that of mechanically conveying politicians' words and actions to the public. Campaign strategists are well aware that journalists detest this role, but many calculate that any journalistic retribution over loss of voice will be more than offset by the candidate's ability to control his or her message most of the time. The open-news strategy gives journalists a wide choice of material from which to select the ingredients of their stories. The hope of this strategy is that, if journalists have ample scope to exercise voice, they will lack the motivation to dig up unflattering information or make negative remarks.

Media negativity toward candidates is, in this view, determined in significant part by the candidate's strategy of news management. When aggressive news management limits journalistic opportunities to express voice, journalists create their own outlets in the form of investigations, critical analyses, and, to the extent they think the public will tolerate it, blunt expressions of sarcasm. Journalists, in effect, substitute their own news, most of which is negative, for that which the campaign has provided. However, what journalists substitute must meet two constraints. First, it must permit politicians some opportunity to speak directly to the mass audience. This is because, as just explained, the public dislikes having any one group dominate communication. Thus journalists cannot offer general commentaries on the election in place of stories that show what the candidates are doing. Second, like a detergent company that wants to get consumers to buy liquid gel instead of soap bars, journalists must offer something that is the functional equivalent of the product they replace, that is, something that provides information about the campaign. Much horse-race coverage—in which, for example, journalists let the candidate deliver a sound bite of the day but then explain how everything said is really just an appeal for votes—meets both of these constraints. So does the clever editing of sound bites to show how the candidate has contradicted himself. More generally, I propose the rule of product substitution as the central hypothesis of this chapter: the more strenuously politicians challenge journalists for control of a news jurisdiction, the more journalists will seek to develop substitute information that the mass audience is willing to accept as news and that gives expression to journalistic voice.

As suggested previously, most of the information that journalists substitute for candidate-supplied information is negative. My expectation, then, is that candidates' efforts at news management will correlate with the amount of media-initiated negativity directed toward them. To test this expectation, it is necessary to make reliable measurements of both news management and media-initiated negativity. I turn now to this task.

Empirical Tests

In this section, I reduce the complexity and drama of sixteen major-party presidential campaigns to numerical scores on a handful of variables, the most important of which are media-initiated negativity and news management style. Having thus measured the key concepts in my theoretical analysis, I test the extent to which they are statistically correlated with one another.

Measuring Media Negativity

In this study, I define media negativity as negative information or opinion that reporters themselves insert into the news. Negativity from other sources, such as the attack of one candidate on another, is outside my definition, which stresses media initiation of the negativity. Like most other scholars, I also exclude horse-race evaluations, that is, statements by reporters about how well or badly a candidate is faring in the competitive struggle. Horse-race statements from ordinary citizens—"soccer moms," "angry white males," and so forth—that include negative comments about one of the candidates are likewise omitted from my conception of media-initiated negativity. In determining the overall amount of media negativity, I calculate it as a fraction of all campaign coverage.

Working with this conception of negativity, I find many instances of media negativity in coverage that contains no explicit negative evaluation. For example, after Gennifer Flowers's allegation of an extramarital affair with Clinton surfaced in a tabloid in 1992, many news outlets reported it as news. Yet few reports offered any explicit criticism of Clinton's alleged behavior. They simply recounted Flowers's allegation and Clinton's response. Thus, without saying anything directly negative, reporters gave Clinton a heavy dose of what I count as media-initiated negativity. Most of what I have classified as media negativity consists, as in this example, of ostensibly straight news about topics that candidates would prefer not to have reported or discussed.

This conception of media negativity differs in important ways from that used in other research. Most scholars, for example, count negative evaluative statements as media negativity but not media-initiated negative information, such as the information in the Flowers story. They also count negative evaluations that derive from nonpress sources, especially the attacks of candidates on one another. Space limitations preclude discussion of these conceptual issues, except to acknowledge them (see, however, Zaller, forthcoming).

I have collected data on media negativity in four media: the *New York Times, Time* and *Newsweek* magazines, and network television news. Coding of the *New York Times* was based on abstracts of campaign coverage, as reported in the *Index to The New York Times,* and coding of the network news was based on the Vanderbilt abstracts. For the newsmagazines, the original texts of campaign and campaign-related stories were coded. Coding was done at the level of individual sentences or, when sentences contained multiple and especially conflicting bits of information, at the level of major phrases.

The following list is a randomly selected sample of the *New York Times* abstracts from three different elections that were coded as instances of media-initiated negativity:

1. "Gov Clinton, stung by recurring questions about his credibility, gives television interview from his mansion in Little Rock, Ark, in effort to control campaign coverage."
2. "Clinton and Bush campaigns have started using paid-for airtime to fling mud, ushering in season of negative advertising."
3. "Gov Bill Clinton and his running mate, Sen Al Gore, have campaigned together on 20 of 52 days since their nomination in July. . . . subtext is to draw comparisons between Democratic package and Republican one, since Pres Bush almost never shares stage with Vice Pres Quayle." (This was coded also as positive for Clinton.)
4. "Newsmen from at least 6 natl pubs and Dem Natl Com agents have been at work for wks searching through data . . . for material on Agnew. . . . probes focus on old charges of conflicts of interest."
5. "Nixon ltr to securities indus leaders pledging to ease Govt regulatory policies disclosed; aide A Greenspan says it was not made pub because it covers 'narrow policy area.'"
6. "Sen Brooke flies to Cleveland to rejoin Nixon campaign; says he is bewildered about Nixon's remarks on school desegregation but stresses he is not leaving the campaign."[4]
7. "Pres Reagan, during televised briefing, says he will meet on September 28 at White House with Soviet Foreign Min Andrei Gromyko . . . denies he has been motivated by election campaign and by criticism that Soviet-American relations have worsened under his Administration and that he has not met with any Soviet leader."
8. "Pres Reagan assails suggestions from some Democrats and news commentators that he showed signs of age in debate with Walter Mondale."
9. "Mayor A Starke Taylor of Dallas insists that Republican National Convention is still the 'free enterprise' convention city leaders said it

would be, even though city's taxpayers will end up paying from $1 million to $1.5 million for convention-related expenses."

All coding was done by Mark Hunt, who began work for me as an undergraduate at the University of California at Los Angeles and now works on a professional basis. As a partial check on his coding, I used his codes to replicate the measure of media negativity in Fig. 2.1 of Patterson's *Out of Order* (1993). The correlation between Hunt's and Patterson's measure was 0.96.

Measuring News Management

As explained earlier, the essence of news management in the context of political campaigns is to control what reporters can report by serving up a limited number of carefully controlled events. All presidential campaigns now engage in such management, but there is significant variation in the extent to which they do so, and it is this variation that I seek to measure.

To do so, I developed a set of 48 codes, each denoting either high (positive) or low (negative) concern for news management. For example, excluding reporters from a fund-raising event is coded as a positive indicator of news management, while taking reporters' questions at an informal press availability is coded as a negative indicator. Similarly, screening attendance at rallies is counted as a positive instance of news management, while taking unrehearsed questions from crowd members is counted as a negative instance. A sample of positive and negative codes, grouped into six subscales, is shown in Table 9.1.

Information on candidate behavior was gleaned from campaign stories covering the period 10–30 September in the *New York Times,* the *Washington Post,* the *Los Angeles Times,* Vanderbilt television news abstracts, and, for elections since 1980, the Associated Press wire. Coding was again done by Hunt.[5] As part of the coding task, Hunt copied the text that he relied on in assigning codes into electronic files, and these files have been put on my Web page. Thus each of the roughly 1100 behaviors coded for the news management scale has a publicly available justification.[6] Further information on the coding and scaling of candidate behavior is available on request.

Converting 48 codes and 1100 candidate behaviors into a usable measure of news management is not a straightforward task. To do it,

TABLE 9.1   Sample Codes for News Management Scale

Message Control
    1. Candidate cancels major rally or event to avoid demonstrators. (Positive)
    2. Candidate responds to specific opponent attacks, excluding debates. (Negative)
    3. Candidate takes questions from group or individual, where questioners have been screened or selected by the candidate himself. (Includes friendly talk show.) (Positive)
    4. Candidate engages in exchange—that is, back-and-forth discussion—with demonstrators or hecklers in crowd. (Negative)
Crowd exposure
    5. Rally or speech takes place in unfriendly territory, for example, Clinton addresses a Veterans of Foreign Wars convention during draft controversy. (Negative)
    6. Rally takes place in controlled setting; audience has been screened or selected by the campaign. (Positive)
Willingness to debate
    7. Candidate refuses to debate with major-party opponent. (Positive)
Interview access
    8. Press conference for national press takes place. (Negative)
    9. There is press availability; that is, candidate meets informally with group of reporters. (Negative)
    10. On his own initiative, candidate engages in light, nonsubstantive banter with reporters. (Negative)
Interview restrictions
    11. No one in the campaign, including press secretary, will respond to queries about sensitive issue. (Positive)
    12. In response to queries from reporters about a sensitive issue, the candidate or press secretary issues a statement, but no one will verbally respond to questions. (Positive)
    13. Candidate has interview with selected print journalists, with restrictions on content. (Positive)
    14. Candidate refuses request from traveling journalists for press conference. (Positive)
Media exclusion
    15. A public or quasi-public event, such as a fund-raiser, is held from which reporters are excluded. (Positive)
    16. Campaign creates impediments to reporting of news; for example, party workers hold up signs to block picture taking. (Positive)

I grouped the 48 codes into six subsets, as outlined in Table 9.1, and gave each candidate a score on each subset of items by adding up positive and negative points. Note from Table 9.1 that three of the subscales refer to behavior of candidates toward reporters and three refer to the management of campaign events independent of reporters. As Table 9.2 shows, scores on these subscales are correlated with negative coverage within each of the four media. When I performed a principal components analysis on the six subscales, all loaded reasonably well on a common factor, as shown in the last column of Table 9.2.

These preliminary results contain two notable pieces of information. Candidates who score high on one facet of news management (such as reluctance to debate) tend to score high on others as well (such as limited reporter access to events and low exposure to potentially unfriendly crowds). Further, each facet of news management correlates with press negativity (albeit somewhat unevenly).

An obvious concern in measuring candidate behavior from media reports, as I have done, is that the reports may be biased in some way. This concern, however, is greater for some subscales than others. For example, one can be confident that when candidates give on-the-record interviews or press conferences, some reference to them will appear in print (e.g., "Speaking with reporters on Air Force One, the President said . . . "). Similarly, one can be confident that when candidates exclude reporters from events, reporters will usually note it (often in the form of a complaint). On the other hand, one cannot be confident that every case in which a campaign screens access to its rallies will be noted; the most one can hope is that there will be more frequent references to such screening for candidates who screen more. In light of this concern, it is reassuring that all six subscales of the news management scale have a zero-order relationship with media negativity, as shown in Table 9.2.

One might also be concerned that, because reporters have focused more on horse-race matters in recent years (Patterson 1993), they would point out more instances of news management now than in the past, even if nothing had changed. However, one might also entertain the opposite worry: that many forms of news management attracted more attention in campaigns during the 1960s and 1970s, when they were newer. One might also be concerned that a liberal media would attribute more instances of news management to Republican candidates, out of prejudice against them. To control for these possibilities, I repeated my main analysis, as described in Table 9.3, after purging the news management scale of the effects of year and party of candidate. The results left the effect of news management entirely unchanged.

TABLE 9.2 Correlations Between News Management Subscales and Media Negativity

| | Correlations with media negativity | | | | | Subscale loading on general news management factor |
	Newsweek magazine	Time magazine	New York Times	Network television news	Row average	
(Limited) interview access	0.18	0.25	0.41	0.44	0.32	0.56
(Un)willingness to debate	0.23	0.29	0.54	0.28	0.34	0.57
Interview restrictions	0.39	0.39	0.47	0.44	0.42	0.39
Media exclusion from events	0.41	0.29	0.57	0.50	0.45	0.66
(Limited) crowd exposure	0.18	0.22	0.37	0.67	0.36	0.54
Message control	0.23	0.30	0.49	0.39	0.35	0.46
Column average	0.27	0.29	0.48	0.45		

NOTE: Cell entries are correlated coefficients based on scores of sixteen major-party candidates from 1968 to 1996. Italicized entries are averages of correlations in the indicated row or column.

Findings

As shown earlier, higher levels of news management, as measured in September, are correlated with higher levels of media negativity, as measured in October. Yet, to demonstrate that these correlations represent a causal relationship, it is necessary to control for potentially confounding variables, as follows:

1. Inspection of the data indicate that, beginning with Nixon in 1968, Republican candidates tended to make more aggressive efforts at news management than Democrats did. This makes it necessary to control for the party of the candidate. Absent such a control, any effect of news management could be a spurious indicator of media bias against Republicans.

2. As Patterson (1993), in particular, has shown, media negativity has increased in recent decades. To control for this general trend, it is necessary to control for the year of the election.

3. In a separate analysis, I have shown that reporters are more inclined to dig up negative information about candidates who are politically strong. I call this the rule of anticipated importance. The idea is that journalists, in serving a news audience that is only minimally interested in politics, concentrate their attention on candidates and causes that have anticipated future importance—that is, they focus on winners rather than losers. Thus, in 1996, reporters investigated Bill Clinton's fund-raising practices but not Bob Dole's. Reporters also ignored Dole's marital indiscretions, despite the fact that *Washington Post* reporter Bob Woodward gathered the information necessary to write such a story. To control for a candidate's anticipated importance, I use the average of his share of the two-party vote in the early October Gallup poll and the final election results.

4. Candidates may resort to aggressive management as a response to media negativity toward them. To control for this possibility, I control for the September level of media criticism. Since September criticism is correlated with October criticism at the level of $r = 0.77$, this is a strong control.

5. The data indicate that reporters are more critical of incumbents. Hence I add an incumbency control.

Using five control variables in a regression having only sixteen observations makes it difficult to show the effect of the variable of interest, news management. Compounding this difficulty is the fact

TABLE 9.3   Effects of News Management on Media Negativity, 1968 to 1996

	(1)	(2)	(3)	(4)
News management (mean = 0, SD = 1)				
β	0.51	—	—	—
b	0.53			
one-tailed p value	0.03			
Reporter management (mean = 0, SD = 1)				
β	—	0.55	—	—
b		0.57		
p value		0.05		
Event management (mean = 0, SD = 1)				
β	—	0.04	0.26	0.34
b		0.04	0.27	0.36
p value		0.44	0.15	0.03
September media criticism[a] (mean = 0, SD = 0.87)				
β	0.18	0.17	0.20	—
b	0.22	0.20	0.12	
p value	0.30	0.28	0.29	
Political strength[b] (range 36 to 62)				
β	0.38	0.39	0.37	0.44
b	0.06	0.06	0.05	0.06
p value	0.03	0.03	0.05	0.01
Year (0 to 7)				
β	0.34	0.38	0.26	0.28
b	0.15	0.17	0.11	0.06
p value	0.02	0.01	0.07	0.04
Democratic candidate[c] (0 or 1)				
b	0.14	0.18	-0.02	—
b	0.29	0.35	-0.04	
p value	0.28	0.34	0.47	
Incumbent (0, 0.50, 1)				
β	0.15	0.12	0.24	0.32
b	0.32	0.25	0.52	0.68
p value	0.25	0.30	0.17	0.04
Intercept	-3.47	-3.63	-3.16	-3.79
R^2	0.84	0.86	0.79	0.78
Adjusted R^2	0.73	0.73	0.65	0.69

NOTE: Estimation is by means of ordinary least squares. Number of cases is 16. All p values are one-tailed. The dependent variable is a weighted average of the October media negativity scores of *Newsweek*, *Time*, the *New York Times*, and television network news. To create this variable, I standardized all four variables; averaged them so as to give equal weight to each type of media, that is, one-sixth weights to each news magazine, one-third weight to the newspaper, and one-third weight to television news (which was already an average across the three major networks); and restandardized the final variable to a mean of zero and a standard deviation (SD) of 1.
[a]September criticism scores from the *New York Times* and television news were standardized and combined. (September scores for *Time* and *Newsweek* are unavailable.)
[b]An average of a candidate's support in the early October Gallup poll and in the final vote.
[c]The nonincumbent nominee of the incumbent party receives a score of 0.50.

that three of the five controls are correlated with news management
at the level of $r = 0.50$ or greater. Nonetheless, Table 9.3 shows that
news management has a significant effect.

The dependent variable in Table 9.3 is media-initiated negativity,
which has been formed by combining negativity scores from all four
media (*Time, Newsweek,* the *New York Times,* and television network news). The key independent variable is news management,
which is a linear combination of the six subscales in Table 9.2, as
weighted by the factor scores from a principal components analysis.[7]
Look first at column 1 of Table 9.3, where the effect of news management on criticism is both statistically significant ($p = 0.03$, one-
tailed) and substantively large. (The standardized coefficient of 0.51
means that a change of 1 standard deviation (SD) on the news management scale is associated with a change of 0.51 SD in press-initi-
ated criticism.) Column 2 of Table 9.3 breaks the news management
scale into two subscales: a three-item subscale that I shall call event
management (crowd exposure, message control, plus willingness to
debate) and a three-item subscale that I shall call reporter management (media exclusion, interview restriction, plus lack of interview
access). In the regression in column 2, reporter management has a
very large and significant effect, whereas event management has almost none. Column 3 shows that, when reporter management is
taken out of the model, event management has a moderate but statistically marginal effect on media negativity.

The latter results suggest that how a candidate treats reporters has
a big effect but that little else matters. Yet it would be a mistake to
accept this conclusion. The two subscales of news management are,
to begin with, correlated at 0.80. In light of the measurement error
that no doubt exists in both subscales, this is a high correlation—
one strongly suggesting that event management and reporter management tap a common syndrome. It is quite possible that the va-
garies of measurement error, in combination with multicollinearity
in a small data set, have made it artificially easier to show effects for
one part of the syndrome than for the other, even though the overall
syndrome, rather than either part alone, is what matters.

A partial test of this supposition is possible. Note that the coefficient for a Democratic candidate is small and statistically insignificant in columns 1, 2, and 3 and, further, that it has the "wrong" sign
in two of the tests. (The positive sign indicates that, contrary to expectation, the media appear to be slightly more critical of Democrats

than Republicans.) These results suggest that party is a superfluous control variable with no real effect at all. Note also that September media criticism was included only to control for the possibility of a reciprocal relationship between media negativity and candidate behavior toward the reporters and that there is little reason to worry about such reciprocity if we are testing the effect of event management by itself. Given this, it is reasonable to omit party and September media criticism as control variables when testing the effect of event management separately from the effect of media control. The results of such a test, as reported in column 4 of Table 9.3, show that event management is both statistically and substantively significant when freed of the need to compete with a set of highly collinear and arguably superfluous rivals.

The conclusion I draw from these results is that attempts by candidates to manage journalists and campaign events are part of a common syndrome and have common effects on media negativity. It may be, as the evidence in column 2 suggests, that reporters are more reactive to attempts to manage them than to attempts to manage campaign events. But it is quite likely, in my opinion, that attempts to measure the former seem more important simply because they are easier to measure accurately.

A final point to notice in Table 9.3 is that both political strength and year have reliable effects on media negativity. The former effect is consistent with my rule of anticipated importance, as described earlier. The latter has no definite theoretical interpretation and could capture any number of temporal developments, such as changes in journalistic norms or the effects of increased competition between media outlets, among other possibilities. As I will explain next, however, I regard the effect of the year variable as an indication of the escalating struggle between politicians and journalists to control the content of political communication.

Discussion

An interesting question is why, if this analysis is correct, do candidates persist in news management techniques that offend the media and result in media criticism? Why not simply ease up and get better coverage in return?

Much of the reason seems to be the belief of campaign consultants, especially on the Republican side, that candidates gain more from the controlled images they get, especially on television, than they lose from the criticism, much of it petty and strained, that journalists visit upon them in return. This belief is on open display in an oft-told tale from Ronald Reagan's 1984 campaign. Frustrated that the Reagan campaign consisted of vacuous hoopla, CBS News reporter Leslie Stahl assembled a repetitive montage of campaign scenes that seemed especially vacuous—cheering crowds, colorful balloons rising into the sky, Reagan smiling and waving—and used it as visual backdrop for an acid commentary about Reagan's supposedly empty campaign. But, as related by Michael Schudson (1995, 115):

> A White House official called [Stahl] soon after the piece aired and said he'd loved it. "How could you?" she responded. He said, "Haven't you figured it out yet? The public doesn't pay any attention to what you say. They just look at the pictures." Stahl, on reflection . . . came to believe that the White House was probably right: all she had done was to assemble, free of charge, a Republican campaign film, a wonderful montage of Reagan appearing in upbeat scenes.

It is hard to believe that media stories about Watergate and Clinton fund-raising were quite as harmless as Stahl's attack on Reagan's campaign style. But I have been able to find no systematic evidence that media criticism during the final phase of the election campaign has any negative effect—and a slight suggestion that it might sometimes help. Consistent with this possibility, I spoke to a Republican adviser who said that the Bush campaign knew in 1988 that it might be criticized by journalists for visiting flag factories but felt that this sort of criticism from none-too-popular journalists could perhaps be helpful with swing voters. No doubt this kind of thinking explains why some campaigns are willing to anger the media.

Another question is why media negativity has accelerated in recent decades. Although, as indicated, I have no strong answer, I regard media-initiated negativity as a defensive response to the increasingly aggressive attempts at news management on the part of politicians. As Ansolabehere, Behr, and Iyengar (1993, 234) observe:

> In a sense, the relationship between reporters and government officials or candidates is akin to a chess game in which each side vies for control. As conditions change, both sides must adapt. Politicians must learn to "game" the system for their own benefit, while reporters must respond in ways that prevent the officials and campaigns from dominating the process.

The relationship between political figures and the media has changed dramatically since the advent of television. Politicians have been much quicker to adjust to these changes than the media. Elected officials, candidates and their consultants have developed intricate strategies for using the media to their advantage. The media, on the other hand, have only just begun to develop counter-strategies for protecting their independence.

What I have called media-initiated negativity—much of it carping complaints about overuse of balloons and patriotic symbols—seems to be the best counterstrategy that journalists have so far come up with.

Conclusion

This chapter has sketched a theory of interactions between politicians, journalists, and citizens and has examined a single testable implication of that theory, the rule of product substitution. The theory has numerous other implications for media politics in both electoral and nonelectoral settings, which I present in a full-length monograph of this material (Zaller, forthcoming). The most important of these implications is that the content of political communication is heavily determined by the disparate self-interests of politicians, journalists, and citizens as each group jostles to get what it wants out of politics and the political communication that makes politics possible.

Notes

I am grateful to Michael Alvarez, Bill Bianco, Lara Brown, Jim DeNardo, John Geer, Shanto Iyengar, Elihu Katz, Taeku Lee, Dan Lowenstein, Warren Miller, Jonathan Nagel, John Petrocik, Tom Schwartz, Jim Sidanius, Michael Traugott, and especially to Larry Bartels, Barbara Geddes, and George Tsebelis for helpful comments on earlier drafts. The research for this article, along with the larger project of which it is a part, has been generously supported by several institutions, including the Center for Advanced Study in the Behavioral Sciences, the National Science Foundation, the Guggenheim Foundation, and the Academic Senate Research Fund at the University of California at Los Angeles. This chapter is reproduced with permission from *The Annals of the American Academy of Political and Social Science*, November, 1998.

1. Professors at research universities, who are the primary audience for this discussion, do not differ much from journalists or other professionals in these matters. Certainly, we are as jealous of our autonomy as any professional group, and more effective in maintaining it than almost any. We

use our autonomy to create and market the most sophisticated product we can—research. We generally consider that the best research is research that does not mechanically report the facts but interprets, analyzes, and theorizes them. Those who are most successful at this derive higher status, higher pay, and perhaps greater intellectual satisfaction than other researchers and colleagues at nonresearch institutions.

2. My colleague Tom Schwartz coined this witty aphorism.

3. Notwithstanding the claim that citizens are attracted to conflict, they often say they dislike it. However, I am more inclined to believe that journalists, who fill their news reports with conflict, know what sells their product than that citizens know their opinions.

4. Reporters were pressing Brooke, a black Republican, to respond to a speech in which Nixon had seemed critical of the Supreme Court's Brown decision.

5. It is a weakness of this research that one person, Mark Hunt, coded both media negativity and candidate behavior. The two concepts, however, are quite different, and the two projects were separated by about a year.

6. These files may be found at www.sscnet.ucla.edu/ polisci/faculty/zaller/data.files/campaign.conduct.files (November 1, 2000). There is a separate file for each election year. The files are in Word format.

7. The alpha reliability of the composite measure is about 0.90.

References

Ansolabehere, Stephen, Roy Behr, and Shanto Iyengar. 1993. *The Media Game.* New York: Macmillan.

Bennett, W. Lance. 1996. *News: The Politics of Illusion.* White Plains, N.Y.: Longman.

Cook, Timothy E. 1998. *Governing with the News: The News Media as a Political Institution.* Chicago: University of Chicago Press.

Downs, Anthony. 1957. *An Economic Theory of Democracy.* New York: Harper.

Germond, Jack, and Jules Witcover. 1989. *Whose Broad Stripes and Bright Stars.* New York: Warner Books.

Graber, Doris. 1984. *Processing the News.* White Plains, N.Y.: Longman.

Grove, Lloyd. 1988. "Goldwater Quip About Bush Reflects Changing Dynamics of Campaign on TV." *Washington Post,* 23 Sept., p. A16.

Halberstam, David. 1978. *The Powers That Be.* New York: Dell.

Jamieson, Kathleen Hall. 1996. *Packaging the Presidency,* 3rd ed. New York: Oxford University Press.

Kernell, Sam. 1997. *Going Public.* Washington, D.C.: Congressional Quarterly Press.

Patterson, Thomas. 1993. *Out of Order.* New York: Knopf.

Schudson, Michael. 1995. *The Power of News.* Cambridge, Mass.: Harvard University Press.

Siegel, Ed. 1988. "A Campaign Dominated by Images, Not Issues." *Boston Globe,*
24 Sept., p. 10.

Zaller, John. Forthcoming. *A Theory of Media Politics.* Chicago: University of
Chicago Press.

Zaller, John, with Dennis Chiu. 1996. "Government's Little Helper: Press Coverage
of Foreign Policy Crises, 1945–1991." *Political Communication* 13(4): 385–406.

ABOUT THE CONTRIBUTORS

Asher Arian is Distinguished Professor in the Ph.D. Program in Political Science at the Graduate School and University Center of the City University of New York and Professor of Political Science at the University of Haifa. Two of his recent books are *The Second Republic: Politics in Israel* (Chatham House, 1998) and *Security Threatened: Surveying Israeli Opinion in Peace and War* (Cambridge University Press, 1995).

Larry Bartels is Professor of Politics and Public Affairs and Donald E. Stokes Professor of Public and International Affairs at Princeton University. He is the author of *Voting Behavior: Essays and Reflections* (University of Michigan Press, 2001), from which his essay in this volume is drawn, and the coeditor (with Lynn Vavreck) of *Campaign Reform: Insights and Evidence* (University of Michigan Press, 2000).

Jay G. Blumler is Emeritus Professor of Social and Political Communication at the University of Leeds and Emeritus Professor of Journalism at the University of Maryland. In addition to *Television in Politics: Its Uses and Influence* (with Denis McQuail; Faber & Faber and University of Chicago Press, 1968), his books based on election communication research include: *The Challenge of Election Broadcasting* (with Michael Gurevitch and Julian Ives; Leeds University Press, 1978), *Television—Fait-Elle L'Election?* (with Roland Cayrol and Gabriel Thoveron; 1978), *Communicating to Voters: Television in the First European Parliamentary Elections* (Sage, 1983), *The Formation of Campaign Agendas* (with Holli Semetko, Michael Gurevitch, and David Weaver; Lawrence Erlbaum Associates, 1991), and *The Crisis of Public Communication* (with Michael Gurevitch; Routledge, 1995). He is also coauthor of "The Third Age of Political Communication: Influences and Features" (with Dennis Kavanagh); *Political Communication* 16(3), 1999, and "Rethinking the Study of Political Communication" (with Michael Gurevitch; in *Mass Media and Society,* Edward Arnold, 2000).

Richard Johnston is Professor of Political Science at the University of British Columbia and, for 2000 and 2001, Visiting Scholar at the Annenberg School for Communication, University of Pennsylvania. He was principal investigator of the 1988 and 1993 Canadian Election Studies and is directing the survey component of the Annenberg School's study of the Year 2000 U.S. Elections. He is coauthor of *Letting the People Decide: Dynamics of a Canadian Election* (Stanford University Press, 1992) and *The Challenge of Direct Democracy: The 1992 Canadian Referendum* (McGill-Queen's University Press, 1996).

Elihu Katz is Trustee Professor at the Annenberg School for Communication, University of Pennsylvania, and Professor Emeritus of the Hebrew University of Jerusalem. He holds honorary degrees from the Universities of Montreal, Ghent, Paris-2, and Haifa, is a member of the American Academy of Arts and Sciences, and is recipient of the McLuhan Prize and the Israel Prize. His interest in the role of media in election campaigns dates to "The Debates in the Light of Research: A Survey of Surveys" (with Jacob J. Feldman; in *The Great Debates,* Indiana University Press, 1962), which led to *Media Events: The Live Broadcasting of History* (with Daniel Dayan; Cambridge University Press, 1992). Recently, he coauthored (with Jerome Segal et al.) *Negotiating Jerusalem* (State University of New York Press, 2000).

Juan Linz is Sterling Professor Emeritus of Political and Social Science at Yale University. He received his Ph.D. from Columbia in 1959 and holds honorary degrees from the University of Granada (Spain), Georgetown, Autonoma de Madrid, Oslo, and Marburg (Germany). He is a member of the Academy of Arts and Sciences, a Foreign Fellow of the British Academy, and a member of Academia Europaea, and winner of the Johann Skytte Prize. He is author of *Breakdown of Democratic Regimes: Crisis, Breakdown and Reequilibration* (Johns Hopkins University Press, 1978); with Alfred Stepan, *Problems of Democratic Transition and Consolidation: Southern Europe, South America and Post-Communist Europe* (Johns Hopkins University Press, 1996); with Arturo Valenzuela (eds.), *The Failure of Presidential Democracy* (Johns Hopkins University Press, 1994); *Conflicto en Euskadi* (Espasa Calpe, 1986); and numerous papers in collective volumes on the party systems of Spain, electoral behavior, public opinion, elites, peripheral nationalisms, fascism, and religion and politics in Spain and other countries. Recently, his book *Totalitarian and Authoritarian Regimes* was updated and reissued (Lynne Rienner, 2000). He is currently writing a book with Alfred Stepan entitled *Federalism, Democracy and Nation.*

Seymour Martin Lipset, retired from Harvard and Stanford, is Hazel Professor of Public Policy at George Mason University and Senior Fellow at the Hoover Institution, the Progressive Policy Institute, and the Woodrow Wilson Center. He has written many books, including *Political Man* (Doubleday & Co., 1959) and, most recently, *It Didn't Happen Here: Why Socialism Failed in the United States* (W. W. Norton, 2000). He is a past president of both the American Political Science Association and the American Sociological Association.

William J. McGuire is Professor Emeritus of Psychology at Yale University, doing research on topics such as persuasive communication, the self-concept, and thought systems. He coedited (with S. Iyengar) and contributed to *Explorations in Political Psychology* (Duke University Press, 1993). In 1999 he received the annual Lasswell Award for Distinguished Scientific Contribution to Political Psychology from the International Society of Political Psychology.

Denis McQuail is Professor Emeritus at the School of Communication at the University of Amsterdam and Visiting Professor in the Department of Politics at the University of Southampton. He recently coedited (with Doris Graber and Pippa Norris) *News of Politics; Politics of News* (Congressional Quarterly Press, 1998).

Michal Shamir is Associate Professor of Political Science at Tel-Aviv University. Her work concentrates on elections, party systems, and public opinion, and has been published widely in American, European, and Israeli journals. Her most recent book, coauthored with Jacob Shamir, is *The Anatomy of Public Opinion* (University of Michigan Press, 2000). She has been conducting the Israel National Election Study together with Asher Arian since 1984; the results of these studies have been published in *The Elections in Israel* series. Work is currently under way on the ninth volume in the series, about the 1999 election.

Merrill Shanks is Professor of Political Science and Director of the Computer-Assisted Survey Methods (CSM) Program at the University of California at Berkeley. He is coauthor, with Warren E. Miller, of *The New American Voter* (Harvard University Press, 1996) and a series of essays on each U.S. presidential election since 1980. He is also responsible for the Survey of Governmental Objectives (SGO), which is based on a general strategy for providing direct measurement of voters' opinions concerning a comprehensive set of potential issues. Initial results from a pilot version of the SGO are discussed in the second half of his contribution, and this general approach to issue-related measurement is used in the Annenberg survey of the 2000 election.

Yael Warshel is a graduate student at the Annenberg School for Communication of the University of Pennsylvania. She was awarded a John Gardner Fellowship for Public Service from the University of California at Berkeley and Stanford University. She is interested in questions of unequal access to communication technology and their interplay with violent behavior. She has conducted research for the Truman Institute for the Advancement of Peace at the Hebrew University of Jerusalem and for the Center for International Development and Conflict Management of the University of Maryland at College Park.

John Zaller is coauthor (with Herbert McClosky) of *The American Ethos* (Harvard University Press, 1984) and author of *Nature and Origins of Mass Opinion* (Cambridge University Press, 1992). He is currently completing work on *A Theory of Media Politics: How the Interests of Politicians, Journalists, and Citizens Shape the News*. He received his Ph.D. in political science from the University of California at Berkeley, in 1984.

INDEX